36178545

D1622368

Subversive Imaginations

Subversive Imaginations

Fantastic Prose and the End of
Soviet Literature, 1970s–1990s

Nadya L. Peterson

WestviewPress
A Division of HarperCollins*Publishers*

Copyright © 1997 by Westview Press, A Division of HarperCollins Publishers, Inc.

Published in 1997 in the United States of America by Westview Press, 5500 Central Avenue, Boulder, Colorado 80301-2877, and in the United Kingdom by Westview Press, 12 Hid's Copse Road, Cumnor Hill, Oxford OX2 9JJ

A CIP catalog record for this book is available from the Library of Congress.
ISBN 0-8133-8920-8

Typeset by Letra Libre.

The paper used in this publication meets the requirements of the American National Standard for Permanence of Paper for Printed Library Materials Z39.48-1984.

10   9   8   7   6   5   4   3   2   1

To Emma, Toma, and Natalie
with love and gratitude

Contents

Acknowledgments

M Y FIRST AND PROFOUND THANKS go to several individuals who have helped to bring this book into existence. Katerina
Clark, without whose initial direction and thoughtful attention
this project would not have materialized, has offered constant intellectual and emotional sustenance. Helena Goscilo, whose work inspired
me and whose friendship helped me to go on, has provided invaluable
criticism and warm encouragement. Janet Rabinowitch, who guided me
through the multiple revisions of the manuscript, has contributed immeasurably to this book. Rebecca Ritke, my indefatigable and brilliant
editor, has been indispensable to the completion of this project. My
most heartfelt thanks go to Ben Eklof, who, with his expertise in all
things Russian, prodigious editorial skills, and unwavering belief in my
work, has been my best critic and my greatest, and selfless, supporter.

   I have benefited tremendously from the generosity of several institutions. The Social Science Research Council supported my participation
in two Seminars on Soviet Literature and Society held at Stanford University in 1986 and Yale University in 1987. A University of Pennsylvania
Research Foundation Award in 1989 and a Women's Studies Summer
Research Grant from the University of Pennsylvania in 1992 enabled me
to make several research trips to Russia. The Center for Russian and European Studies at the University of Pennsylvania provided unfailing
practical assistance related to my research. The staff of the *Slavic Review*, Richard Frost in particular, have offered help and advice. I also
thank some of the important protagonists of this book—the Russian
critic Lev Anninskii and the writers Valeriia Narbikova, Liudmila Petrushevskaia, Nina Sadur, and Tatiana Tolstaya—for their willingness to
talk with me and share their insights about Russian life and literature. I
owe special thanks to my students at the University of Pennsylvania—
Vitaly Chernetsky, Vladislav Todorov, and Vera Zubareva—who partici-
pated in the seminar on contemporary Russian literature and whose
work and intellectual vitality have been a source of great joy and an inspiration. The many individuals who offered support and intellectual
guidance include the participants of the two Seminars on Soviet Literature and Society sponsored by the SSRC as well as Marina Ledkovsky,

Peter Barta, Nancy Condee, Vladimir Padunov, John Bushnell, Alex Riazanovsky, and Elliott Mossman. I also thank my friends Jocelyn Carlson, Digby Baltzell, Ann Armstrong, Gray Read, Elizabeth English, Eva Rotmann, Shelley Nelson, Scott Presti, Gail Felton, and Michael Oshinsky for their support, and the Philadelphians among them for making Philadelphia one of my homes.

My most special thanks are to those named in the dedication to this book, all three of whom have been eagerly following my work and whose presence in my life has enabled me to pursue my dreams and to indulge in intellectual endeavors. My mother, Natalie Peterson, did not live to see the final version of the book, but her love and her steadfast encouragement of my pursuits have made the completion of this project possible. My two daughters, Emma and Toma, who have experienced firsthand the challenges of a dual-career family, gave me their unfailing support and prompted me to higher achievements.

Nadya L. Peterson

1

Introduction

WRITING IN 1996 ABOUT SOVIET LITERATURE, one has, despite the ongoing tumult in Russia, a certain sense of closure. The Soviet Union, after all, no longer exists. As a result, Russian literature is going through a tremendous, and to many, disheartening, moment of transition. The rigid dictates of the state are fast being replaced by the no less harsh rules of the market: writers have to then hawk their wares on the steps of the House of Writers, and readers demand, first and foremost, light entertainment—for their hard-won and scarce rubles. The common cry of the critic is: "Soviet literature is dead."[1]

One can find ample justification for the assumption that Soviet literature can no longer be considered a monolithic whole, if only in the sense that the system of cultural and national cross-pollination within the former Union has been put on hold, if not completely out of existence. It is premature, however, to proclaim that the traditional ways of Russian literature in the Soviet period are no longer operative; in order for that to happen a new generation of writers untainted by Soviet experience would have to appear. Yet the sense of an ending is inescapable.

Russian writers of the late eighties and early nineties have placed the myths of the Soviet state at the core of their works, examined genesis and language of the myths, and then discarded them in a gesture of frustration with failed truths. In this process the rhetoric of the Stalinist culture, and the Soviet culture it spawned, is now brought forth and made visible. This culture, disciplined by socialist realist aesthetics to view history as "a version of nature in the service of the political" where everything is "preinterpreted and events are already foreseen," to postulate the world as knowable and hierarchical, has been deliberately defamiliarized and deconstructed.[2]

In Mikhail Kuraev's *Kapitan Dikshtein* (*Captain Dikshtein*, 1987), for example, historical experience appears as an illusive continuum impossible to transcribe in language. Valeriia Narbikova, Liudmila Petrushev-

1

skaia, and Aleksandr Ivanchenko offer the reader the "new Soviet man and woman," envisioned by socialist realism as the product of an ultimate reconciliation of individual and society, as suffering from profound spiritual malaise—prisoners "of time, of consciousness, of absurdity, of insatiable destiny, of a dehumanized society."[3] In the work of Vladimir Sorokin, Viktor Erofeev, and Evgenii Popov of the 1990s, the language of canonical socialist realism, striving to combine the verisimilitude and coherence of realistic writing with the utopian heroic timelessness of an epic, becomes the material for parody.[4] Narbikova's work posits the entire realm of cultural images shaping everyday Soviet reality and rhetoric as a system of signs in need of decoding. The Soviet cultural and historical experience becomes an entity that can be examined and revalued in literature.

Yet this change in approach to writing came about only as the result of lengthy corrosive processes. Rooted in Khrushchev's Thaw, the transformation of Soviet letters gained momentum in the mid-1970s and early 1980s, fueled largely by subversive fantasy and utopian imagination.[5] It was during that decade (what I call the fantastic decade) that writers used utopian motifs and gestures of fantasy to deal in an admissible form with the issues of social imagination and alternative social constructs, with the limitations of the teleological view of history embedded in Marxism-Leninism, and with the constraints on personal freedom that this vision of the world implies.

With the advent of glasnost in the mid-1980s, Soviet literature launched a much more direct assault on the mythologies of the state. Under glasnost, writers documented the failure of Soviet socialism in quasi-journalistic accounts and offered traditional Russian values as a substitute for the bankrupt ideology of Communism. The writers, labeled publicists because of the topical nature of their work, reacted viscerally to the now offensive content of the myths sustaining the idea of Soviet exceptionality and perfection. The Soviet people were no longer represented in literary discourse as one big happy family. Nationalistic concerns permeated the glasnost works of such prominent Russian and minority writers as Iurii Bondarev, Valentin Rasputin, and Chingiz Aitmatov. The garden of Soviet society was polluted, and environmental problems dominated the writings of such publicists as Viktor Astaf'ev, Rasputin, and Vasilii Belov. The machine of Stalinist society broke down; the generally sad state of the Soviet economy became an important theme of glasnost. Deconstruction of Soviet myths in recent literature mirrors the collapse of the ideological edifice supporting the structures of the Soviet state. It is inevitable that fiction writers of today would bid farewell to the Soviet experience and would search for new experiences and new ways of expression.

This book is the story of the end of Soviet literature and of the emergence of the new Russian literature, through the prism of an increasing engagement with fantasy. I use the terms *fantastic* and *fantasy* broadly, referring simply to any narrated instances that cannot be explained rationally. At one end of the spectrum are events that ultimately find their logical explanation; at the other, supernatural occurrences that are from the beginning established as rationally inexplicable (such as those depicted in the fairy tale and science fiction), but are accepted by the reader, who is provided with a specific framework for understanding the narrative. In the middle lies an area that Tzvetan Todorov views as the true fantastic, that hesitation between "a natural and a supernatural explanation of the events described."[6] One can find the entire spectrum of these fantastic devices in post-Stalinist Soviet literature.

Exploration of fantasy in writing must be seen primarily as a reaction to and a departure from the socialist realist dogma. Andrei Sinyavsky, writing in the late 1950s, articulated Soviet writers' frustration with teleology and with the prescribed verisimilitude of socialist realism when he called for "a phantasmagoric art with hypothesis instead of a Purpose, an art in which the grotesque will replace realistic descriptions of ordinary life."[7] To be sure, the applications, stylistic arrangements, and structural role of the fantastic in Soviet literature of the seventies and early eighties (from science fiction, to supernatural fantasy and to fairy-tale magic) varied as much as did Soviet writers. Science fiction grounded the narratives in the context of contemporary social debates more overtly than supernatural fantasy and magic. Yet the subversive character of the fantastic orientation and utopian motifs, as well as the dialogical relationship this fiction had with the tradition of socialist realism were, nevertheless, common to all contributions.

In a way, socialist realism contained the instruments of its own demise; for the mythological dimension of socialist realism, the official artistic method of Soviet literature, is an embodiment of an impulse to fantasy, of a desire to articulate and represent as real an imaginary world of the future. This is utopian realism that "premembers the future."[8] Novels of canonical socialist realism reenact official myths, actualizing in their narratives various layers of culture, from history to philosophy to literature.[9] The very project of socialist realism is broadly fantastic; here the reality of what is to be appears as the everyday reality of the present, and superhuman heroes function according to the rules of verisimilitude, consistency, and coherence. In this codified representation of "a reality lived," myths, fantasy, and utopia become interdependent, linked in the act of wishing; here myths serve to dramatize the utopian impulse.[10] In canonical socialist realism, time is represented mythically; the sacred tale of what Mircea Eliade termed the "time of origins" lives in the ritual replayed in fiction; and the myths this literature inscribes are "hidden," in that they cannot be perceived as "myths," but, rather must be seen as a lived story of the past.[11]

The gradual disengagement of post-Stalinist literature from the aesthetic of socialist realism occurs when literature, in an irreverent atheistic gesture, begins to disentangle the strands of the sacred story, addressing the components of socialist realist formula one by one, and undermining in the process its epic wholeness. Fantastic fiction contributes to this process of disengagement by isolating and making visible that which is fantastic in socialist realism, now narrating a story rather than reenacting a myth. During the fantastic decade, in the work of Anatolii Kim and Nikolai Evdokimov, for example, the dichotomy of real-unreal becomes the central philosophical theme. The biblical story of salvation and rebirth, basic to the master plot of socialist realism but impossible to convey in the language of Christian faith in the canon, is offered in Nodar Dumbadze's *The Law of Eternity* (*Zakon vechnosti,* 1979) as a precursor of Communist ideology. The utopian vision of a perfect Communist society on earth, the teleology of socialist realism, leads such writers of the fantastic decade as Chingiz Aitmatov and Evgenii Evtushenko to consider and represent in their fictions alternatives to the present social order. In the work of Mikhail Bulgakov's followers (Vladimir Orlov, Marger Zarin', Natal'ia Sokolova), superhuman protagonists are recognized as such, and their exploits become the result of irrational, unpredictable forces or, simply, magic.

During the fantastic decade Soviet writers expressed their desire for change—personal, political, cultural, literary—in the Aesopian language of fantasy. In the most dismal days of the "period of stagnation," fantasy appeared as a means of expressing dissatisfaction with the state of affairs in the country. The reader read between the lines, looking for a subversive message under the veil of improbable occurrences and wondrous transformations. To some writers, then, fantasy was a means to conceal an essentially political message. Others, such as, the authors belonging to a group labeled alternative by critics, used fantastic situations and devices in fiction to assert freedom in literary expression, to write prose "where everything is allowed" in order to portray this "distorted, tawdry, phantasmagoric—reality" and to reveal the "underground of the human soul."[12] Whatever the reasons, for a brief time fantasy became, and was perceived as, the ubiquitous language of public discontent.[13] In this book I shall refer to the literary output in this period of intense and all-encompassing engagement of Soviet literature with the fantastic as fantastic prose or literature.[14]

The political vagaries of the mid-eighties, which, for all practical purposes, liberated Soviet writers from the constraints of censorship, significantly altered the situation. The absence of direct control over literature prompted some writers (publicists in particular) to dispense with overt devices of fantasy. Such authors as Astaf'ev, Belov, Evtushenko, and Bondarev who had employed fantasy in their work of the seventies, chose now to present their message of moral indignation about the state of the country directly. In a continuous dialogue with the traditions of socialist realism, these publicistic writers now addressed the content of Soviet mythologies, juxtaposing myths of the Soviet past with the myth of a regenerated Russia. Comparisons between the fantastic prose and publicistic literature of glasnost throw light on what it was precisely that had been concealed under the cloak of fantasy; such comparisons also point to a pronounced desire and tendency of publicists, still rooted in the aesthetics of socialist realism, to organize chaotic reality in mythological terms.

During the period of glasnost, alternative writers (such as Kim, Vladimir Makanin, Tatiana Tolstaya, Narbikova, Ivanchenko, Nina Sadur) continued, as they had before the advent of glasnost, to employ fantastic devices in their works. These writers persisted in using fantasy as a particular mode of discourse about life, as a philosophical statement on the nature of reality and on the human propensity for creating cultural and political myths. Experimentation with form, the transgressive character of narrative gestures, and a fascination with the psychological and physiological aspects of human life, expressed in a language saturated with fantasy, are still operative in alternative writings. In viewing these works, one can see the elaboration of an approach, the strengthening of a position, rather than a departure from the discourse of fantasy. Narbikova's and Sorokin's use of fantasy, for example, is an indicator of alternative literature's affinity with modernist writing, which privileges "heterogeneity, play, marginality, transgression, the unconscious, eroticism, excess" over "representation, the unitary subject, linear narrative, paternal authority, and Truth with a capital T."[15] This is precisely the direction—the modernist, or perhaps postmodernist, mode of expression—that the alternative stream of Russian prose appears to be moving in.

My focus on fantasy does not mean that other historical narratives about the literature of the period are not pertinent or correct; nor do I wish to imply that other works of literature produced during this period, and not mentioned in this book, are not worthy of attention.[16] What I want to demonstrate through my necessarily limited interpretation are the continuities and discontinuities—of purpose, ideology, representation—with the past that obtain in this body of literature we have designated as Soviet. Fantastic prose of the seventies and early eighties investigated alternative societal structures as a possibility (or impossibility) for Soviet society, questioned the epistemological presuppositions of Marxism-Leninism embedded in teleological socialist realism, and served as a prelude and a bridge to the literature of the Gorbachev period. An investigation of its addiction to the devices of fantasy serves to elucidate Soviet literature's relationship to its own history as well as to make some sense of its closure.

This book places the story of literary change in the context of social change and belongs to a trend in Western criticism that views Soviet literary output in a process of mutual dialectic interaction with various aspects of the dominant culture, including ideology and politics. What concerns me here are the adjustments and compromises that occurred in middlebrow Soviet fiction in response to social change. Transformations in middlebrow fiction (defined by Vera Dunham as "compliant, didactic, grey and routine," "echoing the official views of the moment," "the perishable output of average, 'safe' writers") provide a source for insights into the system's changing values.[17] This approach explains the primary focus of my narrative on surface channels of Soviet literature, including official Soviet criticism, and is responsible for my reliance on the work of social historians and those literary critics who view literature as inseparable from history and culture.

Many important authors whose works were originally published only in *tamizdat* (e.g., Andrei Sinyavsky, Sasha Sokolov, Venedikt Erofeev, Andrei Bitov) are mentioned only in passing or not considered at all.[18] Any attempt to assert that the influences of underground writers were formative for mainstream writers would conflict with the actual literary situation before Gorbachev's thaw, when the work of *tamizdat* authors was still not readily available to the Soviet public. Before Gorbachev, Soviet mainstream fiction moved on "establishmentarian tracks" (the phrase is Dunham's). Soviet writers polemicized with and reacted only to the texts in the domain of the permissible. Because of the limited access to *tamizdat* works, the intertextual polemic between these texts and mainstream fiction, necessary for aesthetic innovation, was virtually impossible before glasnost.[19]

Widely published and reviewed, not yet fully free of socialist realist formulae, mainstream fiction was still operating largely in isolation, in an environment where outside influences were carefully monitored by the establishment, and where literary innovations signaled social change. As a result, literary and philosophical influences outside the sphere of the permissible could appear only as veiled refractions of original positions. Sinyavsky's call for a new Russian literature, published in the West, was an articulation of a shared desire for change; yet, like the work of other *tamizdat* writers, Sinyavsky's own innovative fiction had to wait for decades before it could exert a more direct influence on Russian writing. A qualitatively different Russian fiction emerges only in the late eighties, when official monitoring and control were visibly weakened and writers could react openly to the legacy of Russian underground writing.

The fantastic orientation of Soviet literature appears now as an important stage in the disintegration of the political and cultural myths supporting not only the edifice of socialist realist writing but that of the Party-dominated state itself. What are the links of this literature to the literature of the Gorbachev era and beyond? And, finally, what course is Russian literature taking after the demise of the Soviet Union? Even a partial answer to these questions can help us assess the nature and significance of the changes under way in Russian society and literature.

In the words of one prominent American historian of Russia, "the world of fantasy, like the world of myth and legend, reveals and evokes deep layers, archaic dreams and longings that may better describe the feelings and anxieties [of a society] than some conventional acts of political adherence."[20] In the seventies and eighties the tension between popular utopian vision, administrative utopia decreed from above, and the utopian dreams of the Russian intelligentsia—the heady brew out of which revolutionary change had earlier emerged in 1917—once again pulsed through various currents of Soviet fiction. And, as in the previous century, the literature of this period was able to express best "the feelings and anxieties" of its society.

The following chapters will explore the literary and social roots of fantastic prose, seeking its motivation and purpose in relationship to socialist realism. The basic parameters of fantastic fiction, the dialogic relationship of this fiction with socialist realism and the social factors that made its appearance possible (i.e., the place of fantastic prose in Soviet literary history) are the subject of the first chapter. The rest of the book follows a loosely chronological organization, identifying the first manifestations of interest in fantasy in the literature of Khrushchev's Thaw (chapter 3); tracing the development of fantastic prose in the fantastic decade (chapters 4–7); and evaluating the uses of fantasy under glasnost and beyond (chapters 8–10).

Recent developments in Russian literature and in the literature of the national minorities are a logical extension of processes occurring in the late Brezhnev era. The concentration here is on points of relevance and continuity rather than on the ongoing (swift and often unpredictable) change. Soviet fiction of the last two decades is a literature in transition, aimed at a middle-class public, and still propelled largely by an ideological rather than an aesthetic impulse. It is, above all, a literature with a message, and, precisely because of its intimate connections to social concerns, the assessment of its final decades has much to offer to an "archaeologist of culture," a literary critic, a historian, and even a political scientist.

Notes

1. Viktor Erofeev, "Pominki po sovetskoi literature," *Literaturnaia gazeta* 27 (1990): 8. See more on the effect of the move toward market economy on the arts in Russia in John Rockwell, "Russia's Culture Struggles to Root in Freedom's Stony Soil," *New York Times,* November 9, 1992, pp. A1–B5; also David Remnick, "Exit the Saints," *New Yorker* 70 (July 18, 1994): 50–55.

2. Regine Robin, *Socialist Realism: An Impossible Aesthetic* (Stanford: Stanford University Press, 1992), p. 25.

3. Rufus Mathewson, "The Novel in Russia and the West," in Max Hayward and Edward L. Crowley, eds., *Soviet Literature in the Sixties: An International Symposium* (New York: Praeger, 1964), pp. 9–10.

4. See, for example, Vladimir Sorokin, *Sbornik rasskazov* (Moscow: Russlit, 1992); Viktor Erofeev, *Zhizn' s idiotom* (Moscow: SP "Interbuk," 1991); and Evgenii Popov, *Prekrasnost' zhizni* (Moscow: Moskovskii rabochii, 1990).

5. The Thaw decade (1953–1963) received its name from Ilya Ehrenburg's *The Thaw* (1954), the novel that articulated major points of the de-Stalinization period in Soviet literature. The Thaw, characterized by a greater degree of freedom of artistic expression and spurred on by a relaxation of censorship, generated such important trends as "youth" prose, "village" prose, and *byt* prose. The Thaw also coincided with the revival of Soviet science fiction in post-Stalin literature.

6. Tzvetan Todorov, *The Fantastic: A Structural Approach to a Literary Genre* (Cleveland: Press of Case Western Reserve University, 1973), p. 33. For a succinct and clear review of theoretical approaches to the fantastic, see Neil Cornwell, *The Literary Fantastic: From Gothic to Postmodernism* (New York: Harvester Wheatsheaf, 1990), esp. introduction, pp. 3–41. See also Eric S. Rabkin, *The Fantastic in Literature* (Princeton: Princeton University Press, 1976); Rosemary Jackson, *Fantasy: The Literature of Subversion* (London: Methuen, 1981); Kathryn Hume, *Fantasy and Mimesis: Responses to Reality in Western Literature* (New York: Methuen, 1984); and Amaryll Beatrice Chanady, *Magical Realism and the Fantastic: Resolved versus Unresolved Antinomy* (New York: Garland, 1985).

7. Abram Terts, *On Socialist Realism* (New York: Pantheon, 1960), pp. 94–95.

8. Brian McHale, *Postmodernist Fiction* (London: Methuen, 1987), p. 65. Quoted in Edith W. Clowes, *Russian Experimental Fiction: Resisting Ideology after Utopia* (Princeton: Princeton University Press, 1993), p. 63.

9. Katerina Clark, *The Soviet Novel: History as Ritual* (Chicago: University of Chicago Press, 1981), pp. 3–15.

10. Fredric Jameson, *Marxism and Form* (Princeton: Princeton University Press, 1971), p. 145. "A reality lived" is part of Bronislaw Malinowski's definition of myth: ". . . not merely a story but a reality lived. It is not of the nature of fiction, such as we read today in a novel, but it is a living reality, believed to have once happened in primaeval times, and continuing ever since to influence the work and human destinies. . . ." *Magic, Science, and Religion* (New York: Double-

day, 1954), p. 100. Quoted in David M. Bethea, *The Shape of Apocalypse in Modern Russian Fiction* (Princeton: Princeton University Press, 1989), p. 3.

11. Mircea Eliade, "Sacred Time and Myths," in *The Sacred and the Profane: The Nature of Religion* (New York: Harper and Row, 1961), pp. 68–113.

12. Sergei Chuprinin,"Drugaia proza," *Literaturnaia gazeta*, February 8, 1989, p. 4.

13. See T. Chernysheva, "Potrebnost' v udivitel'nom i priroda fantastiki," *Voprosy literatury* 5 (1975) 211–232; V. Ivasheva, "O granitsakh poniatii," *Literaturnoe obozrenie* 1 (1976): 72–75; Iurii Seleznev, "Fantasticheskoe v sovremennoi proze," *Moskva* 2 (1977) 198–206; Lev Anninskii, "Zhazhdu realizma!," *Literaturnaia gazeta* 4 (March 1, 1978); M. Epstein and E. Iukina, "Mir i chelovek," *Novyi mir* 4 (1981): 236–247; A. Bocharov, *Beskonechnost' poiska* (Moscow: Sovetskii Pisatel', 1982); L. Mikhailova, "Fakt v zerkale voobrazheniia," *Literaturnoe obozrenie* 6 (1983): 9–14; I. Panchenko, "Voproshaia proshloe—zaglianut' v budushchee," *Voprosy literatury* 6 (1983): 83–108.

14. I leave it to other scholars to consider poetry, drama, and cinema, the areas of Soviet literature in which there was a great deal of experimentation with fantasy.

15. Susan Rubin Suleiman, *Subversive Intent: Gender, Politics, and the Avant-Garde* (Cambridge, Mass.: Harvard University Press, 1990), p. 13.

16. Several important books published in the West deal with the literature of the last two decades either in toto or as background for a discussion of one author. Two monographs are of particular interest: Deming Brown, *The Last Years of Soviet Russian Literature: Prose Fiction, 1975–1991* (Cambridge: Cambridge University Press, 1993) and Clowes, *Russian Experimental Fiction*. Both study the final years of Soviet literature, but approach the issue differently. The work of Iurii Trifonov has attracted attention of excellent scholars. Two recent contributions that put Trifonov's work in the context of Soviet literature of the seventies and eighties are: Josephine Woll, *Invented Truth: Soviet Reality and the Literary Imagination of Iurii Trifonov* (Durham: Duke University Press, 1991) and David Gillespie and Iurii Trifonov, *Unity through Time* (Cambridge: Cambridge University Press, 1992). See also the following contributions by Russian scholars: Aleksandr Arkhangel'skii. *U paradnogo pod'ezda: Literatura i kul'turnye situatsii perioda glasnosti (1987–1990)* (Moscow: Sovetskii Pisatel', 1991); Galina Belaia, "O prirode eksperimenta: k sporam o khudozhestvennykh poiskakh v sovremennoi literature," *Literaturnoe obozrenie* 7 (1985): 21–26; also by Belaia, "Pereput'e," *Voprosy literatury* 12 (1987):75–103; "In the Name of Common Culture," *Soviet Literature* 9 (1988): 132–138; and "Ugrozhaiushchaia real'nost'," *Voprosy literatury* 4 (1990): 3–38.

17. Vera S. Dunham, *In Stalin's Time: Middleclass Values in Soviet Fiction* (Cambridge: Cambridge University Press, 1976), p. 29.

18. *Tamizdat* (*tam*, "there" and *izdat*, "publication") refers to works smuggled out to the West for publication.

19. See more on this in Clowes, *Russian Experimental Fiction*, p. 17.

20. Richard Stites, *Revolutionary Dreams: Utopian Vision and Experimental Life in the Russian Revolution* (Oxford: Oxford University Press, 1989), p. 34.

2

Writers, Readers, Society, and Literary Change

Fantastic literature points to or suggests the basis upon which the cultural order rests, for it opens up, for a brief moment, on to disorder, on to illegality, on to that which lies outside the law, that which is outside the dominant value systems. The fantastic traces the unsaid and the unseen of culture: that which has been silenced, made invisible, covered over and made "absent."

—*Rosemary Jackson*, Fantasy: The Literature of Subversion

Connections and Departures

The first post-Stalinist works in a fantastic vein began to appear in the early seventies, when writers were encouraged to broaden the thematic range of Soviet literature and improve its image.[1] Yet, even as the push for change came from the establishment, the transformation of literary discourse (changes in literary techniques, perspectives, thematics) also occurred as a result of the pull of laws inherent in literature itself. The fiction offered for the reader's consumption possessed its own logic of development, its own laws of inheritance.

A widespread interest in the Latin American novel and, in particular, the popularity of Gabriel García Márquez, only partially explain the form that Soviet fantastic literature took in the seventies and eighties. Many writers who figure in this study (Aitmatov, Dumbadze, Rasputin, for example) acknowledged García Márquez's magical realism *(magicheskii realizm)* as a formative influence.[2] The use of native folklore, nationalistic concerns, and resort to the fantastic by these writers could all be attributed to the direct influence of García Márquez's work, and particularly, his *One Hundred Years of Solitude* (published in Russian in 1970).

11

Overall, however, fiction written in the fantastic decade is closer to the fantastic realism of Nikolai Gogol and Fyodor Dostoyevsky than to García Márquez's distinctive style. Features shared by the trend and its nineteenth-century predecessor include a focus on ethical issues, utopian motifs, the use of popular genres, a view of all reality as fantastic, and a belief in the unique importance of Russia for the future of the entire world. To be sure, post-Stalinist literature provided the immediate impetus for the emergence of fantastic fiction, but the themes and concerns of this body of literature were in a sense a reworking of questions embedded in the Russian literary cosmos. The debate about the future of society in the fantastic decade, propelled by the clash of two visions— that of a Communist perfect world and of Russia's idealized patriarchal past—was an echo of the nineteenth-century battles between Dostoyevsky's ideal of the country's spiritual regeneration based on reverence for its religious past and Nikolai Chernyshevsky's scientistic and deterministic theories of a realized utopia on earth.[3] The philosopher N. F. Fyodorov's scholarly reworking of the theological idea of resurrection and redemption accomplished through divine-human collaboration to transform the mortal world into an immortal universe was an idea that had likewise been important in the intellectual development of such nineteenth-century writers as Leo Tolstoy, Dostoyevsky, and Vladimir Solovyov. It shaped the work of the writer Andrei Platonov in the twenties and was later appropriated by writers of fantastic prose (as, for example, Evtushenko and Kim).[4]

The two most important aspects of Fyodorov's work, refracted in Soviet writing of the last two decades, are his confidence in Russia's messianic role in regulating nature and his focus on combining the ideas of the West with those of the East.[5] Fyodorov's belief in the eventual transfiguration of all matter through communal work, his faith in the regenerated feeling of brotherliness, and his distaste for procreation are the ideas that have filtered into both Russian and Soviet literature.[6] The vision of a world evolving toward greater harmony, where the social and the natural phenomena come together as one, is pervasive in nineteenth-century literature and in the works of Aitmatov, Kim, and Belov.[7]

As we will see below, fantastic fiction also responded to and incorporated divergent literary trends current at the time, namely: "village" prose, science fiction, and *byt* prose.[8] Yet a continuous dialogue with canonical socialist realism underlined all these attempts to invigorate Soviet literature. Novels of canonical socialist realism reenact official myths, actualizing in their narratives various layers of culture. By supporting and explaining the workings of the politically dominant forces in society through a continuous performance of the culture's rituals, the socialist realist novel accomplishes a mythological task. In Katerina

Clark's Proppian scheme, the formulaic plot structure of the canonical socialist realist novel (the "master plot") is seen to recapitulate symbolically the society's unswerving path toward Communism.[9] The relationship between myths and rituals is dialectical; but, while the relationship of interaction itself remains constant (the novels will serve as repositories of official myths for maintaining the status quo), the content of these myths is subject to change, as Clark demonstrates in her periodization of Stalinist literature. Ritualized myths of industrialization, embodied in the image of the machine, for example, are replaced in the early thirties by the Stalinist culture's preoccupation with elemental forces of nature. Representation of nature, in turn, undergoes significant changes in subsequent years.[10] Official myths change, but the mechanism of ritualization remains the same.

The proleptic tendency of socialist realism is rooted in the idea that the world has one indisputable meaning and purpose; it is the world that "acknowledges no alternatives to itself."[11] Based on the teleology of Marxism-Leninism, the socialist realist aesthetic rests on the utopian socialist ideal of "dismantling the old order, forging a new world, or constructing a New Man."[12] Yet, as Fredric Jameson reminds us, "the Utopian moment . . . is impossible for us to imagine, except as the unimaginable; thus a kind of allegorical structure is built into the very forward movement of the Utopian impulse itself, which always points to something other, which can never reveal itself directly. . . ."[13] To accommodate "the unimaginable," to represent as contemporary reality the perfect world of the future shaped around the nation's sacred past, is, then, the Herculean project of socialist realism. The result, as Regine Robin has shown, is a monosemy of language, a unitary system of value, and superhuman heroes who function in a transparent, consistent, and coherent authoritative discourse.

But the mutual interdependence of myth and ritual in literature remains stable only if channels of interaction between the writer and the state are rigidly controlled by the strictures of censorship, both imposed from the outside and self-imposed. When, in post-Stalinist Russia, the controls were loosened, expanding the limits of the permissible, when "the story in myth" was no longer accepted as a ritualized performance of a sacred tale but began to be viewed simply as a story, then the mechanism of interdependence between social myths and their actualization in literature was damaged beyond repair. The official directive to enliven socialist realism in the seventies was a belated recognition of the breakdown of the method's epic wholeness and an acknowledgment of the irreversible process of change that began in Khrushchev's Thaw. Disengagement from the aesthetic of socialist realism occurs when writers begin to isolate, play with, and make visible its very components—the insistence on clarity and verisimilitude, the teleological view of history, utopianism, didacticism, and the perfect hero.

Breaking It Apart:
Fantastic Prose and Its Strands

Fantastic prose represented a continuum in Russian letters, but of an innovative kind. Standard socialist realist novels were animated by science fiction subplots, yet could also offer nostalgic accounts of the idyllic past; traditional works about village life (village prose) focused on the sacred past and on the utopian future; chronicles of everyday life of urban dwellers (*byt* prose and "urban" prose) included science fiction, fairy-tale magic, or gothic fantasy. Writers approached the task of invigorating Soviet literature by engaging in intertextual, or intergeneric, polemic that allowed for incorporation of and interaction between various trends in one work. The boundaries between trends were easily crossed; literature displayed the intellectual omnivorousness of an eager young student.

Since the main feature of fantastic prose is its ability to interrogate, by means of incorporation, the various existing literary structures, the task of categorization is a difficult one. I group the four strands of fantastic prose, discussed below, around those literary patterns that predominate in each. Canonical novels of socialist realism, village prose, Mikhail Bulgakov's *The Master and Margarita* and *byt* prose, and, finally, urban prose are the models that Soviet writers of the fantastic decade chose to conduct their experiments in innovation.

Science Fiction and the
Legendary Past in Updated Socialist Realism

A number of novels written during the fantastic decade attempted to update, or make more sophisticated, the basic socialist realist formula by the simple means of temporal and spatial expansion. In the novels of Aitmatov and Dumbadze, for example, the time of the canonical novel was extended into the past and future. Science fiction plots were complemented by legendary plots; issues examined in the future found their parallels in history. This extension of the temporal frame was paralleled by the expansion of spatial dimensions, when the locus of narration shifted between the city, the faraway settlement, and the universe.

The use of science fiction devices and legendary plots in "updated" socialist realism invigorated and then, inevitably, subverted the standard plot. The Stalinist novel and Soviet science fiction are both formulaic literatures whose protagonists "know or discover the laws governing their social existence, and the ultimate outcome of those laws in a Great Society of the future."[14] Stalinist science fiction (with only a handful of titles published in the thirties) was governed by the theory of the near target *(blizkaia tsel')*, circumscribing science fiction's area of thematic concern to include only the technological issues pertaining to the nearest future. To address the issue of alternative social constructs, as Evgenii Zamiatin had done in his anti-utopian novel *We* (1924), for example, would have been a suicidal gesture for an author.[15] As we will see below, it was only in the fifties that Soviet science fiction ventured again into descriptions of other worlds and alternative social and political systems. Its susceptibility to the utopian worlds of incontrovertible meaning and purpose (i.e., the inevitability of teleology in science fiction, as well as the perfect people of the future that populate its static worlds) are the features that Soviet science fiction shares with canonical socialist realism.

Yet the move of Soviet prose to self-reinvigoration, the desire of writers to represent other possible patterns of social practice by incorporating science fiction plots in mainstream novels signaled a profoundly significant change in post-Stalin mentality and literature during the fantastic decade. In their search for alternative models of happiness, Soviet writers of fantasy questioned the urbanist, Marxist-Leninist, utopian vision based on efficiency, industrialization, and technology. As Douglas Weiner has shown in *Models of Nature*, Stalin-era attitudes toward nature had as their source a distinct phenomenology of the human being. According to this view, human beings were seen "as the climax of evolution," as "progressively, relentlessly evolving toward total mastery of the course of life on the planet, becoming a this-worldly god to replace the toppled gods of religion."[16] Thus, nature was "not useful until it was exploited or transformed."[17] As a reaction to this position, for many writers of the fantastic decade (e.g., Aitmatov, Kim, Rasputin, Krupin), the desecration of nature was presented as "unnatural," morally evil, and potentially disastrous. Aitmatov's "updated" socialist realist novel *The Day Lasts More than a Hundred Years* (1980) betrays apprehension of the dehumanizing effects of the machine-oriented society. Aitmatov's utopian vision is based on reverence for tradition and respect for nature. In updated socialist realism the desirable was projected into the future, but the roots of the Communist ideal were also traced into the prehistoric past of myths and legends.

The simultaneous "opening up" of the model from both ends was a device that diversified the socialist realist model and contributed to its eventual disintegration. By supplementing and explicating contemporary plots with legendary tales these novels bared the mythmaking propensity of socialist realism and revealed its vulnerability. And, in spite of its debt to canonical socialist realism, the search to broaden the official norm changed the model to accommodate new concerns of Soviet society. There is a progression, evident in a close analysis of the novels themselves (chapter 3), from an insistence on building a new society at any cost to a questioning of the costs and gains of such a drastic change.

Village Utopians

Another group of works in this period took its departure from the well-established canon of village prose. This post-Stalinist thematic orientation in Soviet literature possessed its own ideological, moral, and aesthetic profile centering around an alienated view of modern society and idealization of Russia's patriarchal past. The post-1956 village prose of Aleksandr Solzhenitsyn, Vasily Belov, Fedor Abramov, Vladimir Soloukhin, Vasily Shukshin, and Rasputin worked against the traditions of the "kolkhoz" literature of Stalinist times, the literature that presented the glorious future of the Soviet village as an accomplished fact. In a violent reversal of value, village prose rejected the future and looked into the past. In fantastic prose the hoary conflicts of this model were infused with fantasy based on Christian legend and pre-Christian myths. In the works of Sergei Zalygin, Rasputin, Vladimir Drozd, and Vladimir Krupin of the mid-seventies the imagined preindustrialized village was celebrated as the true ideal (chapter 6).

For writers in this strand of fantastic prose, the heartless and calculating attitude toward nature, found in socialist realist prose, mirrored the moral vacuum *(bezdukhovnost')* of Soviet society. The notion of transforming humble people into masters of the universe was challenged on religious, historical, ecological, and moral grounds. Village utopians (Rasputin, Zalygin, Krupin) showed the desecration of nature to be a direct result of the loss of Russian traditional (Christian and even pre-Christian) values of reverence and humility toward nature.[18] For these writers, only a return to the golden age of the Russian village can save humankind from spiritual impoverishment.

The issues of mastery over nature and of the consequences of human arrogance toward the natural world were raised in other works of fantastic prose as well, although the village prose writers were, perhaps, the most adamant supporters of the antitechnology view. If, for the village utopians, the ideal future could be found in the past, before the Promethean designs of Soviet urbanists changed the old way of life, for others, the perfect society of the future was one where individual needs were protected, communal values upheld, and technology not allowed to dictate arrangements or despoil nature. One should note here that only a few works (Kim's *Gurin's Utopia*, Aitmatov's *The Day Lasts More than a Hundred Years,* and Evtushenko's *Wild Berries)* included what might be called the true utopia.[19] In most fantastic fiction, utopian ideals served to illustrate other issues, such as the dangers of uncontrolled technological advance and the contradictions inherent in social progress. Yet the attention given to alternative models of social organization in fantastic prose cannot be underestimated or ignored.

The Bulgakovian Novel

If village utopians reacted to the socialist realist tendency to "premember the future," imitators of Mikhail Bulgakov's last novel, *The Master and Margarita,* responded to the escapism of socialist realism and to its superhuman heroes. *The Master and Margarita,* finished by Bulgakov on his deathbed in 1940 and published only in 1966–1967, became responsible for the "Bulgakov phenomenon" in the Soviet Union, a virtual cult of the writer that, in the fantastic decade, led to the appearance of a number of novel's imitations. Bulgakovian novels such as Marger Zarin's *The False Faust* (*Fal'shivyi Faust,* 1981), Natal'ia Sokolova's *Careful, Magic!* (*Ostorozhno, volshebnoe!,* 1981), and Vladimir Orlov's *Danilov, the Viola Player* (*Al'tist Danilov,* 1980) are excellent examples of escapist Soviet literature and are a blend of different genres of popular literature: of mystery, science fiction, and the spy novel (chapter 7). In Bulgakovian novels, *byt* prose was revitalized, and the city, instead of being presented as a source of corruption and evil as was typical of village prose, became a magical place where suppressed desires of common people came true and the protagonist assumed qualities of a superhero, capable of extraordinary achievements.

Stalinist literature of the thirties and forties was also an escapist literature, if not openly so. The consumers of "production novels" are comfortable in their knowledge that the hero will overcome all obstacles and successfully accomplish the task of changing the world. Readers of Valentin Kataev's *Time, Forward* (*Vremia, vpered!,* 1932), a novel celebrating the general increase in work tempos, cannot help but be infected with the enthusiasm of a people striving to accomplish superhuman tasks. Nikolai Ostrovsky's *How the Steel Was Tempered* (*Kak zakalialas' stal',* 1932–1934) is capable of generating strong feelings of compassion and even identification with the hero who, against all odds, pursues his dream of building a new and better society. The appeal of the socialist realist aesthetic lies in its distance from "the opacity and indeterminacy of agents, from the disturbance of narrative functions, from the floating connotators of mimesis"; it is a "readable aesthetic" because it accounts "for the world, for History, for personal experience saturated with history and for hypostatized individual fantasies."[20] Yet this is the aesthetic that couches its fantastic premise in the language of clarity, verisimilitude, and seriousness, all the while reshaping the real to suit the ideal. In contrast to the concealment of the "unimaginable" in socialist realist writing, Bulgakovian novels are overtly escapist in their generic mix and message, addressing the impossibility of superhuman feats for ordinary Soviet people, catering to their fantasies by endowing the ordinary with magical powers, titillating their suppressed eroticism, and vicariously satisfying their desire for a comfortable, middle-class existence.

Fantasy as a Philosophical Theme

The core concerns and aims of post-Stalinist underground meta-utopias—"reinvigoration and reframing of social imagination," analyzing of the "poverty of existing social scripts available in contemporary Russian culture," seeking "social and political alternatives to a long-standing authoritarian culture"—likewise motivated mainstream fantastic prose in the late Brezhnev era (mid-seventies and early eighties).[21] The interest in alternative modes of thinking and social organization, and the questioning of history's predictability and of the human ability to comprehend reality, are the central issues examined in a strand of fantastic prose that posits the fantastic as a thematic-philosophical concern in a familiar setting of urban fiction. In the "alternative" works of Kim, Anar, and Makanin, the fantastic is an expression of the protagonist's and reader's ambiguous vision (chapter 5). The literary language loses its monosemy; and present, past, and future are fused in the vision of a problematic hero, "unsure of himself and of the society in which he lives, born by a narration that has its own way of reinscribing indeterminancy, polysemy."[22]

In fantastic prose the cultural and political myths supporting the Soviet state begin to disintegrate before our eyes. The rituals of mythologized History, played out in literature and culture to the point where they become Nature (automatic and unchanging), are exposed as such. The utopian thrust of most of this literature is directed back into the prerevolutionary past—the Communist utopia has been rejected or ridiculed, humanity's claims to omnipotence have been questioned and discarded, while the perfect future of Communism appears to be unattainable. Now historical change is shown to stem not from design or will but from fortuitous and unpredictable circumstance. This reevaluation of the epistemological suppositions of Marxism-Leninism, which radically upset the "law-governed pattern" (the notorious *zakonomernost*') of teleological socialist realism, was an important contribution of fantastic prose to changes in Soviet cultural and political discourse.

High and Low: On the
Use of Popular Genres in Fantastic Prose

One of the reasons for the broad controversy generated by the appearance of Chingiz Aitmatov's *Day* (1980) was the novelist's use of science fiction plots. Mystery, fairy tale, and science fiction in post-Stalin literature had their own generic niches; supernatural fantasy was a taboo for Soviet writers; and mainstream novels were generally devoid of the overt mix of high and low genres. Incorporation of a science fiction plot in a work by a "serious" mainstream writer signaled an important shift in literary practice and pointed to new areas of social concern.

The utopian aspirations expressed by fantastic prose as well as its incorporation of popular genres such as mystery, the folktale, and science fiction indicate a degree of continuity between pre- and postrevolutionary Russia. Richard Stites has shown that in prerevolutionary Russian society the onset of rapid industrialization brought with it greater interest in utopian dreaming. Another notable feature of the period, pointed out by Jeffrey Brooks, was the fascination of lower-class readers with *lubok*, folk tales, and the adventure and detective stories published in the penny press.[23]

The use of popular genres did not stop at the level of lower- or middle-class readerships; the elite literature of the time was not at all immune to the rhetorical gestures of popular imagination. The nineteenth-century canon of Russian fiction is rich with examples of the interpenetration of "high" and "low." Gogol's dependence on Ukrainian folklore in *Evenings on a Farm near Dikanka*, Tolstoy's insistence on a biblical simplicity in his later stories, Dostoyevsky's use of a mystery to frame his narratives, or Nikolai Leskov's reliance on *skaz* permeated with the spirit of Russian folklore are just a few illustrations of this phenomenon that immediately come to mind. The social and cultural implications of such rhetorical moves of representation are complex. As Dominick LaCapra has pointed out, elite cultures often employ elements of popular cultures to couch a message of resistance to dominant social forces in a language accessible to broader levels of the population.[24] Although this mechanism of spreading the word through the use of the popular seems to underlie both Russian prerevolutionary fiction and Soviet literature, the reasons for the integration were different in the nineteenth century, in Stalin's Russia, and in the post-Stalin period.

Discussions of high and low culture are problematic, because, even if in early modern Russia the gap between Westernized aristocratic culture and the peasant world may have been wide, it was by no means absolute. Moreover, in the second half of the nineteenth century, as modern classes began to emerge and the ascriptive terms of the estate system began to lose their meaning, popular and elite cultures began to assume new forms, as did the interaction between them.[25] Russian educated elites, "who loved not the state and knew not the people," were consumed with a guilty sense of alienation from "the people," striving for reintegration into a broader community of "Russians."[26] Prerevolutionary Russian fiction catered to this longing, attempting to bridge the gap between the folk and the nobility. This cultural bridging was in part accomplished by a conscious employment of elements of popular culture in elite literature. The philosophical underpinnings of this phenomenon are perhaps best evident in Tolstoy's desire "to learn from the people."

The traumatic experience of war and Stalinism, as well as official policies, created a "quicksand" society (the phrase is Moshe Lewin's) with rapid social mobility, the extermination of traditional elites, and a quite radical realignment of relationships among the classes, as well as between social groups and the state. With the emergence of the Soviet middle class in Stalin's time, the educated public, which had once "learned from the folk," or seen its mission as educating and leading the masses, now came to distance itself from folk culture or manual labor. The use of folk elements in the rhetoric of the thirties was only a means to provide a medium to convey the notion of transcendence, "a neoreligious doctrine of salvation and rebirth," central to the culture of High Stalinism and impossible to express in the language of Christian symbolism. Folklore was used as an enabling language and was abandoned in the postwar forties.[27] Science fiction of the time worked within the strict boundaries of the "near target," and the detective novel as a separate genre lay dormant in Stalin's time, although some of its features resurfaced in socialist realist novels (antigovernment plots, spying, murder, and enemies of the people exposed and punished by vigilant Party members).[28]

In the post-Stalinist period, the notion of "high" literature gave way to "mainstream" literature directed at a much broader public; the public changed by the processes of urbanization, industrialization, and universal education, which blurred the societal and cultural boundaries between working-class and intelligentsia cultures. As a result, rigid generic compartmentalizing of Stalinist literature was succeeded by an overt interaction between various literary trends.

The use of popular genres in mainstream literature of the late Brezhnev era was a continuation of the process of disengagement from the aesthetic of socialist realism, already under way during Khrushchev's Thaw. Addressing the very components of socialist realist dogma, writers in the late fifties and early sixties concerned themselves with the issues of alternative worlds, the dissimulation inherent in the portrayal of reality as it should be, and the abandonment of native traditions brought about by the propagation of the notion of progress. During Khrushchev's Thaw, writers examined these social issues in popular genres of science fiction (Ivan Efremov, the brothers Strugatsky) or fable (Belov, Shukshin). In the fantastic decade writers began to use a much broader variety of popular genres and to incorporate these in mainstream novels. This move served several purposes simultaneously: the product was enlivened and made more appealing to the reader as literature began to examine issues central to their society and culture, and the aesthetic of socialist realism was irreparably undermined.

Speaking to the Middle

Soviet literature of the seventies and eighties had to appeal to a new audience—better educated, more discriminating in taste, and deeply dissatisfied with the general state of affairs in the country.[29] Urbanization, industrialization, and universal secondary education left an indelible mark on Soviet readers and set them apart from their prerevolutionary counterparts. By the sixties, observers spoke of a Soviet middle class, and it was, indeed, to the "middle" that writers ordinarily spoke. Moreover, it was the Soviet middle classes who, beginning in the late seventies, began to express strong discontent with the status quo and frustration with the Soviet leadership.

Economic slowdown, environmental despoliation, political corruption, and an aging and inept leadership combined to create a widespread sense of stagnation and drift. The political and social climate of the late Brezhnev era was marked by a gradual erosion of confidence in the Soviet regime within the broader society, and in Brezhnev's political leadership within the broader elite.[30] Under Stalin and Khrushchev the ability of the Soviet leadership to deliver substantial improvements in mass consumption and the growing level of economic welfare led to the congruence of elite and popular values and overall social and political stability—what Vera Dunham has so aptly called the Big Deal.[31] Under Brezhnev, however, a gap emerged between expectations and the capacity of the system to meet them. According to some scholars, Soviet society before Gorbachev was exhibiting potential for serious sociopolitical instability, with stagnation of living standards, declining opportunities for upward mobility, increases in mortality rates combined, and the rise of ethno-nationalism.[32]

Discontent grew, and spread, as society also "began to talk to itself" through informal, horizontal means of communication and as growing contact with the West, as well as with Eastern Europe, fostered perceptions of relative deprivation.[33] Significantly, it was the Soviet middle class that most strongly experienced feelings of pessimism and angst about the future.[34] It was also this stratum that began to formulate reform agendas, and to communicate them cautiously, but insistently, in specialized journals, at academic seminars, and "through channels" in the bureaucracy.[35] In fact, some scholars have argued that before Gorbachev the Soviet Union may have been acquiring the rudiments of a civil society. As Robert C. Tucker has shown, for example, in Khrushchev's time, and later under Brezhnev, a "no-longer-wholly-regimented society" evolved in Soviet Russia, a society "still closely connected with the state, but no longer its mere tool." In this process, the Stalinist period's "monologue of the state with itself" gave way to "a dialogue between state and society."[36] This dialogic view is based on the acknowledgment of a powerful and self-aware middle class acting through informal horizontal associations, as well as on the presence of a large "marginalized" stratum and a significant second economy (providing alternative access to income and status) before Gorbachev came to power.

But who were the members of this Soviet middle class?[37] The boundaries between blue collar and white collar (*rabochie* and *sluzhashchie*, in official Soviet terminology) were porous and marked by several gradations.[38] Richard Stites has shown, too, that a semiofficial "popular culture" brought together elements of the blue-collar work force and "employees" in a shared appreciation of certain types of music and dance.[39] Most important, as Mary McAuley and Viktor Zaslavsky have pointed out, the vast Soviet middle class created by industrialization, urbanization, and education may have been the raw material for a new civil society, but it was also a uniquely Soviet middle class, one shaped, and perhaps distorted, by the policies of the redistributive state.[40] The core of this class was made up of skilled workers, engineers, and scientists who were employed in the military and the space and nuclear industries and enjoyed higher salaries, better housing, and improved medical care. The "state-dependent" middle class, whether employed as engineers in factories, or history teachers in secondary schools, was overwhelmingly loyal to the core values of the regime.[41] Yet increasingly available information about the outside world created status anxiety as well as aspirations to what came to be called, under Gorbachev, a normal standard of living.

Thus, a rather variegated, but also highly dependent middle class felt growing frustration with the economic downturn and political stagnation of the early eighties. Its consumption patterns and expectations had changed profoundly. New patterns of communication were emerging, but the types of association common to a civil society were virtually absent. The concerns of this group conjoined the personal and the political. However, while social agendas were under consideration, no program of reform united all elements of this middle class. As a result, people's hopes and expectations shifted to the private realm, the move that coincided with important "creeping innovations."[42] These innovations included the loosening of controls over religion and culture, where the limits of the permissible were gradually blurred. A quest for alternative sources of values led to a revival of religious activity. Nostalgia for greater order and discipline and growing social conservatism were yet other responses to the general demoralization. The fear of an impending nuclear catastrophe exacerbated the general feeling of pessimism characteristic of some segments of Soviet society before perestroika.[43]

Literature in this period both reflected and contributed to this crisis of confidence in the leadership's ability to find solutions to the country's cultural and sociopolitical problems. More important, it helped formulate agendas (if only implicitly), provide role models, and introduce a new vocabulary. Literature, like society, was shaped by the Soviet redistributive state, rather than by market forces.[44] The print market had been narrowly circumscribed since the October Revolution, and writers negotiated primarily with journals and publishers, all working under the constraints of censorship. But now the public's actual, rather than the invented, cultural preferences began to be validated by the regime.[45] Reader preferences exerted an influence, and, according to readership studies, it was the middle classes who were the principal consumers of mainstream literature.[46] As long as the distinctive relationship persisted between writer, printed word, and audience—a relationship mediated by the redistributive state—the dialogue created and sustained by mainstream Soviet literature continued to contribute to the process of reimagining the Soviet present.

From Fantasy to Glasnost

With the advent of glasnost in the mid-eighties, the language of fantasy and utopian dreaming in which Soviet writers had conducted their dialogue with the state was replaced in publicistic prose by direct expressions of dissatisfaction with social problems and an examination of the failed promises of the myth of a Communist state. Meanwhile, alternative writers continued to use devices of fantasy in fiction, reinvigorating in the process the literary language and social imagination.

Gorbachev's thaw (1985–1991) was unique for Russian literature in that it was marked by the simultaneous appearance of a virtual flood of previously unavailable material—novels, plays, poetry, memoirs, and critical, historical, and philosophical monographs by Russian, Soviet, Western, and émigré authors, written before the Revolution, half a century ago, a decade ago, or after Gorbachev came to power. The literary production under glasnost can be loosely divided into: (1) works written under the first Thaw, revised or continued under Gorbachev, and focusing on "blank spots" in history; (2) publicistic literature of glasnost—fiction by established authors, written under Gorbachev and focusing on the ills of Soviet society; (3) works by alternative writers, with their careful attention to form, penchant for revealing the sexual and psychological "underground" of their characters, and deliberate avoidance of direct social messages.

Writers of the "Thaw" Under Glasnost

As was common in the works of the first Thaw, novels written during the glasnost era that focus on "blank spots" in history—such as Anatolii Rybakov's *Children of the Arbat* (*Deti Arbata,* 1987),[47] Vladimir Dudintsev's *White Garments* (*Belye odezhdy,* 1987),[48] and Anatolii Pristavkin's *A Golden Cloud Spent the Night* (*Nochevala tuchka zolotaia,* 1987)[49]— trace the roots of the hardships experienced by Soviet society to the time of Stalin. Vasilii Grossman's novel *Life and Fate* (*Zhizn' i sud'ba,* 1988) portrays life in the camps and provides explicit comparisons between Nazism and Stalinism.[50] Sergei Zalygin's *After the Storm* (*Posle buri,* 1980–1985) and the work of contemporary playwright Mikhail Shatrov, on the other hand, questioned the wisdom of early Soviet policy before Stalin as well.[51] All the above works were received in the Soviet Union as major cultural events of glasnost, and had fought a long battle with censors to reach the reader.[52]

Overall, affinity with the ideals of the first Thaw was a notable feature of these works of glasnost, since most of them were begun under Khrushchev. Yet these novels went much further in their overt criticism of the Soviet system and focused more directly on the Soviet intelligentsia than their counterparts in the first Thaw. The glasnost novels of Rybakov, Zalygin, and Dudintsev traced various threads in the intricate web of lies and injustices that led to the current collapse of social and moral ideals. Moreover, like works of the first Thaw, some of these novels were, in effect, reactions to the canon of socialist realism, where the formulae of the canon were often simply adjusted to the new demands of glasnost. Dudintsev's *White Garments* is a good example of such hybrid construction, for here the canon of socialist realism is adjusted to accommodate a new political message.[53] The difficulties in adapting to the political demands of the moment become obvious in the seemingly unintended intermixing of phenomena from different temporal periods in one work.

Publicists

In the period just before Gorbachev's thaw, the ideals of Communism (the backbone of socialist realist writing) had been examined in a general way—and found wanting—through the use of legendary plots, supernatural fantasy, and science fiction devices. Under glasnost, publicists examined and criticized the contents of specific myths in narratives approaching, in their immediacy and intensity of presentation, journalistic accounts. Conventional devices of fantasy were mostly abandoned, and these narratives were organized around distinct mythological anchors. Three major overlapping areas of concern in publicistic fiction were: how and why it all went wrong (the historical perspective—the old myths); the specifics of the catastrophic situation in the country (the contemporary perspective); and the possibility of regeneration (the formulation of new myths). In *Day* (1980), for example, Aitmatov had addressed troubling social issues in the language of fantasy—by means of science fiction plots and legends; but paraphrasing through fantasy resulted in considerable ambiguity of representation, and reception, of Aitmatov's celebrated novel. In *The Execution Block* (1986), on the other hand, Aitmatov discusses the same issues directly. The novel offers a journalistic, almost sensational portrayal of the ills of contemporary Soviet society. The tone here is openly didactic; it is a sermon to the reader about one's moral responsibilities in life. Yet Aitmatov places his account of a social catastrophe in the context of the story of Christ, which he uses as a directive for the creation of a new and better community of people.

Most publicistic writers had written works of fantastic prose and that connection could still be felt.[54] Under glasnost, however, they were offered, for the first time, an opportunity to present possible solutions to the problems plaguing their society.[55] The particularistic, antimodernist mythologizing prose of the village writers served as a convenient breeding ground for the formation of new myths, now with a specific focus on ethnic identity. As Thomas Venclova has pointed out, many writers of the glasnost period attempted to offer traditions and myths of their ethnic group as a palliative to the ubiquitous lack of spirituality.[56] According to Venclova, this new mythology was often an artificial construct, a patchwork of isolated fragments of past cultures.[57] In this process, nationalistic concerns were elevated at the expense of the former myth of the multinational unity. As a result, some novels of the period expressed intense anti-urban, nationalistic, and anti-Semitic sentiments.[58]

The openly nationalistic flavor of some glasnost novels, stories, and public (and private) statements by such well-established and respected authors as Rasputin, Astaf'ev, and Belov had prompted some scholars to view the Russophile movement in the Soviet Union of the late eighties as offering "the only cohesive (if not coherent) philosophy, based on a return to an idealized, authoritarian past, freed from the 'bankrupt' schemes of both Westerners and the ethnic minorities, both industry and collectivization, both Brezhnev and Gorbachev."[59]

Alternative Writers

As formidable as the publicistic position appeared to be, one cannot discount the healthy counterweight of alternative literature, concerned with roughly the same issues but professing no ready-made solutions to the problems of Soviet society. This was a position quite different from that espoused by proponents of ultranationalism (Russian or any other kind). In contrast to publicistic prose, with its portrayal of an impending day of reckoning for humanity—a situation blamed now on various policies of the Soviet state and now on particular ethnic groups—a direct moralizing tendency was notably absent in alternative literature. Alternative literature of the Gorbachev period experienced no drastic rupture with the previous mode of representation. Some alternative writers active in the fantastic decade, such as Kim and Makanin, continued, if more intensely and openly, to investigate the limits of human perceptions of reality and the very process of mythmaking. Younger writers (Narbikova, Tolstaya) joined the ranks of alternative literature under Gorbachev and, like their counterparts before glasnost, conducted the search for the "mechanics of illusion" on the level of language and narrative structure. Fantasy remained at the heart of this fiction. Yet post-1985 alternative writing also underwent significant changes. Such writers as Sorokin, Erofeev, Popov, and Narbikova gradually abandoned even partial dependence on mimesis in their work, examining the relativity of meaning in representation and rejecting moralism in literature. The roots of this transformation in literary practice, of the final escape from the strictures of socialist realism in Russian literature, can be found in the literature of Khrushchev's Thaw.

Notes

1. This admission of the need to expand the traditional mode of socialist realism was the major theme of the speech by Georgii Markov at the Seventh Congress of the Writers' Union. See "Sovetskaia literatura v bor'be za kommunizm i ee zadachi v svete reshenii XXV-go s"ezda KPSS." *Doklad pervogo sekretaria*

pravleniia Soiuza pisatelei SSSR G.M. Markova, in *Literaturnaia gazeta* 27 (July 1, 1981): 2.

2. See, for example, Chingiz Aitmatov's formulation of his own style in the introduction to *The Day Lasts More than a Hundred Years* (Bloomington: Indiana University Press, 1983), p. xix.

3. On the emergence of Chernyshevsky's model of perfection and on its subsequent transformation into a new gospel for Russian radical youth, see Irina Paperno, *Chernyshevsky and the Age of Realism: A Study in the Semiotics of Behavior* (Stanford: Stanford University Press, 1988).

4. The issue of Platonov's influence on contemporary Soviet writers is a complex one. Before glasnost, collections of Platonov's prose were published in 1965, 1966, and 1977. It is safe to assume, therefore, a lesser degree of influence before 1965. One should not forget, however, Solzhenitsyn's letter to the membership of the Union of Soviet Writers (at the Fourth Congress of Writers in 1967), in which he mentions Platonov's name in a long list of great and neglected Soviet writers. This presupposes some familiarity with Platonov's work, and, in the case of Solzhenitsyn's village prose pieces, one can argue a certain degree of influence of Platonov's themes and ideas. Sergei Zalygin, writing in defense of Platonov in 1970, highlights similarities between Platonov's work and his own. See Sergei Zalygin, "Skazki realista i realizm skazochnika" in *Literaturnye zaboty*, 3d ed. (Moscow: Sovetskaia Rossiia, 1982), p. 102.

5. For in-depth discussion of Fyodorov and Platonov see Ayleen Teskey, *Platonov and Fyodorov: The Influence of Christian Philosophy on a Soviet Writer* (Amersham, England: Avebury Publishing, 1982); Mikhail Geller, *Andrei Platonov v poiskakh shchast'ia* (Paris: YMCA Press, 1982); Thomas Seifrid provides an interesting view of the impact of Fyodorov's, Aleksandr Bogdanov's and Vladimir Solovyov's work on Platonov in *Andrei Platonov: Uncertainties of Spirit* (Cambridge University Press, 1992), see esp. pp. 20–24. See also Ludmila Koehler, *N. F. Fyodorov: The Philosophy of Action* (Pittsburgh: Institute for the Human Sciences, 1979); Stephen Lukashevich, *N. F. Fedorov (1828–1903): A Study in Russian Eupsychian and Utopian Thought* (Newark: University of Delaware Press, 1977); and George M. Young, Jr., *Nikolai F. Fedorov: An Introduction* (Belmont, Mass.: Nordland Publishing, 1979). In his monograph on the theme of apocalypse in Russian fiction, David Bethea pinpoints shared ideas in Fyodorov's philosophy and Platonov's *Chevengur* (written in 1928 and1929). Those ideas include "the emphasis on genuine brotherhood, the . . . preoccupation with death, the positive sublimation of the sex drive ('positive chastity'), the responsibility toward parents, the . . . need for movement toward a worthy goal, the skepticism toward any society that separates the 'thinkers' from the 'doers,' the belief that Russia provides the ideal historical and geopolitical setting for an undertaking of the grand task" (Bethea, *Shape of Apocalypse*, p. 161).

6. See more on this in Eric Naiman, "Historectomies: On the Metaphysics of Reproduction in a Utopian Age," in Jane T. Costlow, Stephanie Sandler, Judith Vowles, eds., *Sexuality and the Body in Russian Culture* (Stanford: Stanford University Press, 1993), pp. 255–276. Fyodorov's ideas on the unlimited human potential and resurrection were instrumental in the creation of the theory of bio-

logical reconstruction in the 1920s. The preservation of Lenin's body is a direct result of the belief that humanity will at some point be able to resurrect its great dead leaders. Leonid Krasin, one of the organizers of Lenin's funeral, was a staunch believer in biological reconstruction (Related in M. Os'minskii, "Kritich-eskie stat'i i zametki," *Proletarskaia revoliutsiia* 1 [1931]: 149–150). See more on Krasin's role in Lenin's burial and on Fyodorov's disciples (the Biocosmists, whose slogan was "Immortalism and Interplanetism" and who included in their ranks the rocket scientist Konstantin Tsiolkovsky, the earth scientist V. K. Vernad-sky, and Leonid Krasin) in Stites, *Revolutionary Dreams*, pp. 120, 170.

7. The "organic view" of contemporary Soviet fiction and its antecedents in Russian literature are discussed in Charles Rougle's paper "Noospheric Notions: The Search for Harmony in Recent Soviet Literature," delivered at the Texas Tech University Conference on Contemporary Soviet Literature, October 1990. See also Charles Rougle, "On the 'Fantastic Trend' in Recent Soviet Prose," *Slavic and East European Journal*, Fall 1990, pp. 308–321.

8. *Byt* prose (from the Russian word *byt*, "everyday existence") refers to post-Thaw works of literature focusing on the everyday lives of ordinary people. The term village prose (or country prose) refers to a genre of post-Thaw literature that deals sympathetically with rural life and its traditions.

9. Clark, *Soviet Novel*, pp. 10, 252.

10. Ibid., pp. 91–135.

11. Clowes, *Russian Experimental Fiction*, p. 23.

12. Stites, *Revolutionary Dreams*, p. 4.

13. Jameson, *Marxism and Form*, p. 142.

14. Geoffrey Hosking, *Beyond Socialist Realism: Soviet Fiction since Ivan Denisovich* (New York: Holmes and Meier, 1980), p. 18.

15. Patrick L. McGuire, *Red Stars: Political Aspects of Soviet Science Fiction* (Ann Arbor: UMI Research Press), pp. 15–16; Darko Suvin, *Metamorphoses of Science Fiction: On the Poetics and History of a Literary Genre* (New Haven: Yale University Press, 1979), pp. 264–265.

16. Douglas Weiner, *Models of Nature: Ecology, Conservation, and Cultural Revolution in Soviet Russia* (Bloomington: Indiana University Press, 1988), p. 234.

17. Ibid., p. 235.

18. See more on this in David Gillespie, *Valentin Rasputin and Soviet Russian Village Prose* (London: Modern Humanities Research Association, 1986).

19. By a true utopia I mean a narrative that is written in the tradition of previous utopian literary work, that depicts an ideal society, and that advocates (or is taken to advocate) the realization of that society (formulated in Gary Saul Morson, *The Boundaries of Genre: Dostoyevsky's Diary of a Writer and the Traditions of Literary Utopia* [Evanston: Northwestern University Press, 1981], p. 74).

20. Robin, *Socialist Realism*, p. 64.

21. Clowes, *Russian Experimental Fiction*, pp. x, 5.

22. Robin, *Socialist Realism*, p. 266.

23. Stites, *Revolutionary Dreams*, pp. 30, 31. For more on the reading preferences of lower-class readers in the nineteenth century, see Jeffrey Brooks, *When*

Russia Learned to Read: Literacy and Popular Literature, 1861–1917 (Princeton: Princeton University Press, 1985). For a discussion of the same issue both in the nineteenth and twentieth centuries, as well as for a good bibliography of Russian sources, see V. A. Kozlov, *Kul'turnaia revoliutsiia i krest'ianstvo, 1921–1927* (Moscow: Nauka, 1983), pp. 160–173.

24. See Dominick LaCapra, *History and Criticism* (Ithaca: Cornell University Press, 1985), particularly chapter 3, "Is Everyone a Mentalite Case? Transference and the 'Culture' Concept," pp. 71–94.

25. And yet, traditional understandings persisted in the conceptual lexicon. In the second half of the nineteenth century the critical intelligentsia (much of the educated, privileged public) had defined itself in opposition to the state. It was "society," or *obshchestvennost'*, lined up against "the authorities" or *vlast'*. In this struggle, "society" included the *narod*, or folk, for the educated minority "spoke for" the masses. However, *narod* was culturally quite distinct from society; even after the erosion of estate categories the social markers were abundant and clear. See Edith W. Clowes, Samuel D. Kassow, James L. West, eds., *Between Tsar and People: Educated Society and the Quest for Public Identity in Late Imperial Russia* (Princeton: Princeton U. Press, 1992).

26. Stites, *Revolutionary Dreams*, 24.

27. Clark, *Soviet Novel*, 151.

28. See Natalia Il'ina, Arkadii Adamov, "Detective Novels: A Game and Life," *Soviet Literature* 3 (1975): 142–150; Norbert Franz, *Moskauer Mordgeschichten: Der Russisch-Sowjetische Krimi 1953–1983* (Mainz: Liber, 1988); Viktor Terras, *Handbook of Russian Literature* (New Haven: Yale University Press, 1985), p. 100.

29. The classic statement on this is by Moshe Lewin, *The Gorbachev Phenomenon* (Berkeley: University of California Press, 1988). A still useful text is James Bater, *The Soviet Scene: A Geographical Perspective* (London: Edward Arnold, 1989), esp. pp. 244–281. See also Ben Eklof, *Soviet Briefing: Gorbachev and the Reform Period* (Boulder: Westview Press, 1989), esp. pp. 108–132; and pp. 172–187.

30. Gail W. Lapidus, *Gorbachev's Reforms: Redefining the Relationship of State and Society* (Washington D.C.: Wilson Center, Kennan Institute for Advanced Russian Studies, 1988), p. 6. Lapidus further points to the two mutually reinforcing trends that contributed to the process of stagnation under Brezhnev: "an objective deterioration in the performance of the Soviet economy, which brought in its wake a mounting array of social and political problems, and a growing mood of demoralization within the Soviet elite, reflecting a subtle but profound shift in perceptions of regime performance" (pp. 6–7).

31. Gail W. Lapidus, "Social Trends" in Robert F. Byrnes, ed., *After Brezhnev* (Bloomington: Indiana University Press, 1983), pp. 186–249. See more on the political stability in Stalin's time in Seweryn Bialer, *Stalin's Successors: Leadership, Stability, and Change in the Soviet Union* (Cambridge: Cambridge University Press, 1980), especially the chapter on "The Mature Stalinist System," pp. 9–28; and Vera S. Dunham, *In Stalin's Time*, pp. 3–33.

32. On the question of nationalism in the USSR before Gorbachev see David Lane, *Soviet Economy and Society* (New York: New York University Press, 1985),

pp. 202–240 and George W. Simmonds, ed., *Nationalism in the USSR and Eastern Europe in the Era of Brezhnev and Kosygin* (Detroit: University of Detroit Press, 1977), particularly Teresa Rakowska-Harmstone, "The Study of Ethnic Politics in the USSR," pp. 20–37. See also Linda J. Cook, *The Soviet Social Contract and Why It Failed: Welfare Policy and Workers' Politics from Brezhnev to Yeltsin* (Cambridge, Mass.: Harvard University Press, 1993).

33. S. Frederick Starr, "Soviet Union: A Civil Society," *Foreign Policy* 70 (Spring 1988): 31–36; and " Civil Society and the Impediments to Reform," in William Green Miller, ed., *Toward a More Civil Society? The USSR under Mikhail Sergeevich Gorbachev* (New York: Harper and Row, 1989), pp. 304–309; see also Eklof, *Soviet Briefing*, p. 44.

34. John Bushnell, "The 'New Soviet Man' Turns Pessimist," in Stephen Cohen, Alexander Rabinowitch and Robert Sharlet, eds., *The Soviet Union since Stalin* (Bloomington: Indiana University Press, 1980), pp. 179–199; Barbara B. Green, *The Dynamics of Russian Politics: A Short History* (Westport, Conn.: Praeger, 1994), pp. 77–92.

35. Joel C. Moses, "Democratic Reform in the Gorbachev Era: Dimensions of Reform in the Soviet Union, 1986–1989," *Russian Review* 48.3 (July 1989): 235–247.

36. Robert Tucker, *Political Culture and Leadership in Soviet Russia: From Lenin to Gorbachev* (New York: Norton, 1987), pp. 169–170

37. It has sometimes been argued that the Brezhnev regime catered to the blue-collar work force and that the core values of the Soviet regime (patriotism, law and order, the welfare state) excluded, hence alienated, the "middle." In this version, the bulk of the Soviet middle class resembled the old intelligentsia in opposition. Thus, a triangular relationship of *vlast'*, *narod*, and intelligentsia continued to define Soviet political culture and to shape reading patterns. According to this analysis, the Soviet middle class paid more attention to samizdat and dissident prose than to mainstream Soviet literature. See, for example, Green, *Dynamics of Russian Politics*, p. 97; also Cook, *Soviet Social Contract*, p. 4.

38. See David Lane, *Soviet Society under Perestroika*, rev. ed. (London: Routledge, 1992).

39. Richard Stites, *Russian Popular Culture: Entertainment and Society since 1900* (Cambridge: Cambridge University Press, 1992).

40. Viktor Zaslavsky, "From Redistribution to Marketization: Social and Attitudinal Change in Post-Soviet Russia," in *The New Russia: Troubled Transformation* (Boulder: Westview, 1994), pp. 115–142; Mary McAuley, *Soviet Politics, 1917–1991* (New York: Oxford University Press, 1992), pp. 94–95, 120–123.

41. Recent public opinion polls have convincingly demonstrated that a highly diverse society exists in Russia in terms of its values and orientations and that this diversity exists vertically, but also regionally; that this public as a whole shows a commitment to a social welfare state, to the diffusion of political power and to economic reform simultaneously, and that a large minority still adhere to the ideals of the Russian Revolution. See Arthur H. Miller, William M. Reisinger and Vicki L. Hesli, eds., *Public Opinion and Regime Change: The New Politics of Post-Soviet Societies* (Boulder: Westview Press, 1993).

42. Timothy Colton, *The Dilemma of Reform in the Soviet Union*, rev. ed. (New York: Council on Foreign Relations, 1986), p. 19.

43. See more on this in David E. Powell, "A Troubled Society," in James Cracraft, ed., *The Soviet Union Today: An Interpretive Guide* (Chicago: University of Chicago Press, 1983), pp. 317–331.

44. By controlling all resources and in making choices about how to redistribute economic resources, a redistributive state is capable of shaping society much more quickly and directly than in mixed economies (Zaslavsky, "From Redistribution to Marketization").

45. S. Frederick Starr, *Red and Hot: The Fate of Jazz in the Soviet Union, 1917–1980* (New York: Limelight Editions, 1983), p. 318.

46. See, for example, Jenny Brine, "Reading as a Leisure Pursuit in the USSR," in Jenny Brine, Maureen Perrie, and Andrew Sutton, eds., *Home, School and Leisure in the Soviet Union* (London: Allen and Unwin, 1981), p. 264; see also Valeriia Stel'makh, "Kakaia kniga u vas v rukakh," *Literaturnoe obozrenie* 5 (1973): 100–104; A. G. Levinson, "Starye knigi, novye chitateli," *Sotsiologicheskie issledovaniia* 3 (1987): 43–49; S. Shvedov, "Literaturnaia kritika i literatura chitatelei," *Voprosy literatury* 5 (1988): 3–30.

47. *Druzhba narodov* 4–6 (1987).

48. *Neva* 1–4 (1987). For an excellent reading of the novel see Natasha Kolchevska, "White Garments: Retrieving the Past through Science and Literature," Studies in Comparative Communism 21.3/4 (Autumn/Winter 1988): 275–282.

49. *Znamia* 3–4 (1987). For additional information on the history of the novel's publication see Pristavkin's interview with the reporter of *Smena*, Igor' D'iakov, published as an introduction to the book edition (Moscow: Knizhnaia Palata, 1988), pp. 5–11.

50. *Oktiabr'* 1–4 (1988).

51. *Druzhba narodov* 4–5 (May-June 1980); 5 (May 1982); 7–9 (July–September 1985). For immediate reactions on the novel see: Aleksandr Korol'kov, "Zrelost' zrelosti (Filosofskii roman S.P. Zalygina)," *Sever* 5 (1986): 107–113; Nikolai Koniaev, "Vtoraia zhizn' Petra Kornilova," *Zvezda* 7 (1983): 199–201; Aleksandra Spal', "Bremia sud'by i nadezhdy," *Oktiabr'* 3 (1986): 201–203; P. Nikolaev, "Trudnoe vremia: Liudi, sud'by," *Literaturnaia gazeta*, March 30, 1983, p. 4; V. Piskunov and S. Piskunova, "Mezhdu byt' i ne byt'," *Novyi mir* 5 (1986): 238–246; Aleksei Gorshenin, *Sibirskie Ogni* 11 (1982): 168–170; A. Nuikin, "Ot mozaiki k panorame," *Literaturnoe obozrenie* 12 (1982): 50–53; Gennadii Murikov, "Poedinok s sud'boi," *Zvezda* 5 (1986): 191–200; and Evgenii Sergeev, "Poisk schastliveishego sluchaia," *Znamia* (3, 1986): 205–215. See also Yitzhak M. Brudny, "Between Liberalism and Nationalism: The Case of Sergei Zalygin" *Studies in Comparative Communism* 21.3/4 (Autumn/Winter 1988): 331–340.

52. See more on the difficulties of publishing some of these works in *RLRB*, no. 505, p. 88 (Julia Wishnevsky).

53. Kolchevska, "White Garments," p. 277.

54. In some cases the link is obvious in the sequential character of a given writer's plots. For example, Valentin Rasputin's *Fire* (1985) is obviously a continu-

ation of the story begun in *Farewell to Matera* (1976), Iurii Bondarev's *The Game* is the third part of a trilogy about intelligentsia in the Soviet Union, while Chingiz Aitmatov's *Execution Block* (1986) is closely linked to *Day*, both formally and thematically.

55. Several works published in the West address the issue of publicistic literature under glasnost. See Gerald M. Easter and Janet E. Mitchell, "Cultural Reform in the Soviet Union" in *Toward a More Civil Society?*, pp. 79–119; N. N. Sneidman, *Soviet Literature in the 1980s: Decade of Transition* (Toronto: University of Toronto Press, 1989).

56. "Ethnic Identity and the Nationality Issue in Contemporary Soviet Literature," *Studies in Comparative Communism* 21.3/4:322.

57. Ibid.

58. See, for example, Viktor Astaf'ev, "Pechal'nyi detektiv," *Oktiabr'* 1 (1986) and Vasilii Belov, "Vse vperedi," *Nash sovremennik* 8 (1986).

59. Nancy Condee and Vladimir Padunov, "The Frontiers of Soviet Culture: Reaching the Limits?," *Harriman Institute Forum* 5 (May 1988): 3.

3

Fantastic Prose as an Escape from the Literature of Purpose

Khrushchev's "secret speech" on Stalin at the Twentieth Congress demolished the very foundations of the beliefs on which [the Soviet educated public, such as] Sinyavsky and his contemporaries had been reared. . . . The only alternative to despair or cynicism was to set about immediately on the search for a substitute. . . . The collapse of the old had been as total as its continuing pretension to undivided predominance. . . .

—**Max Hayward, introduction to**
A Voice from the Chorus *by Andrei Sinyavsky*

ROM ITS PLACE ON THE LITERARY PERIPHERY, fantastic prose moved into the forefront of Soviet literature in the mid-seventies and early eighties. The social and cultural developments contributing to this move included the de-Stalinization of the Thaw, the dissident trials of the sixties, social changes, and the vicissitudes of the economy, all of which occasioned a growing pessimism about the Soviet future in the Brezhnev era. A questioning of official values, after the brief surge of hope of the Thaw, was important for shaping a literary public, be it the common reader, the writer, or the critic whose job it was to assess the development of Soviet literature.[1]

In literature these developments were responsible for the emergence of themes and literary techniques that stretched the formulae of socialist realism to their limit, and often went far beyond. But the move away from the Literature of Purpose (to use Andrei Sinyavsky's term for socialist realism) started in the polemical and idealistic literature of the late fifties and early sixties. This was a time marked by "a profound revaluation of many simplistic perceptions about individuality, a time of rehabilitation of national history, and of renewed interest in the people and their historical fate."[2] The spiritual crisis experienced by the intelligentsia after the revelations of the Twentieth Party Congress (1956) led to a reassessment of Stalinist ideology.

The ideal of post-1956 literature was true Communism, to be achieved through a rejection of "falsehood" (a euphemism for Stalinism and its repugnant outgrowths). One's attitude toward truth (whether to reveal or conceal it) separated society into conservatives and liberals. In their vision of socialism with a human face, the liberal writers were inspired by an upsurge of socialist idealism and Marxist humanitarianism. Solzhenitsyn's call "not to live by the Lie" *(zhyt' ne po lzhi)* helped to shape the moral climate of the sixties and underscored the importance of the writer in Soviet society. As one historian of the period put it, "writers seemed suddenly to be giving voice to all those who for so long had kept silent because they had no public forum for discussing political ideas, for criticizing the institutions of Soviet life, for a radical and searching examination of all the afflictions of Soviet society."[3]

Post-Stalin Soviet literature went through a series of transformations. It would be overly ambitious to try to present an exhaustive picture of this literature in one short chapter. To find out the springs that fed fantastic prose it is necessary only to focus on several specific trends: Soviet science fiction, which in the Thaw burst upon the literary scene out of the relative obscurity of the thirties and forties; "village" prose; "youth" prose; and "urban" *(gorodskaia)* prose, with its distinctive *byt* branch.[4]

Alternative Worlds and Literary Experiments: Science Fiction of the Thaw

In the late fifties and early sixties Soviet prose was still firmly entrenched in the canonical language of socialist realism. In the decade after the Twentieth Party Congress, Soviet science fiction experienced its second great age (after the boom of the twenties).[5] It was a genre rich in tradition, encompassing an increasing range of subjects, with a highly engaged readership.[6] Characteristically for post-Stalinist literature, the main theme of Soviet science fiction of the late fifties and early sixties was a rejection of the wrong road taken on the way to Communism and a revival of fundamental socialist ideals. Ivan Efremov, the dean of Soviet science fiction, revived the classical utopian and socialist vision of Marx and Chernyshevsky and looked forward to a "unified, affluent, humanist, classless, and stateless world."[7] Efremov's *Andromeda Nebula* (*Tumannost' Andromedy*, 1958) portrays a perfect society on Earth.[8] However, the dynamism of his utopia does not come from lengthy descriptions of Efremov's vision of social per-fection; rather, it is generated out of a conflict with the perfect society's own past.

Two parallel plots in the novel serve to illustrate this conflict: a story of a traveling spaceship and a tale of an experiment to establish contact with a planet located many light years away. Both plots focus on the clash between a static model of happiness and the dynamism of imper-fection. The bulk of the novel is devoted to a description of the gradual road to perfection traveled by earthly civilization. Society, the protago-nist of Efremov's utopia, is presented in its development from a state of spontaneity to that of consciousness. However, the author's utopia evolves in constant tension with its past. In Efremov's anthropomorphic system all life in the universe is similar; the protagonists, bent on bring-ing happiness to other worlds, must constantly struggle with innumer-able variants of their own and society's past. Space travelers witness al-ternate societal models on their voyages. The "perfect people" of utopia discuss their planet's unhappy past, and the vestiges of that past are found in the thoughts and acts of the perfect people themselves. The goal of Efremov's utopians is to mold the environment to suit the sacred ideals of Communism: equality, creative and personal freedom, and lib-eration from all material necessity. The moral implications of such a co-ercion of nature do not enter into Efremov's picture of a brave new world. In this sense, Efremov's work of the late fifties is typical of the op-timistic literature of the Thaw period, with its belief in the proximity of the ideal.[9]

Efremov's work engendered and satisfied a desire for a literature that would assimilate the languages of social science and philosophy. The potential pluralism of the future, hinted at in *Andromeda Nebula* and elaborated in the author's other science fiction works, was a signif-icant assertion in the late fifties and early sixties.[10] In their science fic-tion of the time the Strugatsky brothers also examine possibilities of variant future societies. But the inevitable coercion that an advanced technological society exerts over unsuspecting "dissidents" is central to their writing. If Efremov's utopia is the utopia of perfect people, the Strugatskys' society of the future is peopled with men of action. The perfect society forms an avant-garde of perfect people who reeducate entire worlds of illiterate aliens. In the process, the perfect people have to adapt to and adopt the language of "alien" cultures. Russia's own past is reevaluated and dramatized in the Strugatskys' utopia. As Isaiah Berlin has pointed out, the debate over the dilemma of means and ends is "the deepest and most agonizing problem that torments the revolutionary movements of our own day in all the continents of the world." In Russia, Lenin's policy toward the uneducated masses was anticipated by the Nihilist faction of the Populist movement, who believed that "the educated cannot listen to the uneducated and ignorant masses" and that "the masses must be rescued by whatever means were available, if necessary against their own foolish wishes, by guile, or fraud, or violence if need be."[11] The Strugatskys examine the relationship between a conscious avant-garde and the ignorant masses, stressing the moral implications of benevolent coercion. In his quest to improve an alien society the "perfect man" (and it is always a male hero) uses the language of that society, thereby becoming a ruthless man of action, reminiscent in some respects of the leather-jacketed heroes of the Soviet literature of the twenties.

The Strugatskys' work of the sixties looked upon coercion as a necessary evil. In *It Is Hard to Be God (Trudno byt' bogom)* the perfect people weather the transition into men of action with relative ease.[12] A corrupt society of aliens is gradually and successfully transformed into a more just world, and benevolent reformers enjoy a double life, full of risk and adventure. The latter are Soviet superheroes, capable of changing the course of history of an alien civilization. The plans these superheroes entertain for the alien planet are never questioned in the novel; the result will undoubtedly be personal and creative emancipation, the brotherhood of all people, and liberation from material want.

Soviet science fiction of the Thaw was still the Literature of Purpose. Its proclaimed ideal was the establishment of a just order in the universe, but the application of force that this change necessarily involves was not questioned. If the Stalinist novel of the forties described life as it should be, Soviet science fiction of the Thaw projected the desirable into universal time and infinite space. Like the Stalinist novel, Soviet science fiction was filled with optimism and hope for even more daring achievements.

In spite of its obvious debt to the canonical literature of socialist realism, however, Soviet science fiction of the Thaw was singularly important for fantastic prose. The writings of Efremov and the brothers Strugatsky were a first step away from the Literature of Purpose. One indication of this move was the very presence of alternative future societies. A change in locale of the typical Stalinist novel—from the factory and collective farm to the broad vistas of the cosmos—presaged the expansion of the temporal and spatial boundaries of later Soviet literature. Another important change was an issue that these novels addressed for the first time: social coercion as a necessary (and often unnecessary) evil. Finally, Soviet science fiction of the Thaw introduced various literary genres into its overarching model. (In the writings of Ivan Efremov, for example, one can find "whole reaches of the SF tradition: the philosophical story and romantic etude, classic sociological and modern cosmological utopianism.")[13] By moving into new areas of literary exploration Soviet science fiction of the sixties contributed to a diversification of the model of socialist realism. In the 1970s that diversification would lead to a reassessment (and reworking) of the "official method."

Rejection of the "Kolkhoz" Paradise: Village Prose

The Thaw decade also witnessed the emergence of village prose as a variant on the flight from the Literature of Purpose. While the village literature of the thirties and forties, such as Mikhail Sholokhov's *Virgin Soil Upturned* (*Podniataia tselina*, 1933–1959), was basically a justification of collectivization, village prose of the fifties and sixties was sharply critical of Stalin's methods. Of course, this change of attitude was made possible by Khrushchev's policies. The writers of village prose welcomed the program of the (post-Stalin) Party to decentralize authority on the farms, put an end to management from the center, increase investment in agriculture, encourage local initiative, and improve the overall quality of rural life.[14]

Valentin Ovechkin's series of critical sketches *District Routine* (*Raiionnye budni*, 1952–1956) and Efim Dorosh's *Village Diary* (*Derevenskii dnevnik*, 1958–1963) introduced themes that later became trademarks of the trend, such as respect for peasants and traditional culture and a pronounced distrust of bureaucrats. Jurii Kazakov's story *The Smell of Bread* (*Zapakh khleba*, 1961), a typical work of village prose of the Thaw, describes a woman who returns to her native village long after the death of her mother and experiences profound guilt about her abandoned roots. Alexander Solzhenitsyn's *Matrena's Home* (*Matrionin dvor*, 1963) works with a theme that came to define village prose—an old humble peasant woman as the sole keeper of native Russian traditions.

During the Thaw the social, cultural, and psychological split between town and village became, in addition to anti-Stalinism, one of the most visible themes of Soviet literature. It is in the works of the village writers that we find a shift to a literature glorifying the traditional Russian past.[15] The contrast between the future-oriented and high-tempo works of socialist realism and the slow, past-oriented village prose was deliberate and absolute. As Kathleen Parthé has shown, village prose as a literary movement differentiated itself from "kolkhoz" literature by its sense of time and by the value it placed on memory and the past. The *derevenshchiki* "juxtaposed a somewhat idealized 'radiant past' to a wholly compromised 'radiant future' of 'kolkhoz' novels."[16] Village writers successfully revived the rural theme in Russian literature, raising village prose to the status of an important and influential literary trend.

Rebels with a Cause and Ordinary People:
"Youth" Prose and *Byt* Prose

"Youth" writers of the Thaw (published in the sixties mainly by the journal *Yunost'*) worked with language and themes distinctly different from village prose; yet here too one can observe departures from socialist realist norms. Youth prose had a clearly identifiable Purpose, a movement toward a higher self-understanding for its heroes, who tame their rebelliousness and, when confronted with outside challenges, become useful members of society. In Vasilii Aksenov's *Ticket to the Stars* (*Zvezdnyi bilet*, 1961), for example, the troubled teenage hero turns out to be a rebel with a cause when, upon fleeing the world of the capital in search of adventure, he discovers the true meaning of life in devoted service to the people. Like true heroes of socialist realism, Aksenov's rebel is coached by an older and wiser mentor.

Yet protagonists of youth prose hide their exalted ideals under a rugged and laconic Hemingwayesque idiom. The questioning of certitudes, prompted by the revelations of the Twentieth Party Congress, became a necessary component of a new outlook, the inner lives of protagonists assumed greater importance than before, and the confluence between the authorial point of view and that of the characters was no longer there.[17] The new language, as well as the new independent stance of the hero, signaled the beginning of a breakdown of the epic wholeness of socialist realism.

In the early sixties the work of the "urbanists" (Leningrad writers Andrei Bitov, Boris Vakhtin, Vladimir Maramzin, and Valery Popov) marked a significant shift of focus to a narrower realm. Urban prose described the alienation people experienced in today's world, the disintegration of families, and the subsequent moral confusion. The universality of moral problems and categories became a major theme for the writers of *byt* prose (Natalia Baranskaia, I. Grekova, Jurii Trifonov). Closely allied with the urbanists, *byt* writers focused on the Soviet middle class.[18] Although by its very definition unexceptional and emphatically neutral, almost sober in its language, the *byt* prose of the sixties nevertheless served as a transition or perhaps even a negative force for the fantastic trend. The city is the locus of action, and it is oppressive. Life is full of meaningless routine. At the center of these novels we find people whose inner thoughts and feelings are examined in painstaking detail. However, this examination offers no hope for change; the heroes of *byt* prose are not able to flee their oppressive world. In *byt* prose, the world "as it should be" appears as the unchanging world "as it is."

The popularity of *byt* prose was indicative of a change in the creative atmosphere during the late sixties: from a naive belief in the truth and inevitability of Communism to a rejection of the social in favor of the personal, the intimate, even the claustrophobic. The utopian tendency of socialist realism and the world of the masculine and irreverent champions of the triumphant cause of youth prose of the Thaw period, was now rejected completely. *Byt* prose writers focused exclusively on the psychological perturbations of the daily existence of deeply disillusioned people.

The Seventies: A Change of Course

The seventies signal a significant change of course from the literature of narrow dimension to broader realms of fantastic fiction. The works of *byt* prose were enlivened by the injection of the irrational. Village prose writers of the seventies showed a familiar nostalgia for the past but also betrayed a keen interest in the fantastic. The question of imposition of outside control on a society was examined by some practitioners of Soviet science fiction.

Two writers are important in this move of *byt* prose into the fantastic realm: Mikhail Bulgakov and Jurii Trifonov. The transformation of Russian letters from the classical wholeness of socialist realism to the fragmented portrayal of confusion and alienation characteristic of *byt* literature coincided with the publication of *The Master and Margarita* in the literary journal *Moskva* in 1966–1967.[19] A decade and a half after its publication, Bulgakov's novel had generated a score of imitations, a fact indicating the work's importance for Soviet writers. And, as we will see in a subsequent chapter, it is Bulgakov's framework for projecting the everyday into a fantastic dimension that fantastic prose used for its own, quite different purposes. Trifonov, a distinguished practitioner of *byt* prose, was yet another writer who in the late sixties and early seventies provided a link between the literature of the ordinary and the fantastic literature of the following decade. Trifonov's work "probes the official psychology in decay," with the ideals of the Thaw often reduced simply to a struggle for the good life.[20] Trifonov's heroes are either cynics who do not believe in slogans, or offbeat eccentrics, out of tune with and misunderstood by those around them. Trifonov's male characters are often apathetic observers unable to prevent the powerful predators around them from trampling their submerged ethical ideals. Trifonov's women, on the other hand, are mostly determined opportunists, ready to push aside all moral considerations for personal gain.

All novels of Trifonov's "Moscow cycle" (*Exchange, Preliminary Conclusions, A Long Goodbye, Another Life*) have a protagonist who stands out from the crowd of fortune seekers filling Trifonov's pages.[21] Rebrov of *A Long Goodbye*, Gartvig of *Preliminary Conclusions*, and, particularly, Sergei of *Another Life* all share this quality of "nonacceptance" *(nesoglasie)*, as the author himself calls it: ". . . there was something ineradicable there, encoded in their genetic tree, impossible to cut down or beat down or destroy with time."[22] This "eternally striving loser" does not want to change, "does not want to break that which is inside him, something made of steel, invisible to others."[23] These outcasts of Trifonov's fiction are always involved in creative activity, even when generating discontent. Although Sergei of *Another Life* dies before he can accomplish his ambitious and diverse creative goals, he leaves behind him, in the memory of his widow and acquaintances, the creative energy that sustained his short life. Sergei's theory of history is also his theory of life which, even after his death, is capable of evoking strong emotions and profound musings. Trifonov's protagonist does not believe in the total annihilation of a person after death. In his research into Russian history Sergei is looking for "the threads that connect the past with the even more distant past and the future."[24] For this character, "man is a thread, stretching through time, the most sensitive nerve in history, which can be broken off and isolated."[25] According to Trifonov's protagonist, everything that was and will be is already here; the line into the future and into the past is always open—it is in the people themselves.[26]

The preoccupation of Trifonov's characters with the elastic character of time is shared by fantastic prose. Another link to fantastic prose is Trifonov's interest in the illusive borderline between the real and unreal. Trifonov's *Another Life*, for example, introduces intimations of the fantastic proper into its otherwise realistic narrative. The end of the novel is deliberately cryptic, the border between Olga Vasilievna's dream and reality fluid, and it is not clear whether the character imagines the encounter with her dead husband, or if it really takes place. Significantly, forays into fantasy formed Trifonov's design for future work, the sentiment expressed in one of the last interviews with the author.[27]

Village prose of the period rejected the excesses of modern civilization and looked into the future armed with the lessons of the past—as a "a tribute to their [the writers'] parents and grandparents, and yet at the same time a guarantee of the future, in the sense that a nation which has lost its past cannot conceive of a meaningful future."[28] It was propelled by a utopian impulse because it had an ideal, Christian, or even pre-Christian communion with nature. Several works provided a pool of themes and devices later used by the writers of fantastic prose, and particularly by "village utopians." Vasilii Belov's *Vologda Whimsies* (*Bukhtiny vologodskie*, 1969) is indebted to a traditional Russian fairy tale.[29] The work is a series of short fantastic tales (*bukhtina* is defined by the author early in the work as a mixture of legend, joke, and nonsense) narrated by the hero himself. Like the typical resourceful hero of a fairy tale, Belov's Kuz'ma can easily communicate with animals and is not daunted by the supernatural. One of the tales recounts Kuz'ma's journey into the underworld, where "everyone is equal" and "all sinners have had their rights restored."[30] The hero flees the underworld and, after a brief and disappointing stay with his children in the city, returns to the village. In an ironic twist, however, the authorities forbid him to tell more tales—to preserve the folk heritage from its very practitioner. Belov's use of the fairy-tale pattern and of the supernatural reshapes the history of Soviet countryside agricultural policy, here seen through the eyes of a villager. Belov's peasant, like his ingenuous folktale counterpart *Ivanushka-durachok*, easily adapts to the absurdities of Soviet life.

Vasilii Shukshin's work of the early seventies shows the same belief in the resilience of a Russian peasant. However, the tone of Shukshin's *Before the Cock Crows Thrice* is considerably more critical than Belov's lighthearted satire.[31] Shukshin's last novel describes Ivan the Fool's journey through a fairy-tale country. In the author's updated version of the Russian fairy tale, Ivan does not search for wisdom but for a document verifying that he is "intelligent" (*umnyi*). Prominent characters of Russian literature demand proof of Ivan's intelligence because they do not trust his folk origins. In his journey to the Wise Man, Ivan discovers that even the fairy-tale world is infected by a "diabolical" ideology and cheap mass culture. Ivan is saved in the end by his own ingenuity and resourcefulness.

The theme of the imposition of an alien will on a community, an important one for all writers of the fantastic, was particularly prominent in some Soviet science fiction of the seventies. In the early seventies, the morality of all politically motivated coercion emerged as the most important concern for the brothers Strugatsky. The tension between a "backward," alien community and a "superior," technologically more powerful society had been explored by village prose writers before the brothers Strugatsky attempted to view it on a universal scale in *The Snail on the Slope* (*Ulitka na sklone*).[32] Yet the eventual confluence between the two trends is not surprising. Both village prose and science fiction are literatures intimately linked to the Russian utopian tradition. In both there is a strong predisposition to the "finding of truth," and it is natural that the voices of Rasputin and Belov, for example, were not overlooked by the Strugatskys.

Snail on the Slope attempts to relocate the conflict between a naturally evolved order and its technologically superior adversary into the distant future on an alien planet. The future Prometheuses establish a laboratory in a large alien forest with the intent of subjugating it to their power. The depiction of the forest is deliberately defamiliarized, since it is ultimately foreign to the people trying to penetrate its mysteries. The forest is filled with fantastic creatures—half-men, half-animals—who prey on the scientists; and it is capable of regenerating the dead, who then form their own community there. The deliberately disjointed, Faulknerian narrative carries the action in and out of the forest. The message that gradually emerges is that of the impossibility of conquering an alien world. The only way into the forest is through the adoption of and subjugation to its laws.

Just as the literature of the Thaw ushered in new trends and proclaimed new concerns for Soviet literature, the literature of the early seventies paved the way for the emergence of fantastic prose. The examination of the utopian impulse, attempted in the fifties and sixties by two seemingly opposite movements (village prose and Soviet science fiction), was developed in the following decade to probe the idea of alternative social practices. Village prose looked back into the harmonious past of Russia for confirmation of its traditional values. Soviet science fiction was still directed toward Russia's glorious future, but the moral cost of Promethean experiments became one of its prominent concerns.

In the late fifties and early sixties, post-Stalinist literature moved away from the Literature of Purpose only to find a different purpose in the seventies. Now literature rejected the excesses of an advanced technological society, searched for a revival of traditional Russian culture with roots in the village, questioned coercion, and yearned for freedom from the constraints of everyday living. In the mid-seventies and eighties, these themes and ideas, scattered in different works of literature of the period, were united in fantastic prose.

Notes

1. Lapidus, "Social Trends," p. 238.
2. Belaia, "Pereput'e," p. 80. The translation is mine.
3. Abraham Rothberg, *The Heirs of Stalin: Dissidence and the Soviet Regime, 1953–1970* (Ithaca: Cornell University Press, 1972), p. 15.
4. One should also mention in this regard the work of Valentin Kataev and Veniamin Kaverin; both writers produced work that employed elements of fantasy, and both were influential during the Thaw period.
5. On the science fiction of the twenties, see A. F. Britikov, *Russkii Sovetskii nauchno-fantasticheskii roman* (Leningrad: Nauka, 1970); Darko Suvin, "The Utopian Tradition of Russian Science Fiction," *MLR* 66 (1979): 139–159; Robert Maguire, *Red Virgin Soil: Soviet Literature in the 1920s* (Princeton: Princeton Uni-

versity Press, 1968); Richard Stites, "Fantasy and Revolution: Alexander Bogdanov and the Origins of Bolshevik Science Fiction" in *Alexander Bogdanov, Red
Star: the First Bolshevik Utopia,* ed. Loren R. Graham and Richard Stites (Bloomington: Indiana University Press, 1989), pp. 1–16; Stites, *Revolutionary Dreams,*
chap. 8 ("Utopia in Time: Futurology and Science Fiction"); and Rafail Nudelman, "Soviet SF and the Ideology of Soviet Society," *Science Fiction Studies* 16, pt.
1 (March 1989): 39–48.

6. For an excellent bibliography on Soviet post-Stalinist Science Fiction see
Darko Suvin, *Russian Science Fiction 1956–1974* (Elizabethtown, N.Y.: Dragon
Press, 1976). For an overview of Soviet SF, see Evgenii Brandis, "Fantastika i
novoe videnie mira," *Zvezda* 8 (1981): 41–49; a discussion of Soviet SF in the sixties can be found in Britikov *Russkii sovetskii nauchno-fantasticheksii roman*
and "Sovetskaia nauchnaia fantastika" in *Zhanrovo-stilevye iskaniia sovremennoi prozy* (Moscow, 1971); B .V. Liapunov, *V mire fantastiki. Obzor nauchno-fantasticheskoi i fantasticheskoi literatury,* 2d ed. (Moscow: Kniga, 1975); E. Parnov,
Sovremennaia fantastika (Moscow: Znanie, 1968); A. A. Urban, *Fantastika i nash
mir* (Leningrad: Sovetskii Pisatel', 1972); T. Chernysheva , *V mire mechty i privideniia: Nauchnaia fantastika, eie problemy i khudozhestvennye vozmozhnosti*
(Kiev: Naukova Dumka, 1972); Evgenii Brandis, "Gorizonty fantastiki," in *Neva*
10 (1979): 171–181. On samizdat publications of Soviet science fiction in the seventies and eighties, see a short article and a bibliography by A. Chertkov, "Fenziny, ili samizdat fantastiki," *Sovetskaia bibliografiia* 1 (1990): 114–122.

7. Suvin, *Metamorphoses of Science Fiction,* p. 266.

8. Ivan Efremov, *Tumannost' Andromedy* (Moscow: Molodaia gvardiia, 1958).

9. Efremov's work moved into a new direction in the sixties. *The Razor's Edge*
(1963), for example, provides a different, and more complex, vision of the future.
As Rafail Nudelman explains, "Efremov bases his understanding of history on
the Manichaean view of history as an eternal struggle between Good and Evil.
Evil for Efremov (what he terms the 'Inferno') is most fully represented by the Ju-
daeo-Christian culture's notion of Original Sin and the suppression of eros.
Good, on the other hand, is an exotic combination of the Greek cult of eroticism
and heroism with the mystical and the irrational as conceived by the East. The
motif of a return to the 'first civilization,' close to nature and 'soil,' always appears in the utopian segments of Efremov's SF. He does not, however, reject technology as a whole, nor does he repudiate the hierarchical organization of society; rather, he insists on a reorganization of the world according to new
principles. Constituting the utopianism of his SF is a complex combination of
higher technology and a certain mystical spirituality dissolved in nature (the
'soil'); together, these amount to an almost mystical pathos of technology" ("Soviet SF"), p. 56.

10. Efremov's novel takes place in the four hundred and eighth year of the Era
of the Great Ring, when the inhabitants of Earth established contact with distant
alien civilizations. Although the social organization of alien civilizations is not
presented in the novel in great detail, it is distinctly different from that of the
Earth. Nevertheless, relations between different social systems are based here on
the principle of acceptance and nonintervention.

11. Isaiah Berlin, introduction to Franco Venturi, *Roots of Revolution: A History of the Populist and Socialist Movements in Nineteenth-Century Russia*, pp. xiii, xvii.

12. Arkadii Strugatsky and Boris Strugatsky, *Dalekaia raduga–Trudno byt' bogom* (Moscow: Molodaia gvardiia,1964).

13. Suvin, *Metamorphoses of Science Fiction*, p. 267.

14. Edward J. Brown, *Russian Literature since Revolution*, rev. ed. (Cambridge, Mass.: Harvard University Press, 1982), p. 294.

15. Hosking, *Beyond Socialist Realism*, pp. 52–53.

16. Kathleen Parthé, *Time, Backward! Memory and the Past in Soviet Russian Village Prose* (Washington, D.C.: Woodrow Wilson Center, Kennan Institute for Advanced Russian Studies, 1987), p. 20.

17. One should mention the importance of Ilya Il'f and Evgeny Petrov's work on youth prose; the two writers were one of the most famous satirists of the twenties. Their *Twelve Chairs (Dvenadtsat' stul'ev*, 1928), *The Golden Calf (Zolotoi telenok*, 1931), and *One-storeyed America* (*Odnoetazhnaia Amerika*, 1936) had been very popular with the reader until the "freeze" of the Zhdanov period (1946–1948). In the sixties the novels of Il'f and Petrov were published in new editions.

18. See, for example, Natalia Baranskaia, "Provody," *Novyi mir* 5 (1968); I. Grekova, "Letom v gorode," *Novyi mir* 4 (1965); Jurii Trifonov, "Golubinaia gibel'," *Novyi mir* 1 (1968).

19. Some critics claim that Bulgakov's novel was a turning point in the move away from socialist realism. See Petr Vail' and Aleksandr Genis, *Sovremennaia russkaia proza* (Ann Arbor: Hermitage, 1982).

20. David Joravsky, "Literature and Psychology" in *Russian Psychology: A Critical History* (Oxford: Basil Blackwell, 1989), p. 471.

21. Jurii Trifonov, "Obmen," *Novyi mir* 12 (1969); "Predvaritel'nye itogi," in *Novyi mir* 12 (1970); "Dolgoe proshchanie," *Novyi mir* 8 (1971); "Drugaia zhizn'," *Novyi mir* 8 (1975). For a good discussion of Trifonov's cycle of Moscow povesti see Woll, *Invented Truth*; see also Gillespie, *Iurii Trifonov* and C. J. Partridge, *Yuri Trifonov's* The Moscow Cycle: *A Critical Study* (Lewiston, N.Y.: E. Mellen Press, 1990).

22. Jurii Trifonov, *Povesti* (Moscow: Sovetskaia Rossiia,1978), p. 322. The translation is mine.

23. Ibid., p. 267.

24. Ibid., p. 307.

25. Ibid.

26. On Trifonov's fascination with history see Edward Brown, "Trifonov: The Historian as Artist," in *Soviet Society and Culture. Essays in Honor of Vera S. Dunham*, ed. Terry L. Thompson and Richard Sheldon (Boulder: Westview Press, 1988), pp. 109–123; Sigrid McLaughlin, "A Moment in the History of Consciousness of the Soviet Intelligentsia: Trifonov's Novel *Disappearance*," *Studies in Comparative Communism* 21.3/4 (1988): 303–312; Herman Ermolaev, "The Theme of Terrorism in *Starik"* in *Aspects of Modern Russian and Czech Literature*, ed. Arnold McMillin (Columbus, Ohio: Slavica Publishers, 1989), pp. 96–109.

27. In Trifonov's last interview the author formulated his attitude to the fantastic: "I do not really fantasize *[fantaziruiu]* but strive for a realistic representation of reality. These are the limits I am working within. Although . . . with time I began to attempt to go beyond these limits. For example, in the novel *Another Life* there are such . . . departures into the realm of the metaphysical *[vykhody metafizicheskogo svoistva]*. I will probably continue working in this vein." *Kak slovo nashe otzovetsia* (Moscow: Sovetskaia Rossiia, 1985).

28. Boris Shragin, *Protivostoyanie dukha* (London: Overseas Publications Interchange, 1977). Quoted in Hosking, *Beyond Socialist Realism*, p. 53.

29. Vasilii Belov, "Bukhtiny vologodskie," *Novyi mir* 8 (1969): 158–184.

30. Ibid., p. 179.

31. Vasilii Shukshin, "Do tret'ikh petukhov," *Nash sovremennik* 1 (1975): 28–61.

32. See Arkadii Strugatsky and Boris Strugatsky, *Ulitka na sklone: Skazka o troike* (Frankfurt am Main: Posev, 1972), especially in the exerpts published first only in the West. See also *Les* (Ann Arbor: Ardis, 1981).

4

Socialist Realists in Space

Today we are all together in the same boat—with cosmic infinity astern.

—Chingiz Aitmatov,
V soavtorstve s zemleiu i vodoiu. . .

NINETEEN-EIGHTY WAS AN IMPORTANT YEAR in the development of Soviet literature. The emergence and public acceptance of fantastic prose was signaled by the publication of Chingiz Aitmatov's novel *The Day Lasts More than a Hundred Years*.[1] A revelation to readers and writers alike, the novel had an immediate and powerful impact by engendering considerable public debate, giving rise to a number of imitative literary works, and, more importantly, sanctioning a measure of diversity within socialist realist fiction.[2] That critical recognition of the new trend coincided with the appearance of Aitmatov's novel can be explained by the writer's prominent position in Soviet letters, his distinguished career as a minority writer and, not the least, by his easily accessible and heavily sentimental style of writing.[3] All this made Aitmatov an ideal figure to introduce new trends in mainstream fiction, as was amply demonstrated once again by the publication of Aitmatov's *The Execution Block (Plakha)*—one of the first novels of the glasnost era.[4]

Significantly, however, the new directions in literature mapped by Aitmatov's *The Day* were not so new after all. In many ways Aitmatov's celebrated work was only the culmination of a process already begun in the literature of the sixties. Furthermore, Aitmatov's device of incorporating science fiction and other forms of fantasy into a mainstream novel was presaged by the fantastic dimension of village prose and *byt* fiction.[5] No less important is the fact that by the time *The Day* appeared in print, Soviet critics had proclaimed the "magic" realism of Gabriel García Márquez the new form of realism.[6] Moreover, although *The Day* was perceived by critics and readers as a pioneer work, it was immediately preceded, and sometimes accompanied, by works relatively similar to Aitmatov's in structure and literary device.

The novels discussed in this chapter adhere to the socialist realist model in the way they structure their plots and portray their characters. However, the familiar components of a socialist realist novel are arranged in a slightly different fashion here, accents reshuffled, and a whole score of new themes added to enliven what had by then become a hindrance to some and an embarrassment to most writers. The stubborn, if initially timid, attempts to escape the hold of the "official method" are best seen in the preoccupation with certain, hitherto untouchable, themes and with formal innovations in these novels. Each deals with the subjects of personal and national freedom, memory and coercion; each projects its search for truth and perfection into the past, both legendary and historical, and into the future; and each employs science fiction devices to expand the narrative time frame.

Soviet critics were the first to assign to science fiction an important role in the development of fantastic prose.[7] Some rationalized the importance of science fiction in this process by viewing the genre as a different side of realism.[8] And at times the novels of what I would call "the Aitmatov school" (all sharing the grafting of science fiction elements onto village prose plots and employing as well the familiar conventions of socialist realism) seem to be written to order—to exemplify the rather mechanistic idea that the realism of science fiction (of the future) can be incorporated in Soviet literature "as a principle of addition to the realism of the present and the past."[9] According to this formulation the old definition of socialist realism ("a truthful, historically concrete representation of reality in its revolutionary development") is simply extended into the future to accommodate science fiction. In the case of "the Aitmatov school," such adjustment works quite well and the old formulae of socialist realism are simply rearranged to adjust to the new polemics and dilemmas of Soviet society.

Communists as Aliens: Nodar Dumbadze

In 1980 when *The Day* was hailed by Soviet critics as the first novel of its kind in Soviet literature, Nodar Dumbadze's *The Law of Eternity* had been available to the Russian-language reader for over a year.[10] Dumbadze, who died in 1984, was a prominent and highly regarded Georgian writer whose success story is reminiscent of Chingiz Aitmatov's. Both writers are indebted in their writings to the national symbolism of their cultures, and both were elevated to the status of paragons by the Soviet critics. Still, Dumbadze's *The Law of Eternity*—a very "Aitmatovian"

novel—did not make it as the harbinger of the new age in Soviet literature. One reason was, perhaps, that a more prominent name than Dumbadze's was needed to introduce a new model for updating socialist realism. Another possible reason for the relative disregard of *The Law of
Eternity* might have been Dumbadze's bold insistence, played out in the
novel, on the affinity between Communist and Christian doctrines.

The Law of Eternity weaves together legendary, historical and science
fictional plots. These innovations in structure and style, however, never
violate the prescriptions of the "official method." Rather, in this novel
the sources of "realism in its revolutionary development" are found in
Christian legend, and then extended into the science fictional future.
Bachana Ramishvili, the main protagonist of the novel, a well-known
writer and a devoted Communist, holds an important position in one of
Tbilisi's prominent newspapers and is a man of unshakable integrity.
His life, presented in flashbacks as the recollections of a gravely ill man
(part of the action takes place in a hospital ward), is a story of persever-
ance. Bachana is tried by adversity and, in the end, emerges a better
man and Communist. The main story line is supplemented by two interrelated plots. The legendary plot is presented through allusions to the
Georgian twelfth century epic, Shota Rustaveli's *The Knight in Tiger
Skin*, and through Bachana's visions, replete with Christian symbolism.
The contemporary plot depicts the hero's transformation from a spontaneous youth into a conscious member of society. The science fictional
plot narrates the story of a visit from an alien who reveals the protagonist's secret mission in life.

The novel traces Bachana's life from the traumatic arrest and death
of his parents in the purges, to the aging hero's nearly fatal illness.
Early childhood trauma is responsible for the hero's heightened sensi-
tivities; from the very beginning it is stressed that Bachana is capable
of deep feelings. When Bachana's distant relative is killed by a bandit,
the then fifteen-year old hero takes the law into his own hand and
avenges this murder by killing the bandit. This is a trial which tempers
the hero's will; through it he becomes a "man of action" and a true
leader who is permitted to use force to reach a higher goal. When questioned about the death of his parents in the purges, Bachana admits
his anger but assures his fellow party-members that he has been able
to overcome his resentment. The mature hero now perceives his role in
society as that of a watchdog, "to prevent the people on top from re-
peating the same mistakes."[11]

Bachana's strong commitment to the Cause, balanced by human
weaknesses, links him to the urban dwellers of early post-Stalin fiction,
such as, for example, Lopatkin of Dudintsev's *Not By Bread Alone* (1956)
or Bakhirev in Galina Nikolaeva's *Running Battle* (1957). The emphasis

on societal ills and their rectification is reminiscent of the literature of the late fifties as well. As in the literature of Khrushchev's Thaw, the system itself is never questioned in this novel, nor is the hero's determination to achieve his goal of being a true Communist. Bachana's firm dedication to the Cause, however, harks backs to the unquestioning and self-sacrificing heroes of true socialist realism. The path of the true believer is based on sacrificial love, which is the only way to happiness and earthly paradise, i.e., Communism. Here immortality is achieved through communal sharing, brotherly love and sacrifice.[12] This Christian attitude is qualified by Dumbadze's protagonist, however, who reserves such noble feelings only for the best of men.

Bachana's own exceptional nature is underscored by his visions of Christ and the Apocalypse. To an Orthodox priest, who shares Bachana's hospital ward, the visions of an atheist are the utmost proof of divine forgiveness. For Bachana, they point to the affinity between the Christian world view and the ideals of Communism. The Communist Bachana confesses his belief in Christ, who is for him "an earthly God," while the vision of a Communist society is a modern Gospel. Bachana links himself to the Savior, depicting himself, and others like him, as chosen men, martyrs, ready to serve their fellow men and build a better life for the people.

The science fictional plot is another illustration of the idea that Communists are chosen people who work to bring about the inevitable paradise on Earth. At different stages of the development of human society, alien genes are awakened in some people, who then strive to influence the moral standards of humanity. The list of "born again" humans includes Homer, Cervantes, Rustaveli, Tolstoy, Pushkin and others. Bachana learns that he is one of those humans chosen to protect humankind from its own folly.

Andrew Barratt, in his analysis of Bulgakov's *Master and Margarita*, links the Satanic figure of that novel—Woland—to the tradition of Gnostic religion, in which a supernatural being "comes to earth periodically bearing a message which, if properly deciphered, promises the possibility of divine illumination." This being is named the Messenger, or the Alien. Barratt notes that the most important feature of the Alien is that "he will be recognized only by a very small number of people (or "pneumatics"), in whom the divine spark has not been totally extinguished by the conditions of earthly existence." The closeness of the Gnostic Messenger to Dumbadze's visiting alien is uncanny. I cannot prove or disprove Dumbadze's familiarity with Gnostic beliefs. Dumbadze's knowledge of *Master and Margarita*, on the other hand, can be claimed with much more certainty. What is even more important here is the way the idea of the Messenger and the "pneumatics" is employed in the novel.[13]

The leaders of *The Law of Eternity*, although "of the people" and pro-claiming Christian brotherly love, have the distinction of carrying the "alien" genes. The stress on the benevolence of the powerful few is not coincidental, for this novel is a pure apology for intellectual and political inequality. Dumbadze is perhaps the only writer of fantastic prose who embraces outside control, so deeply despised by the practitioners of vil-lage prose. The chosen men of Dumbadze are superior to the ordinary heroes of *byt* or village prose, and they are aware of it. Their claim to su-periority is "cemented" by the legendary link to Christ and the science fictional link to the aliens.

Dumbadze's novel is a good example of updated, refurbished socialist realism. The hero's progression from a natural state to one of higher con-sciousness is traced through contemporary, legendary and science fic-tional plots. Christian symbolism serves to underscore the basic mes-sage of the novel, which establishes the path to perfection through the hearts and minds of the best. In spite of its indebtedness to socialist re-alism, however, Dumbadze's novel differs from the model in the ease with which the temporal progression opens both into past and future. There is also a measure of pessimism expressed in this work about the chances for achieving social perfection. Another point of departure from the standard Stalinist novel is Dumbadze's overt juxtaposition of Com-munist and Christian dogma.

On the surface, *The Law of Eternity* echoes communal and religious ideals of the village prose when it calls for a Christian brotherhood of all people on Earth. When faced with death, Dumbadze's urban hero turns to the figure of Christ as the ultimate symbol of martyrdom. However, Bachana's belief in communalism and mutual support is a credo that has to be imposed from above by the chosen few who form the familiar "conscious avant-garde" of the Marxist-Leninist doctrine. To prove his point, Dumbadze unblushingly turns to the wealth of Christian tradi-tion, tracing the genealogy for his protagonist from Christ to the con-temporary God-cum-Communist.

Escaping Alien Control: Chingiz Aitmatov

Aitmatov's *The Day* relates the story of a journey of the main hero Edigei to bury his friend and mentor Kazangap at the old cemetery of his Sarozek forebears, Ana-Beiit. The novel shifts back and forth between preparations for the trip, the actual journey and Edigei's memories of his life at the faraway railroad junction of Boranly-Burannyi. There are sev-eral temporal planes in the novel which accomodate several interrelated plots: the present tense of the narrative; the historical past to which Edi-gei constantly returns in his reminiscences; the legendary past, which is intimately related to all the events in the story; and the future of the science fictional plot, set apart stylistically and structurally from the other plots. More broadly, the novel breaks into three interrelated stories: the legendary plot; the story of Edigei's life; and the story of an encounter with an alien civilization.

On his way to the cemetery Edigei is haunted with recollections of his stay at the junction. During his life in the steppes Edigei has endured many hardships: he witnessed the arrival and subsequent unlawful arrest of his good friend Abutalip. He endured his unrequited love for Abutalip's widow, illness, and the lean post-war years. In all his adversities Edigei was sustained by his belief in tradition and by reverence for his own culture. It is only natural that the funeral of Edigei's friend Kazangap assumes symbolic proportions for the hero. After Kazangap's death, Edigei becomes the only guardian of the old tradition, whose duty it is to lay his friend to rest according to the Moslem tradition. However, modern society has intruded into the lives of the simple people of the steppes. The rocket-launching site, built in the vicinity of the old cemetery, is an alien space, threatening Edigei and his way of life. The funeral procession is stopped at the gate of the cemetery. Edigei is denied communion with his ancestors.

Edigei's beliefs are exemplified and supported by the legendary plot of the novel which describes the journey of a mother, Naiman, in search of her missing son, captured by an enemy tribe and robbed of his memory by torture. Naiman's missing son is turned into a perfect slave, a *mankurt* (Aitmatov's term), with no memories and no ties to the living. Naiman is killed by her unsuspecting son who follows the command of his captors.

In the science fiction plot two astronauts, an American and a Russian, encounter a superior alien civilization which offers its knowledge and goodwill to the inhabitants of Earth. After intense bilateral deliberations the offer is rejected, and the astronauts are prohibited from returning to Earth. The legendary future of *The Day* portrays a ruthlessly independent cosmos of Earth, intolerant of outside coercion.

The conflict between technology and traditional human values, city vs. country, so prominent in nineteenth century fiction, Soviet science fiction and village prose, lies at the center of Aitmatov's work. Advanced technology, of which space travel is the ultimate example, is that order of technological advancement to which the tradition-bound characters of *The Day* are yet unable to adapt. The train itself, traditionally a symbol of the inhuman machine, becomes in this novel a sign of continuity and human contact. Yet, the train is also one of the many symbols of technology which brings destruction to Aitmatov's characters. The story of a vixen, which begins *The Day*, epitomizes a shaky truce existing between nature and technology.

The novel grafts science fiction on village prose themes, employing as well the familiar conventions of socialist realism. Edigei's final undoing is the result of a standard village prose conflict between the hero's natural impulse for freedom, his insistence on the right to preserve the past, and the control that custom, society, technology and the political mood of the moment impose on Aitmatov's protagonist. On many occasions the hero laments the loss of ancient rituals. When, after his friend Kazangap's death, Edigei's superior is unable to find fitting words of condolence, the hero mourns the breach of style committed by one who has become an outsider in his own culture. Edigei is unsure that anyone will remain at the junction at the time of his own death to bury him properly. He instructs the members of Kazangap's funeral party to observe the traditional ritual carefully.

The loss of tradition is inseparable in Aitmatov's novel from the loss of human memory and freedom. The legendary story of a mother in search of her lost son stands in the center of the novel's treatment of memory. The evil tribe robs the young son of his memory and brings with this act the destruction of the whole family. The theme of memory is echoed in the contemporary plot. Abutalip is punished by the outsiders for daring to preserve his past for his sons. The national memory of Edigei's people is threatened by technology and Russification.

Encroachment on one's past is the worst sin against a nation, a people, its language, and customs. The evils of Russification and technology are fused in the negative character of Sabitzhan, Kazangap's son, who embraces the values and language of his conquerors. Sabitzhan introduces the second science fictional plot of the novel, clearly indebted to Zamiatin's dystopian novel *We* (1924).

It's true! A person will always do everything in accordance with the central program. It'll seem to him that he acts and lives of his own volition, but in fact he'll be directed from above. And everything will be exact. It you are required to sing, a signal will be sent, and sing you will. If you're to work, you'll get the signal and you'll work—and so on. Stealing, hooliganism and crime—all these will be forgotten; you'll only read about such things in history books. Everything in a man's behavior will be foreseen—all his acts, all his thoughts, all his desires. For example, at the present time in the world there is the so-called population explosion; the people have produced too many children and there's not enough food to go around. What is to be done about that? Reduce the birth rate. You'll only perform that act with your wife when they send you the signal to do so in the interests of society.[14]

Although Aitmatov understandably does not name Zamiatin among the writers who influenced his work (at the time of the novel's publication *We* was still banned in the Soviet Union), the concerns of the two authors are similar. *The Day* rejects, even if not as adamantly as Zamiatin's novel, the enforcement of "particular and temporary values on all human beings as eternal verities."[15] Zamiatin's brand of fantastic literature (which he called "Synthetism") signifies "a compressed style, the union of fantasy and reality, Impressionism, and a significant philosophic synthesis that looked to the future."[16] Similar ideas on the nature of his creative method are expressed by Aitmatov in his introduction to *The Day*:

> As far as the meaning of fantasy is concerned, Dostoyevsky in his time wrote: "The fantastic in art has its limits and laws. The fantastic must so merge with reality that you can almost believe it." Indeed, the mythology of the ancient, the fantasy-realism of Gogol', Bulgakov, or Marquez, science fiction—all of these are convincing in so far as they touch reality. Fantasy highlights certain aspects of reality and, when Dostoyevsky's rules are followed, shows them philosophically generalized, developed to their ultimate conclusion.[17]

Both the anti-utopia described by Sabitzhan and the utopia of the alien planet propose happiness imposed from the outside. Although seemingly harmonious, the alien planet is eager to change another society according to its own understanding of perfection.[18] In the anti-utopia, the question of the imposition of an alien will is brought to an extreme: all people are controlled by a contemporary technological deity who, alone, is allowed to decide what a person needs for happiness.

The theme of coercion is presented dynamically. There are two orders of control in the novel—the self-imposed control of the positive hero acting according to the laws of tradition and coercion from the outside. In the legendary plot the young mankurt's loss of identity is brought about by an evil tribe of outsiders. In the "cosmic" plot the decision to protect Earth from aliens prevents the two astronauts from returning home. But in the story of Edigei's forbidden love for Abutalip's widow the hero's tradition-bound friends send the woman away. This forced solution to a tragic situation brings the hero to the brink of suicide. As if to chastise himself for transgressing the laws of his community, Edigei imposes his will and punishes his unruly camel Karanar who heeds his instincts and runs away in search of love.

The conflict between natural impulse and imposed control is not easily solved. Any community brings with it its customs, beliefs and a certain degree of coercion. And it is the commandments of his culture, developed and refined over centuries, that are embraced by Edigei as the only legitimate ethical guides in life. In the end, however, Edigei's terrified escape from the noise of the launching site points to the inability of

Aitmatov's protagonist to survive under the alien control of Russification, imposed perfection, and dehumanizing technology.

Physicists and Lyricists in a Perfect World of Immortality: Evgeny Evtushenko

Evtushenko's contribution to fantastic prose, *Wild Berries (Iagodnye mesta)* (1981), is (perhaps an unconsious) tribute to Aitmatov and his school of writing.[19] Aptly, if harshly, called by John Updike "a book with a bad conscience, by a writer who wants to feel more than he does," *Wild Berries* strives to appeal to the majority of Soviet readers by bringing together a romantic story, a travelogue, psychological thriller, and science fiction.[20]

Wild Berries is a briccolage of narrative modes shaped around several clearly articulated messages. The now familiar rearrangement of temporal planes is given its due by the switching of epilogue and prologue. The book begins with an epilogue taking place some time in the future and describing a Soviet astronaut's thoughts while in space; it ends with a science fictional prologue about aliens who arrive to observe the earth during the life of the rocket scientist Konstantin Tsiolkovsky. In between, we find a contemporary plot which offers a light mix of recognizable literary models—"youth" prose, post-Stalinist fiction about scientists, and even a bit of village prose. This melange is enlivened by constant changes in locale. The action moves from the Siberian taiga, to the Presidential palace of Salvador Allende, to a rock concert in the United States.

The various life stories of Evtushenko's numerous protagonists in the contemporary plot are punctuated by philosophical conversations— around the camp-fire, in a boat going downstream, in a cafe, at the Palace, and in other similar thought-provoking circumstances. It is in these conversations (and also in his protagonists' internal monologues) that Evtushenko's ideas are expounded. These can be briefly summarized as follows. The earth is an enormous spaceship where all people are travellers in space, joined by the same destiny and responsibilities. In order to preserve the world, people need to perfect themselves through education and ethics. Modern technology must have at its foundation an ethical program created for and by the people, the program worked out as a result of intimate familiarity with the cultures of the world and its moral, philosophical, and literary achievements. Evtushenko's list of important authors and philosophers includes Pushkin, Dostoyevsky, Mayakovsky, Bulgakov, N. F. Fyodorov and Konstantin Tsiolkovsky—a scientist (1857–1935) whose Fyodorovian ideas on the resurrection of the dead show his bold imagination and concern for the good of all humanity. The true intelligentsia (in whom knowledge is combined with love for others) is still in the process of emerging, according to Evtushenko; but when this intelligentsia does appear, it will be "of the people," ready and willing to provide answers to the world's problems.

The novel's main plot—the adventures of a geological party in Siberia in search of precious cassiterite—exists to illustrate Evtushenko's views. In spite of the author's designs at innovation, however, the plot of this novel is suspiciously close to the venerable master plot of the true socialist realism. The task of the geological party is to find cassiterite (which will further the advance of Soviet science), and in the end this task is successfully accomplished, a process which changes the novel's young protagonist, Seryozha Lachugin, into a more aware and mature person.

Yet, as in other novels of updated socialist realism, the components of the standard master plot are reshuffled here. Now it is simple people who teach Lachugin his life lessons. The strong man Kolomeitsev, the leader of the geological party, willing to sacrifice lives to achieve his goals, does not become Lachugin's mentor. The author's true *intelligent* of the past is Konstantin Tsiolkovsky.

Evtushenko does not directly advocate the physical resurrection of dead ancestors, as both Fyodorov and Tsiolkovsky had done, in the main plot of the novel. So it is in the science fictional strand of the novel, set apart from the geologists' story, that the author presents his ideas much more directly. In this plot, two invisible aliens observe Tsiolkovsky at work and arrive at the conclusion that humanity will reach a stage when people will become immortal. As in the galaxy of the aliens, immortality is supposed to provide solutions to all problems. Evtushenko's society of immortal aliens betrays direct influence of Fyodorov's philosophical scheme. After many long centuries of careful experiments, the galaxy dwellers have transformed themselves into a radiant state, giving every atom independent thought, feelings, personality, and the ability to reproduce. They have resurrected their ancestors, learned to communicate with the atoms of trees, flowers, grass, earth, and clouds and awakened their memories, thereby learning much of their history. There is no government in the Galaxy of Immortality, no bureaucracy, no army, no police; everything is coordinated by the consciousness of the tiny fellow citizens, elected for a single term of one year to the Council of Conscience. Most professions have disappeared in this society. Teachers are no longer needed because children are born with a memory of the entire course of history and culture. Doctors are no longer needed because no one is sick. Food, transportation, and housing are no longer needed. Freed of the necessity of earning a living, the denizens develop harmoniously and simultaneously evolve into scholars, poets, musicians, and artists.

Evtushenko's utopia is one of free (and immortal) artists and artistic (and immortal) scientists. Evtushenko's utopian vision stipulates that people like Tsiolkovsky will provide the technological know-how to insure personal immortality of all, but will temper their scientific exploits by the dictates of their sensitive hearts and by their closeness to the people. In contrast to the works of Aitmatov and Dumbadze, *Wild Berries* does not pose the issue of imposed benevolence as a key concern. The visitors from the Galaxy of Immortality do not think that an artificial acceleration of the earthlings' development through external intervention is fruitful and humans are left to fend on their own.

In a nostalgic tribute to the "physicists vs. lyricists" debates of the Thaw, Evtushenko creates his utopia for those people of the future who would combine the features of both—physicists and lyricists.[21] For the author, the careful development of technology based on firm ethical principles and reverence for nature are the building blocks for eventual perfection. As in other works of updated socialist realism,*Wild Berries* addresses global problems, puts forth solutions embodied in a radically transformed society, and asserts the necessity of choice in striving for that ideal.

The Ambivalent Hero in
Search of Perfection: Jurii Bondarev

Choice—intellectual, personal and creative—is one of the key words characterizing post-Stalinist fiction and the title of a novel by a celebrated Soviet writer Bondarev.[22] *The Choice*, published in 1981, elicited enormous critical response, both in its narrative and dramatic form.[23] Adapted as a play and staged at the Moscow Maly theater in 1983, it became an instant critical success. In the words of one Soviet critic: "The play does not instruct but instead sounds a warning through philosophical and global disputes about the problems of duty, fidelity, the search for moral solutions in extreme circumstances. . . "[24] Bondarev's focus on national problems in a larger context of global concerns, his attention to the spiritual malaise affecting Soviet society presage the complex of ideas articulated by glasnost literature.

Like the work of Vasil' Bykov and Bondarev's own earlier work, *The Choice* is an intimate look at the daily grind of warfare. This time, however, it is a memory of the war experience that Bondarev represents as central to the understanding of his characters' choices. The artist Vladimir Vasil'ev and his childhood friend Ilya Ramzin go to the front together. In a fateful encounter with the Germans the regiment, where both friends are officers, is surrounded by the enemy. Vasil'ev is wounded but is able to escape, his friend Ramzin is captured by the Germans. The story begins when Vasil'ev learns that Ramzin survived the battle, is living in the West and wants to come back to Russia.

Ramzin's decision to be captured by the Germans and not to commit suicide, as was required of a Soviet officer, is one of the moral choices examined in this novel. For Bondarev, it is the wrong choice, and Ramzin is made to pay a high price for this breach of honour, condemned to the life of the eternal wanderer expiating a crime of conscience. The loss of homeland is experienced by Ramzin as a painful deprivation, and his final choice is to take his own life. Ramzin's suffering and redemption make him more than the stock negative figure of a war novel. In fact, both friends are portrayed as complex characters whose life is riddled with doubt and agonizing search for the right moral solutions. If Ramzin's agony and punishment make this novel acceptable to the broad contigent of Soviet patriotic readers who devour war fiction and films, Vasil'ev's painful quest for the truth is intended for the more sophisticated audiences. Vasil'ev's Tolstoyan crisis of faith is sparked by his search for the meaning of existence. The painful revelation that his childhood friend is a traitor, the recognition of Ramzin's motivations, and envy of his rediscovered friend's charisma plunge Vasil'ev into a profound depression. His art, which up till then had been fulfilling, no longer provides contentment. On the eve of Ramzin's suicide the main characters of the novel are brought together in a Moscow hotel room where they, in a passionate Dostoyevskian argument, express different views on the question of truth and the meaning in life. The disillusioned Il'ia Ramzin advances an idea that the whole history of mankind is a joke played on the people of Earth by mischievous aliens who left the planet without clear instructions about its further direction. Vasil'ev too believes that a higher power exists in the universe. For him, this power is the "rational energy of the universe" which is there to test human strength and the ability to love. Death equalizes all people and the "tragic weakness of everybody before death" should bring them closer.

The recognition that death is the great leveller is especially poignant during the war. This is why Bondarev's legendary time is relegated to the immediate historical past. It becomes a part of an intoxicating time of happiness, enthusiasm and love experienced by the country just after the Second World War. Both Vasil'ev and Ramzin lament the passage of the golden age, face the complexities and unpredictability of a life neither can explain, and both experience guilt.

Bondarev's novel reverses the customary roles of a traditional Stalinist novel. The more spontaneous questing Vasil'ev is presented as a positive hero. Il'a Ramzin, a born leader, experiences total defeat. Firmness and determination are not rewarded in this novel. Ramzin's mother, earlier portrayed as a saintly old woman, suddenly appears grotesque and cold at the funeral of her son because she is not able to forgive him. Forgiveness, understanding of "human frailty," and spontaneity are positive features of Bondarev's characters.

The four novels discussed in this chapter refurbish models of socialist realism to address new social concerns. Dumbadze's novel transposes the myth of Communism into a legendary future, exposing in this process the connections between the Communist and Christian dogmas. Aitmatov's focus on the conflict between tradition and technology is, to a large degree, a reflection of nationalistic concerns of the minorities. Evtushenko's utopia of immortal artists is an expression of the dissatisfaction experienced by the Russian intelligentsia in the early nineteen eighties and of its yearning for freedom of expression. Similarly, Bondarev's novel, suffused with nostalgia for the clear moral choices of the war and post-war years, points to the prevailing mood of pessimism affecting Soviet society on the eve of perestroika.

Memory and freedom are equally important and interrelated in these novels. Only memory can bring back the Communist paradise of Dumbadze, the communal utopia of Aitmatov, the lode of popular wisdom, as well as bygone experiences of Evtushenko's heroes and their ancestors, and the very personal utopia of Bondarev. Freedom is in remembering, and any attempt to rob people of memory is fraught with disaster. Although Bondarev's novel expands its temporal frame to include the past and the future and deals with questions of memory, freedom and happiness, it stands somewhat apart from the novels of Dumbadze, Aitmatov, and Evtushenko. Bondarev's science fiction plot about alien interference is not developed into an independent story; and his protagonist is an eccentric obsessed with "accursed questions." The work can be viewed as transitional, since urban eccentrics populate another branch of fantastic fiction.

Notes

1. *I Dol'she veka dlitsia den', Novyi mir* 11 (1980). Quotations in this chapter are from the English translation *The Day Lasts More than a Hundred Years* (Bloomington: Indiana University Press, 1983).

2. The following list is just a small sample of Soviet immediate critical reaction to the novel: Viktor Peterlin, "Korni," *Ogoniok* 12 (March 1981): 19; N. Potapov, "Mir cheloveka i chelovek v mire: Zametki o romane Chingiza Aitmatova," *Pravda*, February 16, 1981, p. 7; Iu. Mel'vil', "Trud, gumanizm, kosmos," *Voprosy literatury* 9 (September 1981): 26; I. Vasil'eva, "Stilisticheskoe svoeobrazie romana Chingiza Aitmatova 'I dol'she veka dlitsia den' kak proizvedeniia sovetskoi internatsional'noi literatury," *Russkii iazyk v shkole*, (1981): 79—84;

Mikhail Parkhomenko, "Masshtabnost' vzgliada," *Novyi mir* 6 (1981); E. Sidorov, *Voprosy literatury* 9 (1981): 42–43, 49; Vladimir Turbin, "O khudozhestvennoi fantastike: Iskaniia i mel'tesheniia," *Oktiabr'* 9 (1981); Aleksandr Ovcharenko, "Novyi uroven' khudozhestvennogo myshleniia," *Novyi mir* 6 (1981); A. Latynina, "Tsep' chelovecheskoi pamiati," *Oktiabr'* 5 (1981).

3. On May 5, 1986, a plenum of the Union of Writers of Kirgizia elected Chingiz Aitmatov to the post of the first secretary of the Board of the Union of Writers. At the Eighth Congress of Soviet Writers Aitmatov was elected to the "politburo" of the USSR Union of Writers—the Executive Buro of the Secretariat of the Board. Since 1976, and before the collapse of the Union, he had been on the Boards of the USSR Union of Writers and member of the USSR Supreme Soviet, was a delegate to the last five congresses of the CPSU, and has received many awards. See more on Aitmatov's career in *Radio Liberty Research Bulletin*, no. 204, p. 86 (Ann Sheehy).

4. *Novyi mir* 6, 8, 9 (1986).

5. Aitmatov's novel *The White Steamship* (*Belyi parokhod*, 1970) has elements of fantasy in its plot as well.

6. See, for example, Lev Ospovat, "Oboianie mifa, besstrashie smekha: Zametki o novom latinoamerikanskom romane semidesiatykh godov," *Literaturnoe obozrenie* 12 (1981): 24.

7. See Turbin, "O khudozhestvennoi fantastike," p. 209; Bocharov, *Beskonechnost' poiska*, pp. 49–50; Chernysheva, "Potrebnost' v udivitel'nom i priroda fantastiki"; Seleznev, "Fantasticheskoe v sovermennoi proze."

8. A. F. Britikov, "Problemy izucheniia nauchnoi fantastiki," *Russkaia literatura* 1 (1980): 201.

9. Ibid.

10. Nodar Dumbadze, *Zakon vechnosti* (Tbilisi: Merani, 1979). All quotations come from this edition and the translation is mine. First published in Georgian in 1978, the novel was awarded the Lenin prize for literature in 1980.

11. Ibid., p. 213.

12. Ibid.

13. Andrew Barratt, *Between Two Worlds: A Critical Introduction to the Master and Margarita* (Clarendon Press: Oxford, 1987), p. 171.

14. Aitmatov, *Day*, pp. 45–46.

15. Edward J. Brown, *Russian Literature Since Revolution* (Cambridge: Harvard University Press, 1982), p. 55.

16. Alex M. Shane, introduction to *A Soviet Heretic: Essays by Yevgeny Zamyatin* (Chicago: University of Chicago Press, 1982), p. xvii.

17. Aitmatov, *Day*, p. xix.

18. Joseph Mozur points out that the planet Verdant Bosom (*Lesnaia grud'*) functions as the Earth's double in the novel. As Mozur explains, in the pre-Islamic Kirghiz cult of nature the Earth is referred to as *toshu tuktuu zher*, which is rendered in Russian as *zemlia s pokrytoi rastitel'nostiu grud'iu* (the earth with its verdant bosom). On Verdant Bosom the inhabitants are facing the eventual death of their planet as desert continues to eat up more and more of the planet's inhabitable land. The same situation, of course, obtains on Earth, where the Aral

sea is rapidly shrinking. See Joseph Mozur, "Doffing "Mankurt's Cap": Chingiz Aitmatov's *The Day Lasts More than a Hundred Years* and the Turkic National Heritage," *Carl Beck Papers in Russian and East European Studies*, no. 605 (Pittsburgh: University of Pittsburgh Center for Russian and East European Studies, 1987), pp. 21–22. Seen in this light the Earth's decision not to allow the alien civilization to help the earthlings (and help themselves) is fraught with ambiguity. All compulsion to help another civilization disappears when Earth is faced with the prospect of being controlled from the outside. At the same time the Earth may face the same fate of shrinking living space and resources if mindless technology is allowed to rule.

19. First published in *Moskva* 10, 11 (1981). The edition used here is Evgenii Evtushenko, *Iagodnye mesta* (Moscow: Sovetskii Pisatel', 1982). *Wild Berries* is not Evtushenko's sole experiment with the fantastic. "Ardabiola," a story also published in 1981 (in the collection *Tochka opory*), appears to be Evtushenko's tribute to Bulgakov's fantastic short fiction (e.g., *Diaboliad, The Fatal Eggs*) and relates misadventures of a scientist who invented a cure for cancer.

20. John Updike, "Books: Back in the USSR," *New Yorker*, April 15, 1985, p. 118.

21. In the early 1960s the Soviet press devoted a lot of space to a discussion of the effects of the technological revolution on Soviet society. In a position that undermines Evtushenko's utopian scheme, Valentin Rasputin, remarking on the period, rejects the ameliorative effect the "lyricists" (advocates of humanistic values) were suppposed to have had on the "physicists" (proponents of the technological advance). According to Rasputin, the "debate between physicists and poets, which seemed destined to bathe the physicists in spiritual light, to reveal to the poets the realities of a changing world, and to end in universal benefit, in reality moved from the auditorium to the workplace and changed from a hypothetical point of view to a modus operandi. . . . In less than twenty years the friendly 'physicist,' who had once resembled a hussar, grew into a dangerous and autonomous technocrat maneuvering skillfully among duty, purpose, advantage, and morality." ("What We Have," in *Siberia on Fire* [DeKalb: Northern Illinois University Press, 1989], p. 198.)

22. Jurii Bondarev, *Vybor* (Moscow: Molodaia Gvardiia, 1981). The novel was awarded the State Prize for literature in 1983. All subsequent quotations are from the above edition. The translation is mine.

23. See, for example, V. Bondarenko, "Otchuzhdenie," *Don* 7 (1981): 149–153; Sergei Lykoshin, "Vybor pokoleniia," *Don* 7 (1981): 154–157; I. Zhukov, "Ispytanie zhizn'iu," in *Komsomol'skaia pravda*, December 13, 1980; Al. Mikhailov, "Taina dushi," *Literaturnaia ucheba* 5 (1981): 127–137; A. Bocharov's discussion of the novel in *Voprosy literatury* 9 (1981); and Iurii Idashkin, *Grani talanta: O tvorchestve Iuriia Bondareva* (Moscow: Khudozhestvennaia literatura, 1983), pp. 171–228.

24. Anatoli Aleksin, "Kak zhe ty mog?: 'Vybor' Iuriia Bondareva na stsene Malogo teatra," *Komsomol'skaia pravda*, April 15, 1983, p. 4.

5

Between Fantasy and Reality

If for everything that is unusual, incomprehensible and inexplicable we would try to find a succinct rational explanation and our customary earthly analogies, if we do not accept the thought that the Universe lives not only by laws but also by their absence . . . , if we reduce everything to the inadequate laws of our imperfect reason, then no contact is possible with anybody.

—*Anar,* The Contact

A S IF EXPLORING NABOKOV'S well-known dictum that "reality is a very subjective affair,"[1] writers in this, socio-philosophical, strand of fantastic prose examine the inadequacy of human perception of life.[2] The result is a Soviet novel that has more affinity with its nineteenth-century Russian predecessor and modern Western literature than with pure socialist realism, or its updated, refurbished variant. In the fiction of Anar, Kim, and Makanin the fantastic is a thematic and philosophical concern. Alternative modes of thinking and social organization as well as the questioning of history's predictability and of the human ability to comprehend reality fully are the central issues examined in these works.

A number of authors writing in this vein (Kim and Makanin among them) have been called "the forty-year-olds" or representatives of the "Moscow school." In the fiction of this group of writers, the protagonist is usually an ordinary person, a newcomer from the provinces who has to deal with the pressures of living in a big city. Formally, the work of the Moscow school is characterized by experimentation in style and structure. Most of the writers in the school have used fantasy as well as elaborate structural devices to emphasize the disorientation of an ordinary person in a big city. Experiments in form have earned the fiction of the Moscow school yet another name: alternative literature *(al'ternativnaia literatura).*[3]

In contrast to the customary verisimilitude of socialist realist writing, the world in this prose "seems to be unquestionably ours, yet at the same time, as in a dream, ordinary meanings are suspended."[4] Ideas, objects, and situations "remain hedged round with baffling associations" and "all reassurance or reprieve is illusory in face of the anxiety arising from the knowledge that the familiar can take on, and tends to take on, strange and threatening forms."[5] The thrust of this literature is, then, toward a reassessment of the notion that the moral and psychological nature of a person can be known and that the world around us is knowable in some concrete sense.

Limits of human perception, a profound moral confusion stemming from the disintegration of former certitudes, and the mind's propensity for mythmaking are important themes of this literature. To articulate these themes, writers employed a broad range of the fantastic, from the Russian fairy tale to the fantastic of gothic romance. Inexplicable events are often superimposed on the familiar fairy-tale pattern of a journey into a different, even alien world. Here, however, the object of the protagonist's quest is usually self-understanding, and the magic components of the fairy tale ("dead" or "living" water, the obligatory three stages of endeavors, or the Golden Fish) are used to articulate human impotence in the face of reality. Another form of the fantastic employed by these writers is a borrowing from the gothic novel of the nineteenth century, in which magic, mystery, and chivalry are prominent. The medieval castle of the true gothic novel, with its long underground passages, trap doors, dark stairways and mysterious rooms is transformed into a modern high-rise apartment or an old house in a sleepy provincial town. Science fiction plots make their appearance as well, grounding the narratives in the context of contemporary social debates.

The pronounced utopian impulse of this fiction is articulated through various allegorical representations of the desire for change—the fairy tale, Romance, and science fiction. Aversion to the evils of the big industrialized city is common to most writers of this strand of fantastic fiction. The city is a space the protagonists of this literature try to flee and then transform from the outside. Some search for perfection in the past, others place it in a Crystal Palace of the future, and yet others unexpectedly find it in contemporary time and space, hidden in the deeper recesses of the mind.

The Irrational as Punishment for the Crime of Moral Corruption: Nikolai Evdokimov

The dichotomy of real-unreal is one of the central philosophical themes of Evdokimov's works in the fantastic vein. The author is one of many Soviet writers born in the twenties who survived the war but could never entirely divorce themselves from that experience. Evdokimov wrote his share of works celebrating the glory of socialist labor, but it was his war prose that brought him renown as an important Soviet writer. The author's unexpected move in the late seventies and early eighties from socialist realism and war prose into experiments with the fantastic is indicative of significant and broad changes occurring in Soviet literature at the time. In Evdokimov's fantastic prose, a familiar protagonist of urban prose, whose creativity and zest for life are stunted by mindless and corrupting routines of city life, is confronted with the miraculous.

An Incident in the Life of Vladimir Vasil'evich Makhonin (*Proisshestvie iz zhizni Vladimira Vasil'evicha Makhonina*, 1980) is the story of a middle-aged Moscow school principal who returns to his native town to obtain a copy of his birth certificate and, while there, experiences supernatural events.[6] Makhonin's house is capable of changing its location and at night fills up with the voices of the dead; a notification of Makhonin's own death is on file with the town clerk; a friend who is supposed to have died is actually alive; Makhonin's lover survives a deadly airplane crash and then promptly leaves the protagonist to his own devices.

A tale of Makhonin's search for his roots, *Incident* is written in a confessional mode and portrays one person's trial by conscience. Moscow and the provinces, established as opposite points on a moral scale, are two convenient locales for the embodiment of Evdokimov's moralistic scheme. The Moscow of Makhonin's youth no longer exists. Now the protagonist's life is ruled by numbing routines and enlivened only by occasional extramarital affairs. The provinces, on the other hand, are a place where some spontaneity of existence can still be obtained. Makhonin's town is described as a hallucinatory but revealing space, open and mysterious at the same time, the space where, untainted by the sinful ways of the metropolis, the protagonist can rediscover himself and even ponder the nature of happiness.

Makhonin considers two models of happiness here and rejects them both. The fairy-tale vision of a mythical merger with nature is dismissed by the protagonist in a gesture of cynical disbelief. The populist ideal of living a useful and creative existence in the Russian village is equally unacceptable, the position that puts Evdokimov's protagonist squarely against the village prose writers. Makhonin is a displaced person, vacillating between the city and country, unable to belong anywhere but in the enchanted space of a provincial town. The major source of guilt in the protagonist's mid-life crisis are the moral compromises he made leading a comfortable life in the city. Vigorous self-examination brings back the younger, more natural, and ethically more wholesome self, the self that has long been abandoned.

Confrontation with the irrational forces Makhonin to remember. These recollections alternate seemingly at random, yet this randomness is a deliberate strategy, aimed to demonstrate the inseparability of real and unreal, of past, present, and future. When Makhonin is shown to remember his past, it is as real as the events he experiences at the moment of narration. The supernatural events in the novel can be explained either rationally or through a fantastic model. A rational explanation of Makhonin's hallucinations can be found in his emotional and physical exhaustion. The house, which disappears during the day and reappears at night, might simply be a house with two entrances facing two different streets. The fairy-tale magic believed by Makhonin is but a childish indulgence. But the other, fantastic solution to these riddles, is equally viable in the novel. The point is in the inseparability of the two visions of reality. Makhonin's utopian visions, as well as his layered past, are all part of his reality. However, neither the fairy-tale kingdom nor the idyll of country life can regenerate this character whose lot is in redemption through suffering.

The Rational Hero as Prey for the Aliens: Anar

If Evdokimov's hapless urbanite vacillates between rational and supernatural causes of inexplicable occurrences, Anar's protagonist, also a city dweller, is unable to entertain anything but rational explanations for the miraculous events in his life. Anar, like other writers in this strand, is concerned with human propensity for creating cultural, scientific, and political myths. Fantasy is used to articulate desire for political change. Anar questions the predictability of social and human change and attacks rigidity in thought by portraying the life of his protagonist as a series of baffling supernatural events.

Anar (pseudonym of Anar Rasul-ogly Rzaev) was born in Baku, Azerbaijan, in 1938, the son of a prominent Azerbaijani poet Rasul Rza and his wife, Nigiar Rafibeili, also a poet. The author began his publishing career after graduating with a degree in philology from Azerbaijan State University in 1960. His stories, novels, and articles appeared in such Soviet journals as *Novyi mir, Druzhba narodov,* and *Sovetskaia literatura.* His first works were published exclusively in the Azerbaijani language. However, since 1969, like many regional writers in the Soviet Union, Anar had published novels that are authorized translations into Russian.

Until 1978 Anar was perceived essentially as a writer of *byt* prose, whose typical characters are unexceptional people with undistinguished professions. Anar's novel *The Contact (Kontakt),* however, was a significant departure for an author whose earlier preoccupation with ordinary people and events had earned him solid, if not enthusiastic recognition by the critics.[7] Fantastic devices in this work include allusions to fairy-tale magic, to the gothic Romance, a science fiction plot, and a "hesitation" between the real and unreal. Human reactions to the inexplicable in life is the central theme of this short novel.

The story centers around mysterious events in the life of a student. The protagonist has no name, and is referred to as the Student throughout the work, as if to underscore his conformity to a type. There are very few characters in this story, and the locus is an unnamed city transformed and cut off from the rest of the world by an unusual heat wave. After successful entrance examinations into one of the best institutes in the city, the Student has to find an apartment. In his search for a suitable place to live, Anar's character encounters mysterious people and witnesses strange events.

As if to test the Student's reserves and ability to think rationally, time and space undergo unexpected changes. Rooms in the Student's apartment constantly change dimensions, pictures on the walls are transformed right before the Student's eyes, and the clock on the wall moves in reverse. Mysterious boarded-up doors lead nowhere and disconnected phones ring in the night. The Student, unable to explain these occurrences rationally, fears for his mind until one of the characters provides a suitably logical interpretation of events. Now Anar's protagonist can finally enjoy the comforts of ordinary life, undisturbed by the irrational.

Like Evdokimov's work, this story is a succession of mysteries followed by probable resolutions. The Student tries to preserve his sanity by finding rational explanations for supernatural events, no matter how far-fetched these pseudoscientific explanations might be. Each new explanation, however, is negated by the subsequent one, since the author's goal is not "simply to play a guessing game, not to baffle the reader until the final resolution . . . but to create a world that is different, that exists according to its own laws in order to analyze the behavior of an ordinary person in it."[8] This is the reason for the circular plot, where "each new twist negates the experience gained at the previous stage and, finally, in the solution of the mystery the hero remains at the same spot where he began."[9]

Anar's novel is a laboratory in which an ordinary "rational" person undergoes a series of psychological experiments, and the hero's capabilities, self-reliance, and self-confidence are severely tested by the irrational. The Student is ready to believe in "acceptable" wonders: his good luck in entering the institute, or the most unbelievable but "scientific" explanation of miracles. But to accept the fantastic without some probable interpretation is unthinkable. The Student's lack of contact with people, his alienation, is his secret disease. In this sense the Student is an antihero, punished by near-insanity for his rigidity and complacency.

A final explanation for the mysteries encountered by the Student is provided by an astrophysicist whose apartment the Student is renting. The physicist advances the idea that the intergalactic system of communication may have been built on principles new and unknown to us, and that contacts with alien civilizations can be varied and inexplicable from our point of view. He suggests that these aliens are able to assume control over human minds in ways that are incomprehensible to us, and that they may test our potential ability to perceive the world intuitively. Since all their attempts at contact would basically be efforts to disrupt causal relationships in our minds (and causal relationships are seen as the basis of human civilization), they may have chosen the Student's isolated "contactless" mind as the ideal place for their experiment.

To the Student, an avid reader of science fiction, this is a plausible explanation. What he cannot understand is the physicist's conviction about human inability to comprehend reality fully. The Student's response to the physicist's idea—that "no contact is possible with anybody" if people insist on trying to find "a succinct rational explanation and our customary earthly analogies" for everything that is unusual, incomprehensible, and inexplicable—is a decision to conduct research in the area of intergalactic contacts.[10] While the protagonist remains at exactly the same spot where he started, the reader is given an alternative model that accepts the irrational without simplistic logical explanations.

Anar's work examines and rejects rationalistic approaches to reality, challenging thereby the very precepts of the venerable "law-governed pattern" (zakonomernost') of Marxism-Leninism. The myth of a stable world constantly evolving toward perfection, the world that can be observed and easily made sense of, is assaulted here in the very structure of the narrative. The Contact embodies this intellectual claustrophobia through the negative portrayal of enclosed spaces: the stagnant atmosphere of a city cut off from the rest of the world, the haunted apartment, the suffocating space of the possessed elevator, or, finally, the enclosed mind of the Student himself. The aliens are able to assume control over the Student's mind precisely because of his refusal to open it to the outside world. Furthermore, unlike other protagonists of fantastic fiction, the Student lacks any awareness of his cultural tradition. In this sense, his mind is not only closed, but also blank, an easy target for outside influence. This explains also the hero's easy shifts in explaining the irrational; he does not have the anchor of tradition that sustains Aitmatov's characters, for example. The anti-utopia of alien body snatchers controlling people's minds is a motif prominent in fantastic literature. Anar's work suggests a solution that requires an acceptance of alternative modes of thought.

Perfection as Nonresistance to Evil: Anatolii Kim

If Anar in his work primarily questions the idea that the world has one indisputable meaning and purpose, Kim's work is more complex, subverting in a number of ways the narrative paradigms rooted in the teleologies of Marxism-Leninism. At the center is Kim's problematic (male) hero who fuses past, present, and future in his vision and whose "reality" incorporates both the real and unreal. To portray this protagonist, Kim abandons the transparent, consistent, and coherent discourse of socialist realism, the monosemy of its language, and its unitary system of value. Like Anar, Kim uses the fantastic to assail the preconceived notions about human ability to understand reality fully and to chart humanity's future course. Yet, if Anar's dialogue with socialist realism is essentially conducted on the level of ideas, Kim's rejection of teleological mentality is conveyed also in the very language of his narrative.

Born in 1939 in Kazakhstan, Kim graduated from the Literary Institute in Moscow in 1971. His ancestors were Koreans, but three generations of his family have lived in Russia, to which they migrated early in the twentieth century. He writes in Russian and considers Russian to be his native tongue. Kim's first stories were submitted to the literary journal *Avrora* by the famous actor Innokentii Smoktunovskii and published in 1973.[11] Later collections, *The Blue Island (Goluboi ostrov)* and *Four Confessions (Chetyre ispovedi)* appeared in 1976 and 1978. However, it was his novel *Lotus (Lotos, 1980)* that made him an overnight sensation in Moscow literary circles. The controversial work was awarded the annual literary prize of the journal *Druzhba narodov.*[12]

Lotus, disjointed and kaleidoscopic, brings together three main characters: Lokhov, a successful Soviet artist; his mother; and the collective spirit of the dead, called *My* ("We"). Unfolded in a straight chronological line, the story of Lokhov and his mother becomes the story of a mother and her prodigal son. Lokhov's mother is a woman whose links to the natural world and to tradition are very strong. She survives the death of Lokhov's father in the war and flees the approaching Germans with her infant son, crossing the entire country in search of safety. While in flight, she encounters her dead husband, is raped by the Ukrainian *Polizei*, but manages to escape, finding refuge first with an old nomad, then with her second husband, then with a Korean man, Pak, who takes care of her in her terminal illness. Lokhov comes to see her before she dies and offers her an orange cut in the shape of a lotus. Fifteen years later Pak dies after seeing his wife in the image of a young woman, and many years later Lokhov dies after bringing another orange-lotus to his mother's grave.

The immediate response to the novel underscored both the work's originality and the difficulty of its critical assessment. Kim's rather superficial nod to Buddhism was eagerly seized on by critics unaccustomed to a Soviet writer's venture into the area of immortality and reincarnation, the transformation firmly linked by Kim to artistic creativity.[13] The writer's mythological thinking, uniting East and West in one vision, was still a novelty in the early 1980s. Kim's fascination with the irrational was yet another departure from Soviet "establishmentarian" writing, explained away by one critic not as an exception to the everyday rules of life, but as "a pattern [zakonomernost'] hidden in the depths of being and directly correlated with the essence of things and phenomena."[14] Negative reviews of Lotus provided an even better idea of the work as a radical departure from normative writing. Kim was scolded for naturalism, for symbolism, for viewing death in aesthetic terms, for abandoning realistic style, and for showing off "his refined formal skills."[15]

Like other writers in the fantastic decade, in Lotus Kim engages in intertextual polemic that allows for incorporation of and interaction between various trends. On the surface Lotus is reminiscent of a number of village novels about prodigal sons and daughters who return to the country to ask their parents for understanding and forgiveness. By rediscovering their roots, these people acknowledge their alienation from the city, a realization that takes place in a final encounter with the wise, saintly, and strong peasant woman, usually their mother. Kim's novel, however, grafts onto this basic model the existential issue of the spiritual indebtedness of all children to their parents.

The complexity of Kim's philosophical design is underscored by his innovative form. The portrayal of time and space is fluent. The point of narration shifts from the hero's youth to his childhood, to old age (long after the death of his mother), then back to the time of his last visit. The narrative voice changes constantly—from the voice of the young mother to the voice of the son, to the hero's stepfather's, then to the collective voice of the dead. Stream of consciousness, used for the mother's voice, alternates with highly poetic narration, on occasion crossing the borderline into free verse. Through the voice of the main character, on the other hand, we are offered a deeply psychological portrayal of inner turmoil. As in Tolstoy's prose, a multitude of different stimuli generate the thoughts and emotions of the main character at any particular moment of narration. Against the background of mimetic discourse prevalent before the fantastic decade, Kim's narrative innovations signaled a significant change in Soviet literature.

The linear progression of time in realism is replaced here by what Velemir Khlebnikov so aptly called *vsevremennaia odnovremennost'* ("universal [lit., unitemporal] simultaneity"). Kim is trying to embrace all of reality by condensing and expanding time and space in a single utterance. At times the text eludes the spatial and temporal ordering that any reading imparts to it, as if Kim wants to maneuver the reader "into a 'proper' position from which to perceive the paradoxically hidden, but perceptible, structure of meaning."[16]

Unpredictable shifts in the voice of narration, while keeping the reader in constant tension, also point to the basic idea of *Lotus:* there is no death, only a painful but necessary transition into something different. The idea of a transition from the prosaic to the elevated, from one state to another, is supported by deliberate changes in voice and style of narration. An entire subchapter, written in iambic hexameter, marks a transition, a transformation from the prosaic description of Lokhov's mother to the symbolic tale of Lokhov's encounter with the spirit of his mother. For Kim, art is also a transformation. The lotus, an artificial flower created of something no longer living (an orange), becomes newly alive as a symbol of connections between all things and of the moral responsibility of all people before their ancestors. Kim's hero bridges the gap between himself and his dying mother, his city life and his village roots, with a gift of art.

The issues of ancestral debt and of alternative social scripts for Russia's future play an important role in another of Kim's novels of the eighties, *Gurin's Utopia (Utopiia Gurina).*[17] Iurii Gurin, the main protagonist of the novel, is an unsuccessful actor in one of Moscow's regional theaters who leaves his unhappy marriage, work, and life in the city, and tries Tolstoyan "plain living" *(oproshchenie)* in a distant region somewhere in the northeast of Russia. After a brief stay with his friend, the construction engineer Tianigin, Gurin understands that his attempt at plain living has not succeeded and leaves for Moscow. Before Gurin's departure the two friends witness a miracle—Gurin's unassisted flight through air. Both men are transformed by the event.

Like Evdokimov and Anar, Kim employs a variety of fantastic models here. Gurin's flight and his whole exceptional personality are presented by Tianigin in terms of an alien visitation. Gurin sees himself as a Santa Claus who takes upon himself the task of helping others, and his propensity for fantastic activities brings to mind miracles performed by Christian saints. Gurin's behavior challenges his friend's assumptions about life and helps to transform him from a rational, narrow-minded, and sexually dependent man into a person who professes love for everyone and everything. Gurin, who was able to free himself from the demands of sexuality as well, believes in a Fyodorovian devotion to everything existing on the planet, including the spirits of people who earlier inhabited the earth. Death holds no power over Gurin because he does not believe in the complete obliteration of the human spirit. Reverence for the dead, and, particularly, for their remains is an important feature of Kim's characters. Gurin's middle-aged bachelor neighbor preserves his brother's ashes in his apartment; in Gurin's own literary work, "Utopia," death is a welcome act of fusion with nature and the aged are revered but given control over their own destiny. Kim's characters are more concerned with the catastrophic possibilities of the contemporary world than with their own personal mortality. The result of this concern is Gurin's "Utopia," written as a dialogue between the two protagonists. Tianigin's remarks on the margins of the work are a counterpoint to Gurin's assertions.

Gurin's perfect society is a Crystal Palace built by Utopians in the harsh northern country; it is classless, ahistorical, and structureless, revolving around moral questions—love, death, beauty, moral education, and relations between the old and the young. Gurin emphasizes freedom of choice for the Utopians, who are allowed to explore their sexuality unconstrained by a uniform moral code. As a result of this strategy, untamed sexuality and maternal possessiveness disappear, and children are brought up in large institutions. Education is individual, art is considered to be more important than science, and all Utopians are vegetarians.

In his comments, Tianigin objects to Gurin's neglect of technology and to the Prometheanism of the Utopian idea. The conflict between civilization and native cultures, between technology and nature played out both in Utopia and in the descriptions of "how nature was conquered" is not easily resolved. For Gurin, urban life is the source of all evil, and the only way out of this modern dilemma can be found in natural beauty and art. The perfect society is to be built by eccentrics and dreamers. In a scheme reminiscent of Fyodorov's designs for the future (and of Evtushenko's adaptation of Fyodorov's philosophy), Kim's protagonist calls on benevolent scientists to reorganize nature, while artists are to serve as its protectors.

Several features link this novel to other works of fantastic prose. *Gurin's Utopia* uses a three-dimensional temporal frame: the past of the region before the onslaught of civilization (and the past of antiquity alluded to in the image of the beautiful Elena, Gurin's wife), the present tense of the narration, and the perfect future of Gurin's utopia. The novel addresses the issue of benevolent coercion, which, for Kim, results in a pervasive feeling of anxiety and premonition of a social catastrophe, and examines the dangers of unbridled technological experimentation. The fantastic dimension of reality here serves as a means of positing philosophical and social ideas—ideas heavily influenced by the writings of Platonov, Fyodorov, and Tolstoy.

Kim's first full-length novel *The Squirrel* (*Belka*, 1984) offers variations on the themes and an elaboration of the techniques found in *Lotus* and *Gurin's Utopia*.[18] Temporal and spatial planes are fused, the reader is accosted by supernatural occurrences involving eccentric heroes, and the novel professes a profound concern with moral issues. *The Squirrel* describes four students at the Moscow Art Institute—Innokentii Lupetin, Mitia Akutin, Georgii Aznaurian, and the main protagonist, who does not reveal his true name, but calls himself the Squirrel. The life stories of the three protagonists are sifted through the consciousness of the Squirrel, who is able to transform himself into any one of his friends. The thoughts and feelings of the Squirrel's companions are presented in the form of first person narrative, but the Squirrel's own voice constantly intrudes into the narrative, intermingling with the confessional voices of the three friends. This intentional complexity of form makes the narrative very dense, a coded text in need of deciphering. The Squirrel's "remarks on the margins"—a series of philosophical digressions on the state of his society and modern world—do not clarify, but rather complicate the development of the various plots.[19]

A recurrent idea runs through the inner monologues of the novel's protagonists: the lives of "true" *(podlinnye)* people are endangered by a conspiracy of "men-beasts" *(zagovor zverei)* who are out to destroy the world. Each of the four life stories in the novel is an illustration of this idea. Grigorii Aznaurian falls in love with an Australian millionaire, marries her, and leads a comfortable but dull life of leisure. Grigorii's talent deserts him and in the end he is killed in an accident. Innokentii Lupetin tries the life of a village teacher. His village is dying, however, and there are no children left to teach. Inactivity and depression lead to beastly cruelty toward his own mother, then to insanity and, eventually, to suicide.

Mitia Akutin is murdered by a criminal but comes back to life because his creative gift has not been exhausted and he, the true artist, cannot perish without completing his artistic work. His lover, Liliana, whose alter ego is a bloodthirsty polecat, continues to live with Mitia after he is raised from the dead. Mitia is immortal and capable of what Aitmatov in his *Execution Block* would call historical synchronism— traveling through time and spreading his message of people's moral responsibility for their deeds. Mitia is Kim's true *(podlinnyi)* person of the future.

The Squirrel's fate is no less gloomy. A writer whose aim in life is to describe and record events and warn the world of the conspiracy of the man-beasts, he is also an animal, raised by a squirrel after the death of his natural mother. The main protagonist becomes convinced that it is necessary to destroy the animalistic side of himself to be truly human; in order to accomplish this, he kills the squirrel in himself, destroying that part of his identity, and turns into an ordinary man.

The spirits of the dead, "We," transposed into this work from *Lotus*, proclaim an imminent "grandiose change from death to immortality."[20] The main precondition for this change is the acceptance of "the necessity of each to create [their] life in a human fashion *[po-chelovecheski]*," the effort that will bring about a world "where nobody ever will be capable of murder."[21] In achieving this goal, all should work hard "for the accumulation of the universal energy of the good."[22]

In its belief in the eventual immortality of people based on "the accumulation of the universal energy of the good," in its distaste for animalistic (and sexual) instincts, and in its reverence for the sacredness of all matter, Kim's novel is remarkably Fyodorovian and Tolstoyan. Kim is against violence of any kind, be it the violence of revolution or of war. He blames the predominance of animalistic qualities in people for all their misfortunes and hopes for the emergence of a new human being, a Christ-like figure incapable of cruelty. Direct authorial communications with the reader in *The Squirrel*, its moralistic tone, and a sense of an approaching social catastrophe hanging over its characters presage publicistic literature of glasnost. Yet the novel's basic story line—the conspiracy of man-beasts against "real" people—is paraphrased along the lines of a fairy tale whose intricate magic plot and a pronounced hope for a happy resolution mitigate somewhat the apocalyptic flavor of Kim's philosophy.

Kim's contribution to changes in Russian literature was significant and manifold. He achieved the interrogation of existing social scripts and of "establishmentarian" modes of writing through the use of fantasy, multidimensional characters, and innovative technique. Moreover, Kim's work in the fantastic vein offered the Russian middle-class reader a protagonist whose disaffection was recognizable and shared and whose future was still in the making.

Fantastic Compromise: Vladimir Makanin

Alternately claimed as a member of the Moscow school, recognized as a writer of alternative literature, and embraced by the literature of glasnost, Makanin remains an author whose overall originality locate him outside established trends. This elusiveness was reflected in Soviet critical opinion, for while Makanin's work generated enormous critical response, it also baffled the critics.[23] Contemporary Soviet criticism responded to the challenges of Makanin's writings by constantly, if fruitlessly, searching for the author's attitude ("[Makanin's work] affects critics . . . as a mystery that teases the imagination: one wants so much to find in [his] prose a unifying logic *[skvoznuiu logiku]*, a single meaning").[24] Makanin's narrative, however, is deliberately constructed to resist categorization.

In the works of the mature Makanin it is generally a conflict, situation, or human condition that is supposed to elicit an ironic or a sympathetic response.[25] This same central situation-conflict-condition is examined, or mirrored, in other plots, subplots, and even passages—what might be called the narrative polyphony of Makanin's narrative. The notion of polyphony is helpful here because each narrative unit, although illustrating an aspect of one central issue, is given equal importance and an equal share of narrative interest, whether it takes place in legendary time, the recent past, or at the time of narration. To Tatiana Tolstaya, this structural configuration is reminiscent of a dream in which the core situation infuses *(razlita)* the entire narrative.[26] This is a very apt observation, because Makanin's themes are not merely articulated at the level of surface plot, but actually permeate the very structure of his novels and influence them stylistically.

One can observe a clear progression in Makanin's work from the satirical Moscow stories of the seventies to the philosophical works of the eighties that focus on creative artists and intellectuals in search of their provincial roots. Makanin's stories of the seventies can be viewed as a chronicle of the period of stagnation in Soviet society.[27] Makanin's work of the period is filled with the unsavory details of Moscow life—unfair apartment exchanges, the venality of the black market in books and other consumer goods, bribing for promotion or to get into universities, plagiarism, indifference, and sordid interpersonal relations. It was Makanin's story *The Safety Valve (Otdushina)* that introduced the term *mebel'noe vremia* (lit., the furniture period) to describe the materialistic spirit of the seventies.[28] In *The Safety-Valve* the main character, who actually makes furniture for the new Soviet middle class, offers his lover's favors to a professor of mathematics in exchange for his son's admission to the university.[29] In the novel's one-word Russian title Makanin manages to encapsulate the absurdity of the situation played out in the text. Although *otdushina* literally means "safety valve" the prefix *ot-* implies moving away, distancing oneself from the *dusha* (soul), thus imparting a sense of despiritualization to the title.[30]

Another important influence on Makanin's work of the seventies is Jurii Trifonov, whose carefully restrained descriptions of the everyday life of urbanites elucidated the moral degradation and anxieties of the Soviet middle class. Makanin's prose of the seventies is very much like Trifonov's, but where Trifonov's heroes are often engaged in some spiritual quest, intent on discovering "the threads that connect the past with the even more distant past and the future," Makanin's characters display an astonishing materialism and lack of moral values.[31] Makanin's males are weak and his women are portrayed as ruthless. In *Portrait in the Round* (*Portret i vokrug*, 1978), a novel typical of Makanin's work of the seventies, the writer compares marriage with castration and proceeds to illustrate his thesis by telling the story of a starving young writer who, in his struggle for comfortable family life, finds he has completely and irrevocably compromised his talent and ideals. The "I" of the work is revealed in all its complexity through what is around—the notorious atmosphere of stagnation that envelopes, poisons, and turns the unsuspecting protagonist into an opportunist. A portrait of one character expands into a broad canvas depicting the entire Brezhnev era.

The loss of moral values is absolute in Makanin's chronicle of the Soviet middle class. Like Trifonov before him, however, Makanin is never didactic. Makanin's prose is fused with irony, and his narrator is carefully distanced from the events described in the stories. It takes some time before the reader realizes that all these pleasant people inhabiting Makanin's prose are, in fact, negative characters. The distancing of the narrator is achieved through the use of quasidirect speech or *erlebte Rede (nesobstvenno priamaia rech)*, which allows for smooth transitions from one narrative point of view to another.[32] This device also imparts a lively colloquial tone to the narrative at times approaching the immediacy of *skaz* (highly colloquial first person narration). Makanin pays considerable attention to the structure of his stories.

The mirroring of one plot in another (narrative polyphony) and mystery plots are used by Makanin to sustain the reader's interest as well as to portray various facets of his characters. These devices are particularly important in *Portrait in the Round*, for example, where reader are made to think they are following the story of one character while in fact the novel turns out to be the story of the narrator's own fall from grace. In the same work Makanin devotes substantial space to a discussion of the creative process in general. This theme, together with the device of narrative polyphony, becomes important in his later work.

Makanin's work of the early eighties becomes more involved, filled with increasingly elaborate structural devices, and it is here that we find the writer's first experiments with fantasy as well as his sympathetic characters.[33] One such protagonist is an intellectual and a recent city dweller who abandons Moscow in search of his country roots; another is an eccentric. Perhaps the most effective of Makanin's eccentrics is the one found in *The Forerunner* (*Predtecha*, 1982), a former criminal turned healer able to cure terminally ill patients through touch and persuasion to undergo moral change.[34]

Makanin's work of the eighties moves away from the ironic descriptions of the Soviet urban middle class to the search for an ideal fusion of the old and the new, for a reconciliation of individual and communal impulses. His novel *Where the Sky Met the Hills (Gde skhodilos' nebo s kholmami*, 1984) features an intellectual obsessed with the abandonment of his cultural past.[35] Georgii Bashilov, a renowned Soviet composer, is consumed with guilt, the result of imagined harmful influences that his music had on his native community. When Bashilov left home, became a composer, and began integrating native songs into his works, the inhabitants of his settlement stopped singing. Bashilov thinks that his music has exhausted all the creative energies of the settlement and is obsessed with the notion of repaying his debt to the community. Bashilov returns home determined to create a children's chorus to continue the tradition, but his efforts fail. The newcomers to the settlement no longer have any need for indigenous folk art, instead they passively consume the offerings of mass culture on television and radio. In a farewell gesture to the settlement and its vanishing culture, Bashilov sings the old songs together with a retarded man, the only one left who still remembers them, and is startled by a child's voice joining in: ". . . silently and on its own the Minute (*Minuta*) was approaching them when the darkness and silence would be suddenly pierced by the high-pitched and clear voice of a child."[36]

The origins of Bashilov's pressing need to give back what he has taken lie in his memory of the old settlement, which, not unlike the small island settlement of Matera in Valentin Rasputin's *Farewell to Matera* (1976), is the embodiment of the communal spirit. Bashilov owes everything to the old settlement, including his life and his gift for music. Bashilov's settlement (*avariinyi poselok*) was created specifically for the firefighters who work at a nearby plant. The inhabitants are not afraid of death, since catastrophe (fire) is the norm at the settlement; death is accepted as the natural outcome of a perilous existence.[37] Bashilov's parents died in one such fire and all inhabitants of the settlement contributed to his welfare. Yet, in his description of a harmonious community before the onslaught of mass culture, Makanin does not draw exclusively on village traditions, as writers of village prose would. Although one can assume that the inhabitants of Bashilov's community have peasant roots, it is the life of a settlement that is permeated with the communal spirit here. In a sense, Bashilov is a prodigal son returning to his native country to expiate his guilt. However, Makanin's novel suggests the possibility of forgiveness and of the spiritual union of displaced members of any close community with their native traditions.

Bashilov's settlement has changed, and the disintegration of communal ties coincided with the loss of the gift for singing. For Bashilov to continue his work, it is necessary to restore the traditional pool of folk songs; without that source no creation is possible. But to regenerate the primitive source one has to turn back the wheels of history and return to the community as it was before the invasion of mass culture. Bashilov's music is shown here to obliterate the line between high and folk art, since the composer's classical pieces are transformed into popular songs and, in that form, returned to the people. Still, what he gives back is not what he has taken. The songs the inhabitants hear are Bashilov's own, rather than the product of a communal effort. Bashilov's return, however, as well as his success in drawing out the creative energies of his community, points to a possibility of regeneration.

In *Where the Sky*, as in his works of the seventies, Makanin addresses problems of morality in terms familiar from *byt* prose. This time, and in an obvious dialogue with the tradition of village prose, the focus shifts to the loss of the continuity with communal life, a loss shown to lead to hypertrophic individualism and alienation. These moral issues are approached aesthetically, and the solution Makanin offers is a kind of imaginative omnivorousness, an idealized merger between high art and folk art. This major theme is presented with the help of narrative polyphony, whereby Bashilov's thoughts about the dependence of high art on its folk roots are cleverly mirrored in a succession of narrative sequences.

Makanin's neutral, almost colloquial narration is punctuated by highly theoretical passages on the relationship between folk and classical elements in music. The title of the novel *(Where the Sky Met the Hills)* also points to an ideal merger of the finite and the infinite, the high and the low. The overall organization of the novel is highly influenced by that branch of creative activity that is its subject (i.e., music). The beginning of the novel is, in a way, an overture, where all the major themes of the work are condensed into a single form. These themes include the relationship between classical and folk art, Bashilov's guilt for taking away the creative gift of the settlement, and his prophetic vision of the first singing child. In the rest of the narrative these themes are developed further, each reappearing at approximately equal intervals until the final coda, where Bashilov's dream comes true.

The novel's climax comes when the village fool and the intellectual artist unite to give birth to a new voice. The miracle of birth is prepared for by the novel's circular structure. (In the "overture" Bashilov dreams of a singing child, and the child reappears again in the middle of the novel.) Makanin's vision here seems to be optimistic despite all odds. Although the novel's end is deliberately ambiguous, within the context of the entire work the birth of a new voice is perceived as a cathartic event, the resolution of Bashilov's conflict and the expiation of his guilt.[38]

In *Where the Sky* the loss of continuity with communal life is remedied by the reconciliation between individual and communal principles. This (most fantastic) compromise between the two opposing impulses, embodied in the duet of the two protagonists and in the subsequent birth of a new voice, attempts to bring together the irreconcilable realities of city and country life. In the Gorbachev period (discussed in chapter 9), Makanin's general focus on creativity leads to the examination of language as a generator of mythologies and cultures, a focus shared by other alternative writers.

In contrast to the "Aitmatov school," the fantastic fiction of Evdokimov, Anar, Kim, and Makanin represented a firm break from the certitudes of socialist realist prose. The fantastic here served to articulate philosophical and social concerns of a changing society. Human attitudes to the natural world, to tradition, and to the irrational were placed at the center of this fiction, a strategy that led to the reexamination of materialist epistemology and to a shared social ideal. This ideal is a society of people who revere everything living, preach and practice spontaneous enjoyment of life and artistic creativity, respect their ancestors and their traditions, and aspire to a world where communal impulses will harmoniously combine with individual desires.

Notes

1. Vladimir Nabokov, *Strong Opinions* (New York: McGraw-Hill, 1981), p. 10.

2. In a modified version parts of this chapter appeared in my article "Science Fiction and Fantasy—a Prelude to the Literature of Glasnost," *Slavic Review* (Summer 1989): 254–268.

3. Other writers usually associated with the group are: Vladimir Krupin, Vladimir Orlov, Ruslan Kireev, Vladimir Lichutin, Anatolii Kurchatkin, Aleksandr Prokhanov, Vladimir Gusev, and Georgii Bazhenov. Most of the participants at the first meeting of the Club of Moscow Writers, held on November 24, 1979, were members of the Moscow school. The meeting produced a free exchange of opinions on the goals and shared concerns of the school; its record is, in a way, the school's manifesto. The date of the meeting may be viewed as the official date for the formation of the group. See the record of the meeting in Vladimir Bondarenko's "Avtoportret pokoleniia," *Voprosy literatury* 11 (1985): 79–113. More on the shared themes of the Moscow school in A. Bocharov, "Kak slovo nashe otzovetsia?" *Voprosy literatury* 11 (1985): 115–154.

4. T. E. Apter, *Fantasy Literature: An Approach to Reality* (Bloomington: Indiana University Press, 1982), p. 3.

5. Ibid.

6. Nikolai Evdokimov, *Izbrannye proizvedeniia* (Moscow: Khudozhestvennaia Literatura, 1983), 2:150–232.

7. Anar, "Kontakt," *Druzhba narodov* 12 (1978): 122–155. All subsequent quotations are from this edition. The translation is mine.

8. A. Latynina, "Forma dlia mysli?" *Literaturnoe obozrenie* 7 (1979): 56.

9. Ibid., p. 57.

10. Anar, "Kontakt," p. 155.

11. I am grateful to Charles Rougle for this information. Dr. Rougle's sources are two articles on Kim: Vitalii Kamyshev, "Beskonechnost' sud'by: Zametki o proze Anatoliia Kima," *Dal'nii Vostok* 6 (1989): 142; Peter Rollberg, "Anatoli Kim: Einhornchen," *Weimarer Beitrage* 35.7 (1989): 1174.

12. Anatolii Kim, *Lotos, Druzhba narodov* 8 (1980). See more on the reaction to the publication of the novel in W. Beitz, H. Conrad, D. Kassek, and P. Rollberg, "Prosa und Dramatik der Generation der 'Vierzigjährigen,'" *Weimarer Beitrage* 33.10 (1987): 1701.

13. "Otrazhenie istiny: Molodye kritiki obsuzhdaiut" (Pavel Nerler), *Literaturnoe obozrenie* 3 (1982): 40–41.

14. Ibid., (Arkadii Khvoroshchan).

15. Ibid. (Svetlana Lanshchikova); p. 42 (A. Razumikhin). Natal'ia Ivanova offers a view of Lotus that is appreciative of Kim's aestheticism yet also finds in the novel a danger of "linguistic and cultural eclecticism." See Ivanova, "Iskushenie ukrasheniem, ili 'raskalennaia giena,'" (1984) in *Tochka zreniia: O proze poslednikh let* (Moscow: Sovetskii Pisatel', 1988), pp. 66–70.

16. Linda Hutcheon, *Narcissistic Narrative: The Metaphictional Paradox* (New York: Methuen, 1984), p. xvi.

17. First published in the collection *Nefritovyi poias* (Moscow: Molodaia Gvardiia, 1981).

18. Anatolii Kim, *Belka* (Moscow: Sovetskii Pisatel', 1984). All the following quotations are from this edition. The translation is mine.

19. *The Squirrel*'s complexity of form and unorthodox message have been the points most heatedly debated by Soviet critics. See Vs. Surganov, "Energiia dobra" and Vl. Novikov, "Pod sousom vechnosti," *Literaturnaia gazeta* (February 13, 1985): 4; Elena Iukina, "Dostoinstvo cheloveka," *Novyi mir* 12 (1984): 245–248. For a recent Western view see Peter Rollberg, "Between Beast and God: Anatolii Kim's Apocalyptic Vision," in *World Literature Today* 67.1 (1993): 100–106.

20. Kim, *Belka,* p. 269.

21. Ibid.

22. Ibid., p. 270.

23. See Aleksandr Mikhailov, "Stereotip ili kharakter?" *Literaturnaia Rossiia* 13 (March 28, 1986). For an assessement of varying critical responses to Makanin's work see also Lev Anninskii, "Struktura labirinta," *Znamia* 12 (1986): 218–226. For a short bibliography of criticism on Makanin, see V. Piskunov and S. Piskunova, "Vse prochee—literatura," *Voprosy literatury* 2 (1988): 39. In a modified version parts of the section on Makanin's work before glasnost appeared in my article "Vladimir Makanin's Solutions to the Loss of the Past," *Studies in Comparative Communism,* 21.3/4: 349–356.

24. Piskunov and Piskunova, "Vse prochee—literatura," p. 39. For a comparative look at Makanin, Trifonov, and Rasputin, see Natal'ia Ivanova, "Pereklichka" (1984) in *Tochka zreniia,* pp. 82–107.

25. Tatiana Tolstaia and Karen Stepanian note this quality of Makanin's prose in their dialogue ". . . Golos, letiashchii v kupol," *Voprosy literatury* 2 (1988): 78–105.

26. Ibid., pp. 80–82.

27. On Makanin's early work see Boris Pankin, "Dobrota, nedobrota," *Druzhba narodov* 9 (1982): 249–254.

28. Perhaps the closest English term for this phenomenon is *populuxe*, which refers to the decade from the mid-fifties to the mid-sixties in America, a period in which the affluent American middle class spent unprecedented sums on material possessions designed in either pretentious or poor taste.

29. See Vladimir Makanin, *Golosa* (Moscow: Sovetskaia Rossiia, 1982).

30. I am grateful to Katerina Clark for this observation.

31. Trifonov, *Povesti*, p. 307. The translation is mine.

32. Quasi-direct speech involves discourse that is formally authorial, but that belongs in its "emotional structure" to a represented character, his "inner speech transmitted and regulated by the author." Quasi-direct speech is a threshold phenomenon, where intentions of author and characters are combined in a single intentional hybrid. (See Michael Holquist (ed.) in Mikhail Bakhtin, *Dialogic Imagination* (Austin: University of Texas Press, 1981), p. 433.

33. See more on this in Irina Rodnianskaia, "Neznakomye znakomtsy," *Novyi mir* 8 (1986): 230–247; Anatolii Klitko, "Geroi i ego zhiznennaia pozitsiia," *Literaturnaia Rossiia* (January 14, 1983): 8; Alla Latynina, "Beg v zazerkal'e," *Literaturnoe obozrenie* 9 (1982): 22–26.

34. See Aleksandr Kazintsev, "Igra na ponizhenie," *Literaturnoe obozrenie* 10 (1983): 29–32.

35. *Novyi mir* 1 (1984). For the contemporary critical assessment see Mikola Riabchuk, "Sindrom Bashilova," *Literaturnoe obozrenie* 11 (1984): 43–45; A. Lanshchikov, "Nameki ili metafory?" and V. Skuratovskii, "Real'nost' mysli," *Literaturnaia gazeta*, (June 6, 1984): 5.

36. Makanin, *Golosa*, p. 103.

37. For more on catastrophe as a norm, see Anninskii, "Struktura labirinta," p. 225. In a prophetic anticipation of glasnost, some critics have interpreted the fires in this work as a metaphor for the disastrous economic situation in the Soviet Union as a whole. (See, for example, A. Lanshchikov's negative review in *Literaturnaia gazeta*, June 6, 1984, p. 5). One should also mention a similar critical response to Rasputin's 1985 sequel to *Farewell to Matera—Fire (Pozhar)*. In Rasputin's work the loss of traditions equated with the loss of moral values. In the Soviet press of the time allusions to Rasputin's *Fire* often cropped up in discussions about the Chernobyl disaster.

38. Makanin's closure is possibly an allusion to Thomas Mann's *Doktor Faustus* and to the last line of Aleksandr Blok's poem "Devushka pela v tserkovnom khore" *("i tol'ko vysoko u Tsarskikh vrat prichastnyi tainam plakal rebenok o tom chto nikto ne pridet nazad"),* ["A girl was singing in the Choir" ("Only on top of the Holy Doors then—a child partaking the mysteries was crying . . . and one can never return again")], in Vladimir Markov, Merril Sparks, eds., *Modern Russian Poetry, Anthology* (Indianapolis: Bobbs-Merrill, 1966), p. 159.

6

Peasant Dreamers, Shattered Dreams: Village Utopians

There are no misfortunes on earth that a people cannot overcome if they are properly organized and directed in accordance with the whole flow of their historical progression and their spiritual commonality. And only the following can have extremely serious, even irreparable consequences for any people: the complacency of a generation or of several generations, obliviousness to their roots, and a conscious or unconscious break with the centuries-old experience of the past, all of which lead, through subsequent phases to the loss of national feeling and historical memory, to fragmentation, depersonalization, and homelessness.

—*Valentin Rasputin, "Your Son, Russia, and Our Brother"*

THE PEASANT QUESTION, a source of much utopian dreaming in the twenties, has emerged as an important social and literary issue of the last three decades. In the seventies several prominent writers of village prose published novels in which fantastic and utopian elements combined to glorify the traditional Russian peasant way of life and to lament the fate of the Russian peasant in the Soviet period. The novels discussed in this chapter (all written between 1975 and 1976) cannot be considered full-fledged utopias, for they lack the programmatic bent of standard utopian literature. Nevertheless, a pronounced utopian element is apparent in all these works. When engaged in dreaming, contemporary peasant utopians drew their inspiration from the realm of legend and pagan myths (an element of prerevolutionary peasant utopias as well) and, simultaneously, placed themselves in sharp opposition to the scientific and progress-oriented vision of classical socialist realism. They reworked Christian and pre-Christian myths into a poetic vision of a peasant paradise where Nikolai Cherny-shevsky's Crystal Palace seemed decidedly out of place. Or they used carnivalesque laughter to demonstrate the nightmarish perversion of Chernyshevsky's ideals in the contemporary Soviet countryside. Often these novels urged reader participation in a lament for harmony and natural beauty which, purportedly, characterized the true world of the Russian village. They dreamed about the golden past of the Russian peasantry and rued its inexorable demise.

What unites the work of all the writers examined in this chapter is simply the feeling that, for the Russian peasant, the old way of life was better than the present one. And, as we will see below, it is in descriptions of the preindustrialized Russian countryside that the utopian mentality of Soviet village writers is most forcefully expressed. Another common concern of village prose in general, and village utopians in particular, is that the Soviet state, with its belief in progress and technological miracles, has been responsible for depleting the spiritual reservoirs and natural resources of old Russia.[1] This perception of the harmful role of what many saw as the arrogant Soviet technocracy prompted village writers to resort to parody or to express anti-utopian sentiment in their works. Finally, the most common shared idea of village utopians is that peasants and their way of life are fast disappearing, and have to be re-captured, if only in literature, before they become extinct, and before the spiritual wealth of old Russia is completely lost.

Why does village prose shift into a utopian-fantastic mode in the mid-seventies? The question is a complex one. The desire of village prose to posit its own ideal, one that stands in clear opposition to the precepts of the Marxist-Leninist-Stalinist view of the countryside, has long characterized Soviet writing about the countryside. In the last two decades, however, the need for a return to the ways of the traditional village has been much more emphatically stated in such prose.

One should remember, of course, that an interest in the fantastic, and ventures into utopian dreaming, are characteristic of all Soviet literature of the last two decades and cannot be limited to works of village prose. Literature about the countryside addressed the same issues that had for the last two decades concerned the Soviet intelligentsia in general—environmental despoliation, nuclear war, and the moral disintegration of society. In fact, Soviet fiction of the period was characterized by a kind of migration of ideas, issues, and even devices from one trend to another. If village prose writers of the seventies and eighties (and, most notably, in the period of glasnost) often took on the issues debated in "urban" prose, then the standard conflicts of village prose found their place in other works, not readily designated as village prose. In many ways, all

Soviet fiction of the seventies and eighties was engaged in the familiar debate of city versus country, with the values of the country, however, gaining ever more strength.

In the understanding of village prose writers of the period, resolution of the issues troubling Soviet society hinged on a return to the time-tested traditional values of the Russian village. However, village writers could not fail to recognize that the old village no longer existed. The gradual realization of the collapse of the spiritual foundations of a Russian culture based on the communal spirit of the old village prompted village prose writers to resort to utopian dreaming. Vladimir Nabokov has aptly called censorship the mother of metaphor, and it is obvious that in a culture of censorship illusion is managed very carefully. Before the age of glasnost utopian dreaming was, perhaps, the only way left for village prose to express its anguish and profound dissatisfaction with the situation in the Russian countryside. As we will see below, under glasnost writers of the Russian countryside abandoned all attempts at veiling their message and moved into the arena of publicistic prose, with an open declaration of the demise of the Russian village. Village prose under glasnost, together with the rest of Soviet literature, was involved in documenting the collapse of the Bolshevik utopia, both in the city and the country.

From the Battle of Utopias to the Kolkhoz Paradise

The view that the preservation or reconstruction of the old village is the only path to salvation and spiritual regeneration for the entire country has moved from the periphery (where it lay dormant since the twenties) into the forefront of national consciousness. Village prose of the late fifties, sixties, and early seventies had forced the Soviet reader to re-assess former preconceptions about the backwardness and "idiocy of peasant life," preconceptions formed largely due to the victory, after the "duel of utopias" in the twenties, of the Bolshevik utopian model in Soviet literary and social discourse.[2]

In the twenties interest in the peasant issue was prompted by the desire, on the part of the builders of the new society, to accommodate the peasantry within the traditional Marxist models. The Marxist-Leninist vision of the future was pro-urbanist and antivillage. The transformation of the old village was expected to proceed according to the urban model—through technology, efficient use of resources, fast-paced industrialization, and universal education. As Trotsky saw it, the revolution creates the environment for the emergence of a new person, who, "through the machine will command nature in its entirety."[3] Technology should allow humans to conquer material needs and bring about true equality for all in a perfect future where there is no longer any distinction between rural and urban ways of life.

This utopian model provided the shorings used to prop up the formulae of socialist realism in the thirties and forties. The "road to happiness" envisioned by socialist realism presupposed strict control and manipulation of nature by means of technology and science. In this vision, the city triumphed over the country, and the conscious urban proletariat was called on to bring its new gospel into the countryside—to teach, preach to, and convert the uninitiated, by force if necessary. If Platonov's work of the early twenties attempted to rework the Bolshevik utopia into his own vision of the future transformation of the backward village by means of technology and brotherly love, then the peasant utopians of the twenties offered the traditional Russian village as a blueprint for the future world. The Scythian movement, led by Blok, Bely, Ivanov-Razumnik, and Pilnyak, and included writers of peasant origin, was a popular literary movement in Russia in the first half of the twenties.[4] More pointedly antiurban, the peasant writers among the Scythians (Sergei Esenin, Nikolai Kliuev) saw the society of the future as the apotheosis of the rebellious spirit of the Russian peasantry, who sought to destroy the city and to return Russia to her "natural," pre-Petrine state. Nikolai Kliuev's portrait of Lenin as the liberator of folk legends was typical of the group's belief that the Revolution would usher in a true peasant paradise. Boris Pilnyak articulates this misunderstanding of the Bolshevik goals for society in *The Naked Year* (1922). One of his characters embraces the Bolsheviks, who in his view stand for the peasant truth, and rejects the "Communists," who protect the interests of the international proletariat.[5]

Sergei Esenin's *Inonia* (1918) is typical of the Scythian view of the perfect future as a result of the spontaneous, anarchic, and violent release of the suppressed energies of the Russian peasant. Esenin's utopia is, however, sectarian in spirit. Although revolutionary change brings in a new world based on traditional Russian peasant values, Esenin rejects Christian dogma, with its feigned humility and ossified ritual, and calls for another golden age for Russia, where the new faith is "without the cross and without suffering" *(bez kresta i muk)*. Most of the poem is devoted to a portrayal of the destruction of the old age of injustice by the poet himself, who becomes here the liberator of the popular utopian legend. Inonia *(in-aia strana)* is designated only as "different," but is actually a hauntingly familiar country where people live in harmony with nature and the new order, where "faith is in power" and "truth is in us" (i.e., in representatives of the new order). Esenin's vision is heretical, but heresy and the revolution are embraced as the only true paths to perfection. And Esenin's perfect world is the nostalgic recreation of the poet's own peasant childhood. As with Russian sectarian utopias before him, Esenin's vision is "pastoral rather than urban, and religious rather than secular and Promethean."[6]

The Journey of My Brother Aleksei into the Land of Peasant Utopia (1920) by Ivan Kremnev (pseudonym of Aleksandr Chayanov) is another period piece engaged in prophesying a future peasant utopia, but differs from Esenin's in several respects.[7] First, Chayanov's work disregards the issue of how one arrives at the perfect society. Second, unlike Esenin's poetic vision of the destruction of the old and creation of the new (with most attention awarded to the process of destruction), Chayanov's novel is much closer to classical utopias in the space it allots to the actual workings of the new society.

The Russian commune plays the central role in Chayanov's utopia. The hero of the novel wakes up in Moscow in 1984 to find Russia and the world transformed. Since 1934 power has been in the hands of peasant parties, the big cities have been destroyed, and the population is mainly engaged in a labor-intensive agriculture. After a brief period of world peace, there is a devastating war that divides the world into five isolated social systems. The ideal system, arrived at in Russia, is the only one where work is not separated from creativity. Encouragement of personal initiative promotes individual well-being in the broadest sense, within the framework of a collective economy as well as social and state organizations. Consumer and agricultural societies are formed on a voluntary basis and each citizen has a say in the workings of society. As has been pointed out, Chayanov's utopia shared common ground with Bolshevik utopian dreaming in the emphasis upon overcoming, by means of social engineering and by raising the consciousness of the masses, the chronic cultural backwardness of the countryside.[8]

The utopian movement in the twenties was characterized by its diversity. All groups believed that success in building a perfect society depended on higher political awareness, yet the utopians differed in their vision of how to raise the consciousness of the masses. As Katerina Clark explains:

> The anti-urban utopians and the avant-garde stressed the aesthetic as a crucial factor in raising consciousness, while the Bolsheviks stressed enlightenment, technology, and political and economic factors. The anti-urban utopians insisted that the city should be dismantled as a first step in providing an aesthetic and therefore beneficial environment for future development, while the avant-garde and the Bolsheviks hailed the city as the environment of the future.[9]

The tradition that prevailed in Soviet letters in the thirties and forties is clearly indebted to Bolshevik utopianism, with its belief in enlightenment, technology, and political and economic progress as the keys to the perfect world of the future.[10] The works written under the banner of socialist realism provide their distinctive brand of utopian literature, however. The production novels of the thirties offer an inspiring view of human potential; nothing is impossible for the superhuman proletarians of this fiction, capable of spectacular feats of heroism in their endeavor to build a better and just society. This literature is imbued with the myths and images of the "fantasy state" constructed by the regime:

> Stalin's Soviet Union, a "panegyric utopia," consisted of a myth of well-being, an "iconography of happiness," and a cult of the benevolent ruler. If the reality of the Soviet Union contrasted dramatically with the visions of the revolutionary dreamers and utopians, the myths and images constructed by the regime promoted the fiction that the Soviet people were already living in a kind of utopia, that the conservative stability of the social system and the rigidity of the political structure were "revolutionary."[11]

If the Stalinist novels of the thirties focus on the heroic achievements of their extraordinary heroes on the path to a glorious future, then the works of the "kolkhoz" literature of the forties move one step further in mythologizing Soviet reality when they show contemporary life as paradise regained. Semyon Babayevsky's *Cavalier of the Gold Star* (1947) portrays the Russian postwar village as a harmonious and prosperous community where the only obstacles the hero encounters are brought on by the vagaries of nature. In his own way Babayevsky reconciles the dream of a peasant utopia with the Crystal Palace that the heroes of production novels (and Platonov's novels) were building at such incredible cost. The hero helps to build a hydroelectric station in his village, whose happy community can finally reap the fruit of technological progress.

Of course, Babayevsky's peasants are far removed from Kliuev's or Esenin's "keepers of the old flame"; in fact, they are cardboard figures whose claim to *narodnost'* (authenticity) lies only in their peasant dress and occupation. However, if Babayevsky's heroes do not belong to traditional peasant society, they most certainly fit into the tradition of socialist realism. Both Babayevsky's "proletarianized" peasants and the heroes of production novels are striving toward (and, in the case of kolkhoz literature, are shown to achieve) a common goal—the building of a perfect society.

The Future in the Past: The Utopianism of Village Prose

Contrary to the future-oriented works of kolkhoz literature, post-Stalinist village prose was preoccupied with the past. This fiction projected a vision of the traditional Russian peasant mentality, "rooted in a religious

culture, . . . devoid of Western rationalism (as opposed to simple logic
and economic reason), . . . alien to geometric forms and elegant symme-
tries, and suspicious of growth per se and of central authorities. . . ."[12]
Village prose explored the notions of time, memory, kinship, and the image of the long road "which refers not only to the endless, slow roads of
the Russian countryside but also the long road back to one's own past
and to the past of rural Russia."[13] The time of village prose is different
from that of socialist realism—it is slow-paced, cyclical, and often apocalyptic. The language of village prose is startlingly different as well—full
of dialectisms, proverbs, and detailed descriptions of nature.[14]

Village prose focuses on the primordial setting and the memories of
childhood, but also on all the ways in which the rural life and even the
existence of the small village are coming to an end because of a whole
set of historical and social calamities, such as collectivization, World War
II, the migration of villagers to the city, and the environmental disasters
caused by governmental policies. It rejects the idealized world of
kolkhoz literature and offers two opposing, but connected, visions—the
idyllic village before industrialization, urbanization, and collectivization
and the dying village of today. It digs deeper into the roots of its society,
unearthing and condemning the ideas of positivism, determinism, and
materialism, with their arrogant attitude toward nature and un-Christ-
ian faith in human power—all bringing disaster to the pastoral beauty
and communal harmony of the old village.

The utopian dream of the village prose writers is a rich mixture of
sources—from prerevolutionary peasant utopias to the Scythian vision of
the victorious village to the myths and legends found in Russian folklore
(or invented along the lines of Russian folklore tradition). However, if the
peasant utopias of the twenties were written not to advocate a return to
peasant society or rural life, but rather "to maximize the aesthetic in both
the environment and the inner life of man," village utopians writing in
the mid-seventies want the reader to believe that only a return to peasant
society or rural life can regenerate humans spiritually and revitalize the
aesthetic in their environment.[15] Utopias of the twenties vacillated between a glorious vision of the Communist heaven, dystopian distrust of
imposed perfection, and counterutopias of peasant paradise. In fantastic
literature distrust of technologically manufactured happiness and belief
in the superiority of traditional peasant structures are the predominant
modes of utopian thinking.

Utopia I: Communal Law in the Service of Nature

Sergei Zalygin's *Commission (Komissiia)* was one of the first works of village prose in which utopian and fantastic elements were combined to

draw a picture of the vanishing world of the Russian peasant.[16] This was not Zalygin's first venture into the area of the fantastic; however, the merger of the fantastic and the utopian in the context of village prose was a step in a new direction for the writer.[17] The novel traces the fate of a community of Old Believers, who split from their fleeing parent group of schismatics and decide to return to a spot visited earlier in order to establish a village there. The prehistory of the village of Lebiazhka is related in a series of "folk" tales, invented by Zalygin himself as the first step to working on the novel.[18] The present time of narration is the year 1918, marked by continous upheaval in Russia, with political power constantly changing hands and the villagers uncertain about who is governing the country.

The inhabitants of Lebiazhka take matters into their own hands and establish a commission for the protection of their most valuable resource, the forest. The commission is formed from the ranks of the villagers themselves, and its credo is similar to the position of prerevolutionary sectarian utopians, who taught or practiced common landownership in a prosperous economy where everyone worked, where there was social equality, and where "social relations [were] bound together by religion rather than by oaths, laws or law enforcers."[19]

However, the inhabitants of the village are made to violate one important precept of the unwritten code of peasant utopians—they have to establish and enforce the law for the protection of the forest. This law is based on the communal law of the old village, but is modified by Sergei Zalygin's very modern ecological concerns: nature is there for everybody, but one has to be protective of nature. In this case nature is symbolized by the forest, which the commission is formed to protect, both from plundering outsiders and from the unthinking villagers themselves. Initially, the commission succeeds, by persuasion, in protecting the forest from destruction. The interests of the small, closely knit community are protected, the outsiders in need of timber are mollified, and order is restored. Capping the activities of the commission's initiative is the building of a new school in the village. Harmony is threatened however, both from the inside and the outside.

The mythical portion of the novel (the "folk" tales relating the prehistory of Lebiazhka) focuses on the process of unification and harmonization of two very different tribes—the schismatics and the people who had settled in the area before the schismatics arrived. The conflict between two very different sets of beliefs—those of Old Believers and Orthodox Christians—is resolved through intermarriage, love, and the establishment of family ties. However, as is prophesized by the founding schismatic father of the village, only unity and love can protect Lebiazhka from disaster. The last of the folktales in the novel is a retelling of a prophesy predicting that Lebiazhka will perish if one segment of the tribe rises against the other.

Zalygin places the end of Lebiazhka in a context of disunity, showing how both discord within the community and external forces (in this case, the White Guards and their Czech supporters) can annihilate the perfect world of the old village. Erosion of the communal spirit of Lebiazhka's inhabitants is linked to the individualistic impulses of some villagers. One of the members of the commission exhibits all the characteristics of a leather-jacketed hard Communist of the literature of the twenties. Deriabin is ready to declare war on anybody who threatens the Revolution. Grishka Sukhikh, on the other hand, passionately possessive of his share of the communal pie, is the personification of the individualistic spirit of the Russian peasant. The old village knows how to deal with him—with polite indifference—but the new, changing village, does not. Some unknown people (including, possibly, Deriabin) burn Grishka's homestead and turn this man into a sworn enemy of the village. The good man of Zalygin—his name, Ustinov, brings together two important Russian words, *istina* (truth) and *ustav* (law)—is a synthetic figure combining the ideals of East and West. Ustinov reveres nature but is aware of the advances of technology in agriculture. He is ambivalent about killing people, even in war, but is ready to sacrifice his own life to preserve the forest. Ustinov is highly intuitive but values learning.

The triad of Zalygin's protagonists represent the forces active in the village before collectivization. In this novel the roots of the community's demise can be found in two opposing, and corrosive, ideologies—those of the proletarianized peasantry abandoning its traditional ideals, and those of violent individualists unwilling to give in to communal impulses. The perfect man of the old village—Ustinov—is doomed to destruction by forces beyond his control. The idealized world of the old Lebiazhka is annihilated, together with all the members of the commission. In the end, the blame lies with the outsiders who compel the villagers to protect the forest, and the integrity of their society, by force. The uncompromising stance of the proletarianized peasant Deriabin, whose views are inherited from his experience at war, further exacerbates the situation. Deriabin sheds his allegiance to communal values, and, decrying all compromises, alienates such peasants as Grishka Sukhikh. It is the same war mentality, exhibited by Deriabin and shared by his White Guard and Czech adversaries, that, in the end, is responsible for the fulfillment of the prophecy about Lebiazhka's fate. The perfect community of Zalygin perishes before our eyes.

Utopia II: Perfection in the Past

In *Farewell to Matera* (*Proshchanie s Materoi*, 1976) Valentin Rasputin addresses the issue of the legitimacy and consequences of people's efforts to supplant traditional, organically evolved society with their own manufactured model for happiness. In the time-honored fashion of literary dystopia, Rasputin's novel portrays the inevitable destruction of a perfect society on Earth. In an effort to build a hydroelectric station, the island and the village of Matera are to be flooded by the waters of the diverted Angara River. The slow-moving plot focuses on the thoughts and actions of a few remaining villagers who have to grapple with this catastrophic upheaval in their lives.

Rasputin openly establishes two opposing camps in the battle for Matera's survival: Matera's old inhabitants and the outsiders. This opposition is symbolic; it stands for the clash of two antagonistic sets of values: a Pelagian quest for eternal harmony steeped in tradition versus the Promethean exploits of a technological society. Preference is clearly given to the traditional values of Matera's inhabitants. However, as in a true tragedy, the outcome of the conflict is certain. Rasputin's idealized world is inexorably headed toward destruction. The doomed island is described by the author in terms approximating biblical descriptions of the Promised Land:

> The island lay quiet and calm. This was the island destined [to them] by fate itself and even more dear, because it had firm borders beyond which there began not land but water. And from one end to the other, from one shore to the other shore there was plenty of space, wealth, beauty, and wilderness, and all kinds of beasts in pairs. Having separated itself from the continent, it had everything in abundance. Perhaps that is why it appropriated the glorious name Matera.[20]

The novel's opening paragraph establishes the tragic conflict between the vernal regeneration of nature in Rasputin's idealized world and the island's impending and senseless death. The destruction begins with the symbolic act of desecrating the island cemetery. The outsiders have received an order to remove the crosses and monuments from the soon-to-be flooded cemetery—to prevent foreign tourists from witnessing the spectacle of crosses floating down the Angara after the island is submerged. Within the symbolic context of the novel this is the ultimate act of desecration. Rasputin's villagers believe in strong ties with and personal accountability before their dead ancestors. To desecrate the grave of a relative is to attempt to break the thread linking the living and the dead and to perpetrate an unimaginable insult against the living. Rasputin's characters can communicate with their dead ancestors. The boundary between life and death is often crossed in the villagers' dreams. The supernatural dimension of this communion with the dead is an integral part of Rasputin's work.

Rasputin's tradition-bound characters welcome death as a natural outcome of life. Everything on this Earth has been arranged by God to work in harmony. Aging, death, and decay are all part of an endless chain of existence. This natural order is disrupted by people who imagine they have God-like powers. In their relentless quest for power over nature, people forget humility and lose awareness of themselves as members of a community, not only of the living but of the dead. They also lose their ability to communicate with nature, which is both life and death, thought and feeling, rational and irrational things, everything that is visible to the eye as well as the supernatural. Only those who really belong to the world of Matera, the old and faithful protagonists of Rasputin, are capable of perceiving this other reality in which people are always immersed. The mythical spirit of the island, its omniscient Master *(Khoziain)* and the powerful Larch, another master of the island, are seen through the eyes of Rasputin's woman character Daria.

Rasputin's positive ideal is rooted in tradition. Matera, nurtured by this tradition, pays the price for human arrogance with its own destruction. Will anything remain of this Garden of Eden? The answer is ambivalent. For Rasputin, history is sharing in the "collectivity of the spirit, of the ideal, which alone can bestow meaning on the existence and dignity of the personality."[21] When the villagers get together and sing, Daria's son Pavel acutely perceives this collectivity of the spirit, *(sobornost')*. Rasputin's spirit of collectivity naturally presupposes the existence of a close community that shares thoughts and actions. With the disappearance of the old way of life the collective spirit will undoubtedly lose its source of power. That "something for which generations of people have lived," the spiritual core of the country, is being destroyed.

Rasputin's conclusion to the novel provides a glimmer of irrational hope. On the eve of the island's demise, nature provides an escape for the doomed land when it shrouds Matera in a dense fog. Within the context of the novel, Matera is protected from evil forces. Perhaps it will forever be concealed from the "unclean" hands of modern industrialists and appear only to the initiated and righteous, like the Kitezh-gorod of folk imagination.[22]

Rasputin's characters are able to cross the border separating tangible reality from the supernatural. The time of the novel stretches in one uninterrupted line from the prehistoric to the present and even to a future, envisioned by the mythical characters in the novel. Death is not the end of existence, the dead are still living in the minds and hearts of their descendants and are an integral part of communal life.

The spirit of community is the all-important concept for Rasputin and his characters.

Farewell to Matera returns the disenchanted readers of the seventies to an idealized world of truth and harmony, only to plunge them immediately into the despair of ineluctable catastrophe. Rasputin is unequivocal in placing the blame on the destructive, alien forces of technology. As in Zalygin's *Commission,* and contrary to the usual pattern of dystopia, the seeds of destruction are not found within the communal society, but are sown from the outside.[23]

Utopia III: The Legendary World of Childhood

If Rasputin's work focuses on "last things," Vladimir Drozd's *Irij* is a peasant utopia of "first things."[24] *Irij* is a collection of short lyrical reminiscences of the fairy-tale land of Irij, sifted through the consciousness of the narrator. Irij is the land of the narrator's childhood. It is a Gogolian magic world where people can fly, tears cause floods, and where trees express their feelings in words:

> Irij is a fairy-tale land where it is never winter, where the sun spends its days and nights on the bright green hills, where carp crawl out onto the sandy banks in the evening and peacefully converse with pike, where she-wolves nurse their kids and foxes look after chicks so they don't get lost in the woods; Irij is a country where birds fly every autumn and where they return in the spring to spend their summer, like city dwellers returning from their dachas; it is a country from where the warm wind blows, bringing with it a thaw during the fiercest winter cold. . . . Irij is a country where an idyllic life truly exists—a life so wonderfully described in books and by teachers on the first day of school—it is a country of milk rivers with honey banks. . . . Irij is the country of your future.[25]

This brief paragraph summarizes the entire novel, a work that offers a curious blend of literary influences. On the one hand, Drozd's utopia is located in the remembered past of the narrator. On the other, it is projected into the future. It appears that the action of *Irij* takes place in a village, and that assumption is supported by the closeness of the narrative to fairy tales, folk legends, and the stylized "popular" genre of Gogol's *Evenings on a Farm near Dikanka* (*Vechera na khutore bliz Dikan'ki,* 1831). However, the narrator's vision of the future includes a Chernyshevskian Crystal Palace, where people are supposed to reject falsehoods and "live in white houses with spherical glass ceilings, through which the stars peek into their apartments."[26]

Drozd's science fictional touch is deliberately ironic. The narrator's life in the utopian Irij is far from sterile; it is brimming with life, magic, and adventure and is an embodiment of the most cherished ideals of writers of village prose. Drozd's belief in the superiority of patriarchal values of village life is unquestioning. The city is corrupted, the future of a Promethean society aseptic, barren, and unproductive. The life of a closely knit community, the village of the narrator's childhood, is his answer to the question of how one must live. This utopia is propelled by a desire to return to the world of childhood, viewed nostalgically as the mythical golden age of the Russian village.

Utopia IV: Carnivalesque Reversal

Vladimir Krupin's peasant utopia in *Living Water* (*Zhivaia voda*, 1980) is yet another reminder of the disappearance of the traditional peasant way of life, this time offered without the morbid seriousness characteristic of most novels in this genre.[27] *Living Water* embroiders on a legend about Viatka peasants, told by the main character, Aleksandr Kirpikov, to his granddaughter. The peasants do not know they live badly until a passerby comments on their sad situation and recommends an infusion of "living water" to cure their ills.[28] The peasants decide to ask God if they really live worse than anybody else and if living water would help. Kirpikov, a child at the time, is sent as a messenger to God. He forgets to ask if they live worse than anybody else but inquires about the living water given to him by the apostles; it turns out to be nothing more than cheap liquor.

The plot of the novel is an embellished version of the legend. Kirpikov, who makes his living by tilling the private plots of the settlement's inhabitants, asks himself the existential question of the legend, and on the basis of the answer decides to change his life. Like a medieval saint, Kirpikov sheds his bad habits—smoking, drinking, and swearing—shuts himself up in the cellar, and starts his belated education by reading his children's school books. He refuses to accept money for his work (before he was paid with liquor), attempts to write a journal, and comes out of his self-imposed incarceration to preach beauty and the necessity of doing good for others. In a reenactment of the legend, Kirpikov becomes a messenger to his people.

Kirpikov's essentially Orthodox beliefs are modified by his own version of the doctrine of the First Cause. According to Kirpikov, God was there in the beginning, arranged all things to his liking and then let the people do as they please. The hero goes so far as to proclaim that he is his own God and removes his wife's icon from its place of honor in the room. Yet Kirpikov's innate reliogiosity is emphasized by the author at every opportunity, and it is in the process of rediscovering his lost faith that Krupin's character gradually becomes a leader in his community.

As if in answer to Kirpikov's call for moral regeneration, his settlement is graced by a miracle—a spring with "living water," which rejuvenates anybody who tastes it. Krupin's miracle, however, is more of a test than a reward for a people lost midway between the urban and village cultures. The loss of ethics is shown to stem from the loss of native language and mores, and from the consequent need for cheap and easy substitutions—television, radio, and vodka. Living water turns out to be a divine joke on the inhabitants. The liquid rejuvenates them, but does not imrpove them spiritually. They fight over the profits from the sale of the water, abandon their beliefs for the gift of youth, cheat on their wives and husbands, and become indistinguishable from one another. Fighting over the water continues until, in a spectacular eruption, the living water changes into alcohol, and the spring disappears underground.

Only Kirpikov, who has been able to rejuvenate himself by drinking from the fount of the peasant and Christian tradition, does not need the living water. The liquid (named, in an obvious allusion to Chernyshevsky's utopia, Crystal Water) is a symbol of quick solutions to long-standing problems. However, nothing can change, according to the protagonist, until people are willing to change internally. Kirpikov's advice to his fellow villagers fits in with the ideas of village prose; prescriptions for change focus on the rediscovery of natural beauty and ancestral ties, on finding joy in communal work, and on brotherly love.

The apocalypse on a small scale, the eruption of the evil liquid and the spectacular disappearance of the spring are a transparent social allegory. The peasants, with their wholesome work ethic and their firm religious beliefs, are dying out along with with natural life, squandered by unthinking or immoral members of a modern machine-oriented society. The machine tore the peasants out of the natural rhythm of their work and thus changed their existence. The only thing left to the peasant is the glass building of a local pub *(stekliashka)*. The Crystal Palace of the Promethean future is transformed into an evil den of dissipation. The machine utopia celebrated in the canonical works of socialist realism will destroy the last vestiges of Russia's spiritual wealth and turn everybody into an undifferentiated gray mass.

The pessimism of the novel's outlook is counterbalanced by the success story of its main protagonist. If in the beginning Kirpikov is portrayed as the laughingstock of the settlement, a permanently drunk, illiterate peasant whom everybody addresses familiarly, in the end he wins their respect. The fantastic here comes to the rescue of a sinner embarking on a spiritual quest, making it possible for him to demonstrate the evil ways of civilization and Sovietization to his fellow sinners and former villagers. Kirpikov is shown to become a saintly figure who succeeds in self-perfection even when he fails to achieve utopia for others or improve his neighbors spiritually. Kirpikov is also a chosen person, allowed to understand and demonstrate that the Russian peasants today are not ready for a peasant utopia because they are spiritually impoverished. The didacticism of *Living Water* is mitigated by humor. The novel's language is a lively exercise in heteroglossia; it combines fairy-tale magic, journalese, contemporary songs and biblical allusions and evokes the atmosphere of a continuous carnival. Krupin mocks the official utopia of the Crystal Palace and the official Church; he is laughing at vodka-guzzling former peasants who are no longer true members of a village community, and at a government willing to impose drastic measures on the countryside to achieve quick solutions to intractable problems. Kirpikov himself, who refuses to come out of the cellar and dismays his household with his newfound religion, is not spared Krupin's laughter.

In village prose of the seventies the city was rejected and the old village idealized, while its inevitable end was simultaneously lamented. The manufactured happiness of the future-oriented Bolshevik utopia, with its reliance on the engineering of souls and environment and its belief in progress, was shown to destroy the very foundations of old Russia. Village utopians believed that the ideal of reverence for nature, beauty, and tradition was allowed to disappear together with the love for the Russian soil. Old peasants of this village prose were presented as ideal men and women—full of wisdom, in touch with nature and history. However, their time was running out, and the new people of the village were unable and unwilling to preserve the tradition.

The plight of displaced villagers rapidly losing their spiritual foundations—treated in apocalyptic terms in Zalygin's *Commission* and Rasputin's *Matera*—is approached in playful fashion in Krupin's *Living Water* and Drozd's *Irij*. Here village life is revived with an injection of humour, the powers that be appear in an absurd light, and the dream of a Bolshevik utopia is ridiculed. This lightening of the message was not an isolated phenomenon in Soviet prose of the period. The drudgery of urban life—the stuff of *byt* prose—is transformed into a fairy tale of the city in the works of Soviet followers of Mikhail Bulgakov.

Notes

1. See more on this in Gillespie, *Valentin Rasputin and Soviet Russian Village Prose*; also in Robert Porter, *Four Contemporary Russian Writers* (New York: St. Martin's Press, 1989), pp. 11–51; Günter Hasenkamp, *Gedächtnis und Leben in der Prosa Valentin Rasputins* (Wiesbaden: Harrasowitz, 1990), pp. 142–176; and Kathleen Parthé, *Russian Village Prose: The Radiant Past* (Princeton: Princeton University Press, 1992).

2. On the "duel of utopias" in the twenties see Katerina Clark, "The City versus the Countryside in Soviet Peasant Literature of the Twenties: A Duel of Utopias," in Abbot Gleason, Peter Kenez, and Richard Stites, eds., *Bolshevik Culture: Experiment and Order in the Russian Revolution* (Bloomington: Indiana University Press, 1985).

3. Leon Trotsky, *Literature and Revolution* (London: Allen and Unwin, 1925), p. 252.

4. For more on Pilnyak as a Scythian, on his attitude to the peasant question, and on *The Naked Year* see Gary Browning, *Boris Pilnyak: Scythian at a Typewriter* (Ann Arbor: Ardis, 1985), pp. 114–127.

5. For more on the clash between the two postrevolutionary visions of the perfect society see Mikhail Geller, "Utopiia v sovetskoi ideologii," *Revue des etudes slaves*, t. 56, f. 1 (1984): 105–113.

6. Stites, *Revolutionary Dreams*, p. 18.

7. Aleksandr Vasil'evich Chayanov (1888–?) was a pioneer agronomist who introduced multicrop rotation to the Russian peasant communes. He opposed collectivization of agriculture and advocated a cooperative system under which farms should operate individually as public enterprises linked to the state by a cooperative framework. He believed deeply in the compatability of the commune and modern technology. He was arrested in 1929 as a leader of the "Trudovik-wrecker" faction and was executed after a famous trial. See Heinrich E. Schulz, ed., *Who Was Who in the USSR* (Metuchen, N.J.: Scarecrow Press, 1972), p. 104. For a discussion of Chayanov's trial see Aleksandr Solzhenitsyn, *The Gulag Archipelago, 1918–1956* (New York: Harper and Row), pp. 49–50.- See also Viktor Danilov, introduction to *The Theory of Peasant Co-operatives* by Alexandr Chayanov (London, 1991).

8. Clark, "City versus Countryside," p. 181.

9. Ibid., p. 182.

10. More on this in David Shepherd, *Beyond Metafiction: Self-Consciousness in Soviet Literature* (Oxford: Oxford University Press, 1992).

11. Stites, *Revolutionary Dreams*, p. 247.

12. Ibid., p. 15.

13. Kathleen Parthé, "Time, Backward!" p. 1.

14. Parthé observes that the most important kinds of time in village prose are historical, cyclical, literary, generational, and apocalyptic. See Parthé, "Time, Backward!" p. 2.

15. Clark, "City versus Countryside," p. 181.

16. First published in *Nash sovremennik*, nos. 9–11 (1975).

17. See, for example, such "fantastic" novels of Zalygin as *Os'ka, the Ridiculous Boy (Os'ka—smeshnoi mal'chik*, 1973) and *The South American Variant (Iuzhno-amerikanskii variant*, 1973). For more on the use of fantasy in Zalygin's prose of the seventies see David Wilson, "Fantasy in the Fiction of Sergei Zalygin," Ph.D. dissertation (University of Kansas, 1988). For a thoughtful discussion of Zalygin's *Commission* see A. F. Lapchenko, *Chelovek i zemlia v russkoi proze 70x godov (V. Rasputin, V. Astafiev, S. Zalygin)* (Leningrad, 1985).

18. The name of the village, Lebiazhka, evokes images of softness, comfort, and pleasure (in Russian *lebiazhii pukh* means "swansdown").

19. Stites, *Revolutionary Dreams*, p. 17.

20. Rasputin, *Farewell to Matera*, p. 232.

21. Lev Anninski, "Tochka opory," *Don* 6 (1968): 179.

22. The closeness of Rasputin's tragic vision to that of the brothers Strugatsky *(Snail on the Slope)* is, perhaps, startling, but natural. Strugatsky's forest is another Matera, a complete and organic cosmos, impossible to change without causing its total annihilation. Like Rasputin's idealized community, it is capable of regenerating its dead and offers an insurmountable challenge to those who want to destroy it. Unlike Rasputin's utopia, it is viewed from the outside, by the proud would-be conquerors. Ultimately, both visions converge: Rasputin's Matera and the forest of the brothers Strugatsky are out of reach for the intruders.

23. In his public statements before glasnost, Rasputin was always careful to stress that he is not opposed to "electrification" (i.e., technology) but is against the merciless destruction of "the roots of human existence" and supports their careful transplantation. See "Eto stanovitsia traditsiei (Valentin Rasputin v MGU)," *Vestnik Moskovskogo universiteta* 3 (1977): 84. However, in *Farewell to Matera* the life of the inhabitants of Matera is so deeply tied to the island itself that it would be impossible to imagine any such successful "transplantation."

24. Vladimir Drozd, *Irij* (Moscow: Molodaia Gvardiia, 1976). All quotations come from the above edition. The translation is mine. The division into narratives about "first things" and "last things" is Kathleen Parthé's.

25. Ibid., p. 172.

26. Ibid., p. 219.

27. Though the novel was written in 1976 (the year of the publication of Drozd's *Irij* and Rasputin's *Matera*) it was first published in *Novyi mir* 8 (1980). For more details on the history of publication of the novel see Vladimir Korobov, "Poiski 'stsepleniia': Vladimir Krupin: Ozhidanie novykh vstrech," *Literaturnaia ucheba* (1982): 153. All quotations come from the journal edition. The translation is mine.

28. In Russian fairy tales "living water" is a substance capable of returning the hero from the dead.

7

Mikhail Bulgakov's Disciples
in Soviet Literature

. . . fantasy characteristically attempts to compensate for a lack resulting from cultural constraints; it is a literature of desire, which seeks that which is experienced as absence and loss.

—*Rosemary Jackson,* Fantasy: The Literature of Subversion

WHEN MIKHAIL BULGAKOV'S NOVEL *The Master and Margarita* first appeared in the literary journal *Moskva* in 1966–1967, it created an unparalleled wave of excitement. In a prophetic, and almost retributive, realization of Bulgakov's dictum "manuscripts do not burn," *The Master and Margarita,* written at the height of Stalin's purges of the late thirties and finished in 1940, shortly before Bulgakov's death, had not only survived but even reemerged as part of the literature of de-Stalinization.[1] The cult of Bulgakov and his work was an extension of the overwhelming desire of the Russian reading elite for its own cultural heroes, not manufactured by Soviet doctrine. Museums devoted to Bulgakov's life and work opened in Moscow and Kiev, Bulgakov graffiti appeared on the walls of many Moscow buildings, and quotations from *The Master and Margarita* became a part of intellectual conversations.

The degree of Bulgakov's influence and, particularly, the impact of his last novel, *The Master and Margarita,* can be measured in the spread of Soviet graffiti inspired by the novel. As John Bushnell has shown, in the late seventies and eighties there emerged a distinct genre of "Bulgakov" graffiti. Quotations from and illustrations to *The Master and Margarita* adorn the walls of Bulgakov's Moscow apartment house. As Bushnell points out, the quotations from *The Master and Margarita* which do become graffiti are mainly taken from the contemporary fantastic plot of the novel dealing with the pranks of the devil's companions in Moscow. This selective approach to the novel by the graffiti writers could perhaps be explained by the fact that Bulgakov's Moscow apartment was used by the writer as a set for the activities of the devil's retinue.[2] Pilgrimages to Bulgakov's Moscow apartment were yet another proof of Bulgakov's unmatched popularity.[3] In addition, a number of Soviet novels of the mid-seventies and early eighties slavishly imitated *The Master and Margarita*. Under glasnost, the issues of Bulgakov's influence on Soviet writers and of the overall importance of his work became weapons in the fight against the policy of banning certain literary works.[4]

The Master and Margarita is a complex work that has been justly compared to a Mennipean satire because of its tiered structure, sharp criticism of contemporary life, and lampooning of established norms of social behavior.[5] The plot of the novel focuses on the fate of an unsuccessful Soviet writer (the Master) and his unpublished manuscript. The Master's manuscript, a reworking of the biblical story of the Crucifixion, serves as a link between the legendary and contemporary plots.

The contemporary plot contains a series of adventures of the devil and his entourage who descend on Earth, tempt earthlings and help the Master to reconstruct the manuscript he burned in desperation. In his descriptions of the devil's retinue Bulgakov uses the stock figures of fairy tales—werewolves, mermaids, and talking cats. Medieval romances, gothic novels, and the Faust legend provide Bulgakov with a pool of characters and situations. In spite of its numerous literary allusions, the novel is innovative in structure and ideas and presents a sober, if not pessimistic, assessment of the human condition.

Bulgakov's last novel has generated extensive scholarship both in the Soviet Union and abroad.[6] It is appropriate here only to point to those aspects of the novel that Soviet writers picked up and used. It was perhaps inevitable that *The Master and Margarita* would exert a major influence on Soviet readers and writers.[7] First, the novel was perceived as a skillful satirical portrayal of Stalin's society and that perception alone could ensure the novel's immediate and later success. (Some scholars take issue with the idea of the novel as a satire of life in Stalin's Russia. Andrew Barratt, for example, argues quite persuasively for the novel's "center of gravity" being in the twenties, not the thirties.[8] Yet Bulgakov's work was perceived in the context of de-Stalinization as a satire of Russia in the thirties).

Second, as Vladimir Lakshin has pointed out, *The Master and Margarita* "catches into its net readers who differ in their educational level, age and taste, which is one of the reasons for the novel's unparalleled success."[9] In Lakshin's view, some of the novel's features, particularly its plot of mystery and adventure, make it possible to be appropriated by mass culture. The playfulness and the sadness of the story, its puzzles and game playing with the devil on the border of faith and disbelief, the elements of romantic love, the mockery of both dogmatism and "common sense," and its wealth of eminently quotable aphorisms are, in Lakshin's opinion, the reasons for the novel's broad appeal.[10] The new possibilities in ideas, language, and structure that Bulgakov's work offered for Soviet literature also contributed to the novel's exceptional popularity.

The Soviet "Bulgakovian" novel employs features of *The Master and Margarita* in two ways. Formally, writers borrow the novel-within-the-novel technique and use different temporal dimensions. The style of contemporary sections in Bulgakov's work, with its playfulness and fantasy, is equally influential. Thematically, the focus of Bulgakov's imitators is on the social message gleaned from *The Master and Margarita*'s satirical plot. Their protagonists are generally creative people, and the locus of their activities a metropolis. Taken in isolation, these aspects of contemporary Soviet writing might not appear to stem from Bulgakov's novel. Seen together, however, they necessarily evoke it.

In spite of their debt to Bulgakov, the authors of Bulgakovian novels used their model selectively and for their own and quite different purposes. If *The Master and Margarita* is carefully balanced to include a religious plot that offsets the "happy ending" of the central love story, the new novels latched onto the optimistic fairy-tale resolution and left no place for ambiguity. In *The Master and Margarita*, fairy-tale elements are employed to express "Bulgakov's belief in an absolute morality and in the existence of a just God" as well as "to affirm Bulgakov's belief in the magic power of art."[11] In the hands of Bulgakovian novelists, however, the fairy tale became a convenient vehicle for escape from the oppressive drudgery of everyday life.

By the same token, the religious-philosophical plot line of *The Master and Margarita* was generally ignored by the Bulgakovian novel of the late seventies and early eighties. Only in glasnost literature, characterized by a search for God and a quest for moral salvation, did direct allusions to Bulgakov's religious plot come to the fore. In Aitmatov's *The Execution Block*, Bulgakov's intricate plot configuration, with its mixture of fantasy, satire, and legend, is abandoned, and the influence of *The Master and Margarita* is limited to easily recognizable quotes from the novel's religious plot.[12] As we will see in the next chapter, Bulgakov's interpretation of the Christian myth was reinterpreted by Aitmatov to fit a different social agenda of glasnost. Aitmatov's approach to Bulgakov's legacy is quite different from the one found in Bulgakovian novels that celebrate escapism through creativity and use fantastic-satirical devices from *The Master and Margarita.* The world of a Soviet citizen, according to the Bulgakovian novel, is a fascinating place filled with good and bad spirits, demons, femmes fatales, extraordinary occurrences, and magical metamorphoses. Quite unlike the setting evoked by Bulgakov, the world of this fiction is bursting with energy and optimism. The protagonists are (always) men who love their work, good food, games, and beautiful women. They are artists at what they do, and often are real artists as well—writers and musicians, frequently endowed with extraordinary powers. They fight evil in the name of virtue, get into dire situations, but are always rescued at the eleventh hour by some miraculous force. These omnipotent protagonists, close relatives of the mighty characters of Soviet science fiction and descendants of the powerful and single-minded heroes of socialist realism, have nothing in common with Bulgakov's tormented Master. Goethe's Faust, the Faust of legend, and Bulgakov's Woland are, perhaps, more obvious sources for this character, who is energetic, bold, and possesses magical powers.

In structure, Bulgakovian novels are patterned after fairy tales and the links to fairy-tale magic are made obvious or "bared." All the mysteries are fully explained in the end, and the explanation is that all enigmatic events are perpetrated by magical means. Every baffling event has only one source and one (magical) explanation. This quality of the fantastic is responsible for the optimistic flavor of the Bulgakovian novels, placing them closer to the future-oriented canonical works of socialist realism, or science fiction, than to Bulgakov. As Sona Hoisington has shown, Bulgakov does use fairy tale but in a variety of other models.[13] Exclusive reliance on the fairy-tale model robs the reader both of disbelief and of the suspense associated with some fantastic literature. In compensation, the suspense is provided by a mystery plot set against the background of the picaresque, a strategy aimed at animating one-dimensional characters throughout formulaic literature, from fairy tale to science fiction.

Fantasy as a Prosthetic Cultural Memory: Marger Zarin'

One of the first novels in the Bulgakovian vein was not originally written in Russian. Marger Zarin', the author of *The False Faust (Fal'shivyi Faust)*[14], is a renowned Latvian composer, who had the distinguished title of People's Artist of the USSR and received the State Prize of the USSR for his achievements in music. After his literary debut in 1960, Zarin' gained considerable popularity in Latvia. However, he remained relatively unknown to the Russian reading public until the appearance of the Russian translation of his *False Faust* in 1981.

The protagonist of Zarin"s novel is one Christopher Marlowe, a poet and a musician, whose adventures take place in Riga in the late thirties, just before the Second World War. The Latvian Marlowe is a composite portrait, stitched together out of several easily recognizable literary personages. On the one hand, he is a contemporary reincarnation of the Elizabethan dramatist Christopher Marlowe, who, in this novel is able to remember his encounters with Shakespeare and Ben Jonson.[15] Like Mephistopheles, the Marlowe of this novel also has the power of rejuvenation. Finally, Marlowe's pursuit of the beautiful Margarita and his quest for knowledge bring to mind Goethe's Faust.

When Marlowe first appears in the novel, he is purchasing the *Revised and Appended Culinary Book* from its feeble and aged author, Janis Trampedakh, in exchange for the gift of youth. The deal is signed in blood, and Trampedakh is rewarded, in addition to his rejuvenation, with a beautiful Latvian Margarita. Marlowe falls in love with Margarita and pursues her to the capital. The protagonist's adventures in Riga allow Zarin' to describe in brilliant colors the delightfully decadent atmosphere of a Latvia then enjoying complete independence from its powerful neighbor. As becomes evident later in the narrative, the novel we are reading is Marlowe's memoirs, written from his sickbed in the clinic of the swindler Dr. Jonson. They describe Margarita's murder, Marlowe's confrontation with Trampedakh, his capture by the Germans, imprisonment in a concentration camp, his near execution, and liberation by Russian soldiers.

As in Bulgakov's novel, the Faustian theme and the stress on creativity are at the center of Zarin"s plot. Like the protagonists of Bulgakov and like other literary Fausts, Marlowe is in touch with the demonic; in fact he possesses demonic powers. Stylistically, Zarin"s book is extraordinarily rich, perhaps as rich as its model. Linguistic diversity here is achieved through the incorporation of language seldom explored by writers—culinary recipes written in an archaic but opulent medieval dialect. Besides introducing some intriguing recipes and a variety of exotic ingredients, this language imparts a sense of abundance, of unrestrained and joyous indulgence, absent from the everyday lives of Latvians before the war.

For the Latvian reader, Zarin"s pointed portrayal of Riga in the thirties performed an archival function in which a prosthetic cultural memory was constructed against the threat of erasure of the nation's folkore and language. That period was perceived by surviving Latvians as one of the most abundant and culturally vibrant times in the life of the country, and nostalgia for the golden days of the affluent past is present in *The False Faust* in spite of its superficial political message. Unlike Bulgakov's novel, *The False Faust* concludes with a straightforward "happy" ending. Marlowe's unusual powers are shown to shape a political dénouement, the establishment of a just (i.e., Soviet) order in Latvia. Marlowe prevents Trampedakh from giving his newly invented *preparat smerti* (a lethal chemical compound) to the Nazis to use against the Russians. The good magician conquers his evil counterpart and brings happiness to the fairy-tale kingdom.

Vladimir Turbin has noted yet another function for the recipes in the novel: recipes (prescriptions, lists of ingredients, instructions) are used by the doctor, the cook, and the magician. Christopher's adversary, Trampedakh, is a doctor and a cook. Like Marlowe, he is also a magician, and "magic and the occult in the novel are blended in a mysterious fashion with politics."[16] The implication is that the victory of the Soviets was cooked up by means of magic, and that the political dimension of the novel might be ironic. However, it is difficult to determine whether the irony is there and, if so, whether it is intentional. As with other Bulgakovian novels, the underlying fairy-tale pattern places its own strictures on plot development. Good has to conquer evil, and the way the ultimate good was portrayed in a Soviet novel before glasnost was determined by considerations other than literary. In the end, however, the lively spirit of independent Riga achieves much more prominence in this novel than does its politically correct message.

The Fairy Tale of the City: Natal'ia Sokolova

The subtitle of Natal'ia Sokolova's *Careful, Magic!* (*Ostorozhno, volshebnoe!* 1981), *The Fairy Tale of a Big City*, fits other Bulgakovian novels that place the source of creativity, liveliness, and dynamic action in a modern metropolis.[17] Urban life, portrayed in *byt* prose of the sixties and seventies as robbing people of spontaneity, youthful energy, and the ability to enjoy life, is suddenly capable of revitalizing and transforming the protagonist. The cosmopolitan character of Riga before the advent of socialism in Zarin''s novel, or the richness and unpredictability of life around Sokolova's characters, are accentuated. Only life in the city can provide the dynamism necessary for true creativity.

In addition to ordinary people, Sokolova's city is inhabited by good and bad spirits who fight over the soul of Nikita Ivanov, a highly skilled worker and a proud young man unwilling to believe in miracles. Nikita, who states that everything can and should be logically explained in this world, presents an irresistible challenge to both good and bad spirits who tempt him throughout the novel. The hero is too rational to believe in the fantastic and too self-centered to love other people. The good spirits put Nikita on trial and give him an opportunity to correct his ways. Nikita abandons his rational ways, acts on an impulse, and saves the life of a little girl. This heroic act tilts the scales in the ongoing war of good and bad spirits and saves the entire world from disaster.

Playfulness, links to the fairy tale, literary allusions, and humor, all found in the lives of city dwellers, point to the fantastic-satirical plot line of *The Master and Margarita*. But the narrative progression here is linear: protagonists successfully and predictably advance to a happy resolution. Sokolova's character achieves personal liberation from the constraints of totally rational behavior, is humanized in the process, yet does not become a prosaic person. Like Marlowe, he remains emphatically exceptional. The fate of the entire world hinges on Nikita's decision to release himself from the rigidity of his rational beliefs. The destiny of his native country is intimately bound up with Marlowe's actions. The exceptionality of Bulgakovian protagonists is a direct result of their creative powers. Zarin"s hero is a composer, writer, and superb cook. His adversary is a writer, alchemist, doctor, and also a great cook. Nikita Ivanov of Sokolova's novel is an uncommonly creative precision-tool worker whose reluctance to believe in the fantastic is more a feature of his time than of his creative personality.[18]

It is revealing to compare these omnipotent characters with their counterparts in canonical works of socialist realism. A character like Pavel Korchagin of Nikolai Ostrovsky's *How the Steel Was Tempered*, for example, can be classified as a superhero because of the superhuman scope of his achievements. The source of Korchagin's power is his boundless faith in the cause of Communism. Korchagin's view of the world is limited by his narrow-minded obsession with his goal. The punishment that Korchagin's body takes for its host's beliefs is essential for the creation of the saintly aura enveloping superheroes of socialist realism. Bulgakovian characters share with their canonical counterparts the determination to do good for their society. However, the source of that power is a creativity that enables the character to be in touch with the "other world." This, essentially Romantic concept of the artist as a medium between the finite and the infinite, is very much alive here. If the superheroes of socialist realism are elevated by their simple-minded faith into the ranks of the saints, the artists of Bulgakov's followers have direct access to spirits of light and darkness. In order to achieve this, they do not have to be "tempered" physically. Rather, they have to heed the call of their genius and be creative. Denial of one's creative powers is the worst sin that this Soviet hero can commit. This theme can be traced directly to Bulgakov's work where the Master is not granted light as a result of his decision to stop writing.[19]

Demons in the Service of the People: Vladimir Orlov

In Bulgakovian fiction, artistic creativity and diversity of interest and belief are linked. Although the protagonists can hardly be considered "rogues" in a picaresque style, they are full-blooded individuals whose adventures take them far out of the realm of the traditional Soviet novel. Vladimir Orlov's *Danilov, the Viola Player* introduces a character whose appetites range from making love to a demonic woman, to swimming in storm clouds and diving into lightning.[20] The protagonist is a viola player in a Moscow opera house and an experimental composer. The son of a human mother and a true demon exiled for his love for a human, Danilov is both man and demon. As a result of the intervention of his father's powerful friends, Danilov is brought up as a demon. After graduation from the classical school at the Office of Cognition, the hero is supposed "to know, feel, and see everything, and, by that token, to despise everything human."[21] Danilov, a capable student, learns quickly to feel, see, and know everything in space, time, and "deep down in human souls"—whether in the past, present, or eternity—all at the same instant. However, Orlov's character often consciously rejects these possibilities. It seems much more appropriate to him not to use his omniscience but to discover everything anew, the way human beings do. Similarly, he cannot hate people.

The human plot of the novel is propelled by several events. Danilov's valuable viola is stolen, which generates a lengthy search. Finally, it is found and Danilov is offered an opportunity to perform a new, experimental composition. The novel's demonic plot centers on Danilov's love affairs with demonic women, his travels, and his attempts to help humans. Danilov's life as a viola player in an opera house is filled with petty jealousies, with intense competition for lucrative tours and creature comforts, and with a general lack of discipline.[22] Several of Danilov's colleagues are members of a society of *khlopobudy* (a conflation of *khlopotat' o budushchem*—to be actively concerned with or intercede in the future). For the majority of the people, who come to the *khlopobudy* for predictions, however, knowledge of the future is merely a tool for personal advancement.[23] A substantial portion of the contemporary plot is devoted to the protagonist's love and appreciation of good food. Danilov's high esteem for the joys of the palate, shared by his friends, is shown to be related to his creative abilities.

Danilov's adventures in Moscow show the Soviet middle class in a gently ironic light; his journey in hell, on the other hand, is a veiled satire of Soviet bureaucracy and of Marxism's claims of omniscience. (This Aesopean quality explains in part the astonishing popularity of Orlov's novel). Fear of regimentation and manipulation becomes visible when benevolent surveillance turns into a malicious desire to control for gain. Danilov, the familiar chosen man of Soviet fiction, eager to protect people from disaster, discovers that humans do not need too much protection, for they seem to flourish even after disasters induced by demons. Omnipotence and omniscience make one arrogant and less resourceful.

Yet what is celebrated here is the apotheosis of the superman, not the common person. Like the American comic-book superheroes before them, Bulgakovian characters are a pure expression of escapism, a vehicle for the playing out of the pent-up desires of the Soviet middle class relishing the freedoms denied to the protagonists of socialist realism—travel to exotic places, erotic adventures, a comfortable life, and personal freedoms.

Through the use of a sensationally popular model and skillful combination of high-brow and popular genres, the Bulgakovian novel—devoid of rough edges, entertaining, and mildly satirical—tried to reach and amuse different levels of the Soviet reading public. The popularity of certain types of fiction in the seventies hinged precisely on "a strong recreational and amusement element in the reading of novels, rather than a desire for aesthetic and cultural development."[24] Combining popular genres with a more traditional narrative provided a safe way of insuring the accessibility and popularity of this fiction to an audience ranging from teenagers interested in science fiction to older readers of romance and war adventures. Bulgakovian novels embodied the desire of the Soviet middle class to enjoy life in all its aspects, and played up to the intelligentsia's insistence on freedom of creative expression. This literature accepted control from above, but mediated the harshness of that message through the depiction of benevolent and powerful protagonists. It seems at times that it envisioned and sanctioned the appearance of the new, young, and benevolent Soviet ruler.

Notes

1. In a twist that Bulgakov would have probably found amusing, there was a struggle going on in Soviet literary circles over who was going to edit Bulgakov's complete collected works, when its publication was announced in May of 1987. Iurii Bondarev engineered an attempt to exclude three of the most prominent Soviet Bulgakov scholars—Vladimir Lakshin, Marietta Chudakova, and Konstantin Rudnitsky—from the editorship of the project, this for allegedly passing on Bulgakov's archives to Ellendea Proffer of Ardis Publishers. See more on the controversy in *Sovetskaia Rossiia*, September 6 and September 13, 1987.

2. This information comes from John Bushnell's article "A Popular Reading of Bulgakov: Explication des Graffiti," *Slavic Review* 47.3 (Fall 1988): 502–511 and from personal correspondence with him. See also John Bushnell, *Moscow Graffiti: Language and Subculture* (Boston: Unwin Hyman, 1990), chap. 5, "Graffiti and Cultural Critique: An Appreciation of *The Master and Margarita*," pp. 173–204.

3. On this topic see *Literaturnaia gazeta*, August 27, 1986, p. 7; "Sadovaia 302-bis," in *Iunost'* 6 (1987): 81, *Iskusstvo kino* 4 (1987): 49.

4. The formerly conservative Oleg Mikhailov used *The Master and Margarita* as an example of a work that, although not socialist realist, has enriched the

country's spiritual life and influenced Russian literature. See *Literaturnaia gazeta*, July 8, 1981, p. 3.

5. For a brief discussion of this see Elendea Proffer, *Bulgakov: Life and Work* (Ann Arbor: Ardis, 1984), p. 531; and for a detailed comparison of Mennipean satire and Bulgakov's last novel see Proffer, "The Master and Margarita," in E. J. Brown, ed., *Major Soviet Writers* (New York, 1973), pp. 390–392; Nadine Natov, "Structural and Topological Ambivalence of Bulgakov's Novels Interepreted against the Background of Baxtin's Theory of 'Grotesque Realism' and Carnival-ization," in *American Contributions to the Eighth International Congress of Slav-ists* (Columbus, Ohio: Slavica Publishers, 1978), pp. 536–549.

6. Andrew Barratt devotes many pages of his study (*Between Two Worlds*) to the discussion of various responses to the novel, both in the Soviet Union and in the West. Another good source for bibliographical material on the novel is R. L. Busch's article "The Contexts of Bulgakov's Master and Margarita," in Arnold McMillin, ed. *Aspects of Modern Russian Literature: Selected Papers of the Third World Congress for Soviet and East European Studies* (Columbus, Ohio: Slavica Publishers, 1989), pp. 55–78.

7. For examples of Soviet criticism of the trend see Dmitrii Urnov, "Bor'ba ili igra so zlom?" *Literaturnoe obozrenie* 5 (1983): 43–45. Also see Lev Anninskii, "Mne by vashi zaboty!" *Literaturnoe obozrenie* 9 (1980): 41–44 and V. Lakshin, "O dome i o mire," *Literaturnoe obozrenie* 9 (1981): 38–43. For a positive assessment of Bulgakov's influence see V. Turbin, "I igra i bor'ba," *Literaturnoe obozrenie* 5 (1983): 45–49.

8. Barratt, *Between Two Worlds*, p. 88.

9. V. Lakshin, "Mir Mikhaila Bulgakova," *Literaturnoe obozrenie* 11 (1989): 23.

10. Ibid.

11. Sona Hoisington, "Fairy-tale Elements in Bulgakov's *The Master and Mar-garita*," in *SEEJ* 25.2 (1981): 53.

12. See *Novyi mir* 6, 8, 9 (1986).

13. Hoisington, "Fairy-tale Elements," p. 53.

14. The novel was first published in Latvian in 1974. The Russian translation used here is Marger Zarin', *Fal'shivyi Faust ili perepravlennaia popolnennaia po-varennaia kniga* (Moscow: Sovetskii Pisatel', 1981).

15. The real Christopher Marlowe's authorship of *Faustus* is not mentioned in the novel. This deliberate omission can provide one explanation for the word *false* in the title of the book: the novel that Zarin''s hero is writing has already been written by the historical Marlowe.

16. Turbin, "I igra i bor'ba," p. 46.

17. Natal'ia Sokolova, *Ostorozhno, volshebnoe!* (Moscow: Sovetskii Pisatel', 1981).

18. See more on this novel in Vsevolod Revich, "Eta real'naia fantastika," *Liter-aturnaia gazeta* (February 9, 1983): 4.

19. The issue of Master's "punishment" or "reward" has been heatedly de-bated by critics. Here, however, I am not proposing an interpretation of Bul-gakov's novel, but rather of the novels of his followers, which posit the denial of creativity as a fault.

20. This novel was first published in *Novyi mir* 2,3,4 (1980). The text used here is Vladimir Orlov, *Al'tist Danilov* (Moscow: Sovetskii Pisatel', 1981).

21. Orlov, *Al'tist Danilov*, p. 27.

22. One should also mention the obvious stress on music in both novels. It has been suggested that *The Master and Margarita* can be read as "an operatic novel" in which "the music is too loud and too persistent to be ignored" and that "at the very least, Bulgakov has provided us with a musical score or background music for the novel." See Rudy Lentulay's paper "The Master and Margarita: An Opera-Ballet in Prose," presented at the MMLA Conference in Minneapolis on November 3, 1978, p. 5. The same point has been argued in B. Gasparov, "Iz nabliudenii nad motivnoi strukturoi romana M. A. Bulgakova 'Master and Margarita,'" *Slavica Hierosolymitana* 3 (1978): 198–251. It is clear that in his own novel Orlov attempts something similar to Bulgakov's "orchestration" of plot.

23. The subplot about the *khlopobudy* is a thinly veiled satire on the popular movement of contemporary Soviet futurologists *(futurologi)*, whose stated purpose is to predict the course of the future according to scientific methods.

24. Jenny Brine, "Reading as a Leisure Pursuit in the USSR," p. 264.

8

Envisioning the End:
The Apocalyptic
Novels of Glasnost

I knew the years would pass no longer,
That the twenty-first century would never come,
That time had ceased to exist—interrupted
In the middle of the word. . . .

The earth turned hollow like a dry nut,
And someone in heaven was singing:
"You worm, little man, bug,
What a planet you have devoured!"

—*Andrei Voznesensky, "A Dream," 1987*

HE TRANSITION FROM THE FANTASTIC trend into the literature of the Gorbachev period may, at first glance, appear as a revolutionary rupture, a vociferous departure from the principles that had guided Soviet literature before glasnost. The changes this literature underwent with the advent of glasnost were truly momentous; it would be rash, however, to call them revolutionary. What in fact becomes clear from a comparative look at the literary production immediately preceding Gorbachev's thaw and the literature of glasnost is a continuity of concerns and themes. Even though some authors writing in the glasnost period chose new ways to promote their messages, the pool of philosophical ideas, ethical positions, and political solutions remained virtually unchanged. It is this essential continuity of message, if not always of representation, that can be most readily seen through the prism of the new literature's sustained engagement with or its seeming

disengagement from the fantastic. Under glasnost the refurbished socialist realism of the "fantastic decade" gives way to the apocalyptic literature (written by the same authors, now labeled the publicists). In publicistic fiction the dire consequences of the practical realization of the
Communist myth are documented in painstaking detail, and fantasy, if
used at all, is a quick prop to a moralistic message. Writers of alternative
literature in the Gorbachev period, on the other hand, do not abandon
their focus on the fantastic nature of reality. And it is in alternative literature where a genuine change in orientation and literary practice finally
occurs—in the fiction whose aim is to deconstruct the very language of
Soviet socialism.

The widely used term *literature of glasnost*, designating the literary
output of the new thaw, is a broad category embracing a score of different styles, periods, and positions. Works written from ten to fifty years
before, published by samizdat or abroad, begun under Khrushchev and
finished under Gorbachev, or written and published during or shortly
before Gorbachev's liberalization have all been included in this elastic
category. The word *glasnost*, however, is an indicator of this literature's
common denominator. What had been impossible to voice before was
now given a broad forum, what had been formerly suppressed was now
allowed to appear, and what had been concealed under the guise of fantastic devices now often emerged in harsh and openly proselytizing
statements about the dire state of Soviet society.

Julian Graffy has identified four areas of liberalization in Soviet literature of the Gorbachev period: (1) bold new Soviet writing; (2) works by
living Soviet writers previously unpublishable at home; (3) works by great
Soviet writers of the early twentieth century never previously published
in the USSR; and (4) works by living émigrés.[1] Add to this list works by
Western authors, banned before Gorbachev, and the impressive menu of
glasnost literature is complete. In this and the subsequent chapters I will
address bold new Russian writing (which actually often includes category (2), above), and focus, within this category, on its two important
manifestations—publicistic prose and alternative prose. Publicistic
prose, novels written by established authors in the Gorbachev period,
takes its name from its direct attacks on previously unmentionable social
problems.[2] The umbrella term *alternative literature* is somewhat problematic; it unites very different authors under its wide canopy and, significantly, was used even before glasnost to characterize the Moscow school
of the fantastic trend (see chapter 4). In fact, some alternative prose published under Gorbachev was written in the previous decade.

The continuity in the critical perception of alternative literature is not
the only reason for seeing alternative writers as a group. In very broad
terms, what they offered (before, during, and after Gorbachev) was what

Siniavsky had wanted Russian literature to become all along: "a phantas-magoric art with a hypothesis instead of a purpose, an art in which the grotesque replaces realistic descriptions of ordinary life." In contrast to the publicistic trend, alternative literature carefully avoids taking stands. It is written in the tradition of posing questions, rather than placing blame; it purports to show, rather than tell; and it is inclined, in Roland Barthe's words, to set "snares" for the reader, rather than to spell every-thing out. Alternative literature avoids mimetic representation in favor of the grotesque, hallucinatory, and ironic.

Both trends can be considered in light of their different attitudes to the fantasy principle in fiction; both feature writers active during the fantastic decade of the seventies and early eighties. The writers of pub-licistic prose tend to avoid overt manifestations of the fantastic, deni-grate the myths of Soviet society in factual, journalistic accounts, and attempt to create new myths. Publicists, still not fully free from the utopian mentality of socialist realism, substitute the now-compro-mised vision of Russia's glorious future with the ideal of a perfect past.[3] The writers of alternative prose, on the other hand, focus on the phan-tasmagoric nature of reality, continuing their investigation of the me-chanics of human illusion—by means of the fantastic. All mythological thinking becomes suspect in alternative fiction; and it is this close in-vestigation of language as a generator of cultural myths that will propel the younger generation of alternative writers into a qualitatively new stage in the development of Russian fiction, the stage marked by the cheerful interment of everything Soviet, including literature.

Publicists Under Glasnost: The Mythological Laboratory

Publicistic literature is an extension of two distinctive orientations of the fantastic decade—village prose that had idealized the Russian rural past, and refurbished socialist realism that had tried to broaden the scope of Soviet literature by incorporating fantasy into the standard so-cialist realist model. However, if before Gorbachev the concerns articu-lated by those trends were allowed to appear only on the periphery of public discourse, under glasnost they were thrust forward into the light—to be exposed, revalued, and debated. Technocratic utopianism, examined and rejected by the fantastic trend under the guise of legends and fairy-tale magic, was permitted in publicistic prose to manifest all its ugly economic and ecological consequences. The spiritual void *(bez-dukhovnost')*, the grand malaise of Soviet society—hinted at in the works of the fantastic trend but counterbalanced there by the inevitable presence of positive heroes—was now openly shown to stem from the social engineering of Marxism-Leninism, from its rejection of religious beliefs, from urbanization and bureaucratization. Multinational unity, the issue cautiously probed and questioned in the works of the "fantastic decade," was now seen as a goal that is not only impossible to achieve but as the one pursued at the expense of national identity. In short, the new publicistic literature attacked—directly—virtually all the myths informing Soviet society before glasnost.

Publicistic fiction is a literature engaged in a desperate search for a new organizing and explanatory pattern of existence, a different set of guiding myths—radically opposed to the Soviet version of Marxism-Leninism but as mythologically potent as the latter. The movement here is two-pronged: first, there is a rejection of the evil associated with the profane past of postrevolutionary Russia, the evil whose outgrowths are examined in painstaking journalistic detail; and second, a substitute pool of values is introduced, values whose centrality is justified by the reference to an alternative sacred past (that of the preindustrialized village, traditional Russian family, and Christian myth).

In this new "story of reality lived" (to use Bronislaw Malinowsky's definition of myth again), society has to cleanse itself of the evil, repent, suffer, and, through that suffering, achieve forgiveness and dispensation. Protagonists of this fiction, who often serve as stand-ins for their authors, must be martyrs, sacrificial lambs to the new myth, who preach the new Gospel and then perish, prefiguring by their fates, and by the fates of those around them, the inexorable apocalyptic catastrophe and the eventual possible regeneration yet to affect their worlds. Consequently, the writer's position as a public figure becomes increasingly more apparent under glasnost, and literature exhibits a much greater tendency toward monologism than during periods of relative social stability. The ironic stance of writers toward their heroes, characteristic of some literature of the preceding period, is absent in the new publicistic fiction. The new positive hero speaks the writer's language; the confluence of the writer's and the hero's point of view is complete.

The idea of the writer as spiritual guide and martyr informs Evgeny Evtushenko's *Fuku!* (1985), which treats such previously forbidden themes as Soviet neo-Nazism and the Kolyma labor camps.[4] Evtushenko's poetic memoir and testament is a reenactment of the author's typical poetry reading, where each poem is introduced by a narrative passage describing the circumstances of and the poet's state of mind during the poem's composition. Evtushenko rejects "all those who sowed the hunger of body and soul" by refusing to name them. (*Fuku* is the word used in the poem for the evil people of this world, whose names have become taboo). The poet himself (his life and understanding of his own place in history) figures most prominently in the poem. Evtushenko as an emissary of peace, a generous giver of himself, a sufferer, and a passionate accuser of dictatorship in any form overshadows everything else. Here the new monologism reaches its peak, and the poet himself becomes the martyr, ready to be sacrificed at the altar of the new myth.[5]

If, then, in the works of the fantastic decade, the future publicists largely used the accoutrements of the fantastic—fairy tale, legends, science fiction—as discreet paraphrasing devices aimed at signaling areas of social concern, now publicistic narratives become propelled by the mythological impulse. It is in this process of mythological revaluation that publicistic prose acquires a distinct affinity with apocalyptic fiction. Defined broadly by David Bethea as "a subset of the modern novel which takes the core elements of the biblical genre and adapts them to its own hybrid form," the apocalyptic novels of glasnost tread the familiar ground of Russian literature.[6] The following (virtually all) features of modern Russian apocalyptic fiction noted by the critic are shared, to some degree, by the publicistic prose of glasnost: an individual is seen to be free to choose between good and evil in a story determined by some higher power; the pattern of crisis-judgment-vindication, found in Revelation, becomes an organizing narrative vehicle; epic past, a long-lost period of grace and innocence, is shown to guide future personal and national history; finally, this fiction is concerned with a search for the meaning of the Russian (or, perhaps, Soviet) apocalypse, which establishes a connection between personal death and the end of national, even world history.[7]

One could observe the emergence of constituent parts of this new mythological construction in village prose and the refurbished socialist realism of the fantastic decade. Both trends were predisposed to representing reality in mythological terms. Refurbished socialist realism alluded to the myth of a perfect Communist society, the worthy if unattainable goal of its self-sacrificing protagonists. Village prose used Christian and pre-Christian beliefs to juxtapose its own version of the sacred past with the profane present, leading to the end of native cultures. And, in some cases, there was a curious intermixing of these seemingly contradictory visions in one work (as, for example, in Aitmatov's Day or Dumbadze's The Law of Eternity).

In publicistic literature the impulse to shape representation around an explanatory myth becomes the central organizing force. In this process, the myth of the Communist paradise is universally rejected, in fact "retold" in apocalyptic language, with former standard heroes of the Soviet state represented as the embodiments of the Antichrist, and the demise of positive protagonists seen as prefiguring the fall of Soviet society and the end of its history. To sustain itself in the customary role of ethical guide to life, the new publicistic literature latched onto the myths of preindustrialized Russia, Christianity, the family, and native traditions. Yet the forging of new patterns of being by the disillusioned writ-ers for a bitter and suspicious audience was often fraught with a sense of the endeavor's futility.

Aitmatov's *The Execution Block* and the Martyrs of Perestroika

Chingiz Aitmatov's celebrated novel of glasnost, *The Execution Block*, is a thorough depiction of the dire consequences the myth of the Great So-ciety has left in its wake.[8] The novel's "gripe list"(the term is Katerina Clark's) includes a discussion of drug production and trafficking, the break-up of families, lawlessness and cynicism both in the city and country, the plundering of the environment, the wholesale extermina-tion of wildlife, even the murder of innocent children. Aitmatov con-demns the values that have informed his society and offers a substitute for the bankrupt official ideology, a substitute myth constructed out of native traditions, pagan myths, Christianity, and Rousseauesque "nat-ural values."[9] Aitmatov employs some elements of fantasy in this novel (e.g., time travel); yet, overall, the narrative is tilted, much more than his previous work, toward a factual account of social problems in the entire country.

The Execution Block consists of three interrelated plots, each docu-menting the disintegration of Soviet society: the story of Avdii Kallis-tratov, a former seminary student and a quixotic figure bent on chang-ing the world around him; the story of the two wolves forced to wander because of the destruction of their habitat; and the story of Boston Urkunchiev, a successful *chaban* (shepherd) at a collective farm, whose life is destroyed by a coworker. On another level, the three plots of the novel can be seen as elaborations of the three im-portant, and overlapping, areas of concern for the author: the spiri-tual (the story of Avdii), the natural (the wandering wolves), and the traditional (Boston's story).

Avdii Kallistratov (named for the Old Testament prophet Obadiah) is a proponent of the new religion Bog-sovremennik ("God as our contem-porary") which, in Avdii's opinion, will "free the human soul from the power of evil."[10] In his attempts to root out evil in people Avdii plunges himself into the lower depths of Soviet society. He preaches to the col-lectors of the drug *anasha* (marijuana), who throw him off a train for his efforts. He tries to reform a band of outcasts (who try to earn a quick ru-ble by killing *saigaki* in the Moinkum savanna) and is crucified by them. Avdii's search for a new ideology of Man-God ends in his death on a makeshift cross, yet this martyrdom is absolutely indispensable for Aitmatov's mythological scheme. In order for his society to understand the profound nature of its spiritual decay, Avdii, an embodiment of Man-God, has to perish in the service of the people. (When asked why he focused on Christianity instead of Islam in this novel, Aitmatov replied that he needed a martyr.)[11] The Christian myth is used by Aitmatov as the repository of important moral values. To Avdii Kallistratov, only profound personal change can lead to the arrival of Man-God, who, in turn, can save humanity from disaster. And humanity's hope lies in moral regeneration through suffering.

With the help of "historical synchronism" (time travel) Avdii witnesses Jesus' conversation with Pontius Pilate. Aitmatov's rendition of the biblical story was perceived by some critics as the novel's major weakness. There are a number of factual mistakes in this portion of the novel, such as the discussion of Doomsday (long before the historical emergence of the idea), the wrong form of address (Pilate's wife calls him Pontii on a number of occasions), and, generally, a historically inaccurate and simplistic portrayal of Pilate as the embodiment of malevolent power. Some passages lack biblical grandeur and clarity and appear to be taken from contemporary issues of Soviet periodicals.

Curiously, Aitmatov does not go to the biblical source for the story of Jesus' encounter with Pilate, but borrows it from Bulgakov's *The Master and Margarita*. There are too many similarities in setting, imagery, and structure between Aitmatov and Bulgakov here to warrant any other conclusion.[12] But in sharp contrast to the lightly entertaining Bulgakovian novels, this attempt to absorb Bulgakov's heritage in literature focuses on the religious philosophical plot of *The Master and Margarita*. When asked about the affinity between *The Execution Block* and *The Master and Margarita*, Aitmatov admitted the importance of Bulgakov's work for his own:

> Of course I had Bulgakov in mind in a sense that [Bulgakov's] Pontius Pilate and Ieshua and my Pilate and Jesus of Nazareth are the same people who find themselves in the same situation. However, I hope that the discerning reader will notice that although I tried to resolve this situation analogously, I attempted to introduce something essential into the dialogue between Pilate and Jesus. A certain period of history has passed since Bulgakov's portrayal of the encounter. We are living in a somewhat different temporal dimension. I wanted to introduce something new, that which we are learning today, and, in particular, I wanted to say something about the global vulnerability of humanity.[13]

Since one can safely assume that Bulgakov's rendition of the story was more familiar to the general Soviet reader than its biblical source, Aitmatov deliberately used the model most accessible to his audience. This is not to say that Bulgakov's narrative is transposed into Aitmatov's novel lock, stock, and barrel. *The Execution Block* is a tendentious, didactic piece of literature rigidly controlled by its overarching idea of the moral responsibility of people for their deeds in the world. Bulgakov's vision of Jesus and Pilate is necessarily transformed in Aitmatov's presentation of their encounter. Bulgakov's Pilate is an unwilling tool of fate. He wants to save his newly acquired friend from death on the cross but is unable to do so. In *The Execution Block*, Bulgakov's complex psychological portrayal of the conversation between Ieshua and Pilate is reduced to a duel between accuser and accused. In Aitmatov's version of the encounter, Pilate is the embodiment of a destructive power that crushes everything in its path. If in *The Master and Margarita* Pilate's feeling of guilt and a vague premonition of his eternal infamy is just an unarticulated feeling, in *The Execution Block* it is Jesus who warns Pilate that his name will remain in history, and Pilate is flattered by the remark! Most Soviet critics tried to soften the unorthodox God searching of this part of the novel by pointing out that the encounter is seen through the eyes of Avdii Kallistratov, an immature, idealistic man who has not even completed his seminary education.[14] It is obvious, nevertheless, that Jesus—the embodiment of good—serves here as a mouthpiece for Aitmatov's own ideas on the future of humanity, Pilate represents satanic power, while Avdii's role in the narrative is akin to that of the martyred saints of Russian hagiography.

Avdii's personal end foreshadows the possible end of his society, indeed, of the entire world. Aitmatov offers the following interpretation of the spiritual plot of the story:

> I do not at all insist on interpreting Doomsday literally as the nuclear end of the world. However, it is exactly the realization of this threat that forced me to try to prove that one should not be apprehensive of a fictional, mystical end of the world but of that which we ourselves can do, of that which can become a terrifying reality.[15]

Aitmatov's work marks a new step in the assimilation of Bulgakov's legacy into the Soviet literature. Bulgakovian novels of the late seventies and early eighties treated Bulgakov's legacy as a treasury of style and structure. The popularity of those novels resulted from their selective borrowing from the source.[16] It was the lightness of tone, the playfulness of action, and the unpredictability of wondrous adventures that Bulgakov's followers seized upon for their own very successful escapist novels. Aitmatov disregards the fantastic-satirical aspects of *The Master and Margarita* and zeroes in on the religious-philosophical conflict of the relationship between representatives of power and common people. Aitmatov "quotes" from Bulgakov to warn of the possible tragic consequences of modern spiritual impoverishment for Soviet society and the world at large.[17] Both the science fiction device of time travel and Bulgakov's rendition of the Christian legend serve to motivate and promote Aitmatov's vision of his disintegrating society and its possible regeneration.

The story of Avdii is linked to the other important plot line of the novel—the story of two wolves doomed to a life of eternal wandering because of humans' senseless games with nature. Every time the two wolves, Akbara and Tashchainar, settle down to raise cubs, humans encroach on their territory and they have to flee. If Avdii represents the spiritual realm of Aitmatov's mythological construct, the wolves are the embodiment of the natural. They are inseparable from their environment; they are a harmonious part of nature and obey its laws. They are free and powerful in their habitat, and their natural impulses for procreation and physical freedom are respected by Aitmatov. It is only when people, bent on conquering nature to suit their immediate needs, disrupt the laws of nature that the wolves—the "noble savages" of Aitmatov's novel—lose their sustaining power, become vulnerable, and, in their vulnerability, become dangerous.

The wolves provide the only connecting link to the third plot of the novel, which otherwise stands apart from the rest of the narrative. Boston Urkunchiev, a shepherd on a Kirgiz state farm, is dismayed at the apathy and cynicism of his coworkers. He fights hard to improve the work of his unit and is not ashamed of being a true *khoziain* (master). But his efforts to change things at the farm are futile. In a tragic turn of events, Bazarbai, a shepherd on Boston's farm and his enemy, takes away Akbara's cubs, brings them to Boston's house, and then sells them. When all her attempts to find the cubs fail, the she-wolf Akbara steals Boston's son. The child's father hunts down the she-wolf and accidentally kills his own son. When he realizes what has happened, Boston goes to the shepherd who started the horrible chain of events and fatally shoots him.

Aitmatov's focus here is on the realm of the traditional, with the themes of nature and culture playing an important part. Like Aitmatov's other positive heroes, such as Edigei and Abutalip in *Day*, Boston is initially depicted as a person in whom the pulls of native tradition, nature, and culture (understood here as the culture of socialism, with its insistence on productivity and commitment to one's work) are harmoniously balanced. His closeness to the realm of nature is underscored by his name—which alludes to the hero's membership in the clan of the wolves *[boston]*—as well as by his carnal passions. Boston's insatiable desire for his wife and his virile appearance stand in sharp contrast to Avdii's emasculated image. (The use of the name Kallistratov, with its suggestion of castration, is no coincidence.) Observance of local customs points to Boston's reverence for the traditional ways of life. His achievements at work are an indication of Boston's mastery of the language of socialist culture—different from the traditional nomadic ways of the Kirgiz people—and even the language of perestroika. Motivated by the need to improve the lot of his village, Boston advocates private land management and individual control of flocks. Boston's innovations, opposed by the local party leaders, have been shown to mirror the proposals of Gorbachev and his supporters to decentralize the economy.[18] However, as in the story of the wolves, this hard-won balance is disrupted, and Boston becomes another victim of the technocratic utopians, as well as of his own fate.[19]

From the very beginning Boston is portrayed as a person with a singular and difficult destiny.[20] Even though it can be seen as a just retribution for his child's death, the act of murder, unthinkable for someone like Avdii, puts Boston completely apart from other people, destroys him both spiritually and emotionally. The final events of the story, Boston's private "end of the world" are prefigured by the rest of the narrative. Disruption in the laws of nature leads to personal tragedy.

Aitmatov's *The Execution Block* is, in spite of all the sensationalist journalese of its elaborate plots, a variation, or a set of variations, on the themes already present in his novel *Day*. Furthermore, as before, Aitmatov is skillfully juggling various literary models in one work. His is truly an attempt at a "synthetic novel," drawn from all current forms of literary discourse—Bulgakov's novel, the fantastic novels of Kim and Evdokimov, the detective novel, village prose, and investigative reportage. Nor is Aitmatov afraid to borrow from his own store of literary conventions. The use of animal characters to emphasize other conflicts in the novel is a familiar device for him, as is the use of legend to illustrate the unchanging nature of the human condition as well as to provide the narrative with its own epic past.

Avdii's ability to travel through time and his quixotic eccentricities bring to mind Bulgakov's Ieshua and the fantastic eccentrics of Kim, Anar, Makanin, and Evdokimov. Aitmatov mines the religious plot of *The Master and Margarita* for the constituent parts of a new mythology; the fairy-tale magic of Bulgakov's satirical plot, however, does not answer Aitmatov's very serious needs. That is why Aitmatov's characters differ from the omniscient superheroes of the Soviet Bulgakovian novel. For the latter the miraculous is a gift enabling the protagonist to enjoy life in its fullness and then help others—through simple magic. For the fantastic eccentrics, on the other hand, the miraculous is an indication of humans' spiritual disorientation, impossible to "cure" by fairytale transformations. In both cases the miraculous is proof of the exceptionality of the hero: both Bulgakovian superheroes and fantastic eccentrics are intent on changing the world around them. Only the latter, however—and Avdii Kalistratov is their true heir—see moral regeneration as the sole means of affecting this change.

Aitmatov's novel is a good example of the transition from fantasy to glasnost in Soviet literature. The issues, presented in deliberately ambiguous form in *Day*, are spelled out in *The Execution Block*. The mindless use of technology and the danger it poses to the environment, the loss of native cultures and the toll it takes on the spiritual well-being of the nation, and, finally, the very real threat of nuclear war are the issues addressed in both novels. In *The Execution Block* the ambivalence of the authorial position is absent, and the message is clear and urgent, almost shrill. As Carol Avins has pointed out, the earthly paradise promised at the end of the path to Communism is pointedly characterized in *The Execution Block* as an illusory third alternative to narcotics and money, on the one hand, and God, on the other. The promise of a socialist perfection is not achieved in Aitmatov's society and cannot be achieved "by means of old ideological tools."[21] New ideological constructs are needed, and Aitmatov is ready to offer his own, a patchwork of beliefs to fill the spiritual void.

As before, Aitmatov demonstrates acute sensitivity to the political needs of the moment and undeniable skills of formulating those needs in fiction. It is hard to doubt Aitmatov's sincerity; one has only to admire his mastery and intuition in skirting the limits of the politically permissible. Aitmatov's novel heeded the leader's call for providing loyal opposition to the Party; in fact, it came dizzyingly close to rejecting a system seen as responsible for destroying its best people.

The Russian Intellectual as the Only Hope
for Russia's Salvation: Bondarev's *The Game*

Aitmatov's vision of the disintegrating social, cultural, and moral structures of his society was shared by a score of prominent writers of publicistic literature. Jurii Bondarev, another establishment figure and the darling of conservative critics (branded by Igor Zolotusskii a "decorated palace scribe" [*dvortsovyi pisatel' usypannyi nagradami*]),[22] offered his version of an apocalyptic novel in *The Game*.[23] Bondarev's work portrays the last days of Viacheslav Krymov, a successful Soviet film director. Krymov's behavior is under scrutiny by the police because of the unexpected and mysterious death of Irina Skvortsova, the leading actress in his last picture.[24] Krymov's wife is devastated by the rumors of a love affair between her husband and Irina. Krymov's old war buddy betrays him to the authorities, disclosing the details of the director's association with the young actress and Krymov's frank conversations with an American film director, John Grichmar. Irina's father accuses Krymov of seducing his daughter and causing her untimely death. In the end Krymov is completely alone, misunderstood even by those who are close to him. The pressure is overwhelming; the hero succumbs to it and dies.

This brief compendium of the troubles of a leading Soviet film director does not exhaust the novel's complexity, nor does it explain the real reasons for Krymov's demise. Bondarev's protagonist is an intellectual and a martyr who, by his death, is made to demonstrate the approaching end of his world and of the world at large. Like Aitmatov's Avdii, Krymov must die in order to stir people to action, his death yet another sacrifice at the altar of the myth of Russia's resurrection. Krymov and the American Grichmar—both film directors and good friends—are the chosen people engaged in assessing Russia's past and warning about its possible future. (Bondarev deliberately emphasizes the elite character of his protagonists by pointing out that Krymov's and Grichmar's concerns are of no interest to the average person.) Grichmar, the son of Russian émigrés, is profoundly pessimistic in his view of modern civilization in general and of the Russian example in particular, and Krymov is allowed to concur. The American remains virtually unopposed when he says that the entire history of Russia is a tragedy, that here nonentities have destroyed all intellect and talent, and that the spirit of the Russian people has been annihilated, together with their cathedrals and religion.

As is characteristic of publicistic prose, the writer's own ideas on Russian culture and nature mirror those of his protagonists. In his speech at the Eighth Congress of Soviet Writers in June 1986, Bondarev talked about the need to stop the destruction of historical monuments and the environment. According to Bondarev, if "a moral explosion does not occur in science and criticism, then one day we will wake up and see that the national culture of enormous Russia, her spirit, love for the fatherland, her beauty, great literature, art, and philosophy have been murdered and have disappeared forever."[25] The destruction of the constituent parts of the heroic myth of Russian greatness is what Bondarev also saw as the worst side effects of perestroika. In his speech to the Nineteenth Party Conference the writer compared perestroika to a plane that had taken off without knowing whether it could land. Bondarev accused "the knights of extremism" of seeking to assume dictatorial control of the press and of subjecting everything to doubt: "morality, courage, love, art, talent, family, great revolutionary ideas, the genius of Lenin, the October Revolution, and the Great Patriotic War."[26]

It is true that Bondarev's concerns are essentially nationalistic. Contrary to someone like Solzhenitsyn, however, the writer is not willing to dispense entirely with the "great revolutionary ideals" or to doubt "the genius of Lenin." In his view, formulated both in *The Game* and in Bondarev's public statements, all moral foundations and communal structures of a formerly powerful Russia have been allowed to disappear after Lenin's death. The perpetrators of this evil deed are the arrogant technocrats, thoughtless engineers of the future, builders of inhumane socialism, atheists. The Soviet brand of socialism, with its environmental and spiritual engineering, and American technology, in the service of consumerism, are both blamed for the disaster in Russia.

In Bondarev's *Choice* the placing of blame was camouflaged, and the science fiction model of alien manipulation was hinted at the issue that in *The Game* is spelled out directly—the Russian people are being destroyed, together with their religion and cathedrals. As in Aitmatov's *Execution Block*, it is the spiritual void that Bondarev identifies as a chief symptom of a pernicious moral disease in a socialist state gone wrong.

To counterbalance the image of the total dissolution of Russia's moral and spiritual shorings and to advance a program for saving humanity from destruction, Bondarev employs several complementary myths: the messianic view of Russia, the view of nature as a dispassionate reconciler of all differences and an eternal source of moral and physical rejuvenation, and the myth of a savior who, through his suffering, will put the country and the world on the right course.

Bondarev's protagonists agree that the time has come for Russia to save civilization just as it did in the Second World War because "the conscience of the whole world is programmed in Russia."[27] Thus, the country's most recent heroic experience in the war is presented as an immediate sacred past, the time of an inhuman sacrificial communal effort on the part of all Russians—in the service of the entire world. In this scheme, Russia remains the last hope for the regeneration of humanity. But that profound change can be affected only if people learn to respect nature, which has for so long been plundered for immediate profit. The task of saving nature (and in Bondarev's work reverence toward the natural realm is inseparable from adherence to the traditional Russian ethical norms of communal support, humility, and divine guidance) is bestowed on a new Soviet person who would stir up the people by focusing on the most urgent issues of the day as well as on philosophical, "eternal questions" *(vechnye voprosy)*. Even if at first greeted with scorn and laughter, this new quixote alone is capable of opening people's eyes to the sad fact that the forests are being mercilessly plundered, the rivers being turned into sewers, and the sky into a junkyard.

Clearly, Bondarev's Krymov is this new Soviet person capable of preventing the catastrophic slide of his country into the abyss. Krymov's last film, *Undeclared War* is about the mindless plundering of nature and the immorality of the undeclared war as opposed to the one in which he fought. The opposition of a declared, just war and an undeclared, unjust one is significant, since it is part of the formal lexicon of war literature, where the undeclared, unjust, war stands for the one waged by the Nazis. Krymov is now, as he was then, a soldier in a just war—this time against the violators of the natural realm. He is also a quixotic figure, scorned for his convictions, yet willing to spread the word of Russia's greatness and her possible demise.

Krymov dies calling for thousands of "patient preachers" to come and propagate the idea of the need for change. In his last moments he sees the archpriest Avvacum (leader of the Old Believer schism in the Russian Church of the mid-seventeenth century and author of an auto-biographical "Life") and hears a sweet, mysterious voice, full of forgive-ness and absolution. The appearance of Avvacum is as crucial for Bon-darev's mythological scheme as is Krymov's premature death. The two men are linked through their almost fanatic belief in the need to return to the true (as opposed to false) time—before the crystallization of the perfidious dogma. Thus, Partriarch Nikon's reforms of the Russian Church are equated here with the experiments of socialism.[28] Krymov and Avvacum are also martyrs and self-proclaimed outsiders (the men-tion of the Crimean peninsula, *Krym* in Russian, is an allusion to the former's name).

It has been noted that the genre of a saint's life as exemplified by Av-vacum permits the author to present the hardships he endured in the service of his ideals as a sign of his election and as a justification for his role as a national spokesman, and even a "precursor to God in judgment at the Second Coming."[29] Avvacum's martyrdom was a necessary path toward his conversion and was meant to demonstrate that repentance is inseparable from the fulfillment of the national destiny—for Russia to rise from the ashes and prosper.[30] Krymov's death, his sins, his sense of a profoundly important personal mission, as well as his suffering, are equally fraught with meaning. In Bondarev's view people like Krymov offer the only remaining hope for the salvation of Russia and the world. Like Avvacum, and like other protagonists of publicistic prose, the au-thor must suffer and perish for thousands of like-minded people to come in his stead.

Reverence for nature, anti-Western sentiment, Christian motifs, anxi-ety about disappearing traditions, and a belief in the divine destiny of Russia put *The Game* much closer to village prose than any of Bon-darev's previous novels. Of course, Krymov is very different from the characters populating the run-of-the-mill village prose novel. He is not a keeper of the old communal tradition, neither is he a repentant city dweller returning to his roots. Krymov belongs in a big city, his village surrogate is his country dacha. But, as an intellectual and an artist, he is made to see and understand more than the average citizen; he can articulate that which intuitive, "natural" heroes of village prose can only feel. In this readjustment of standard components of village prose its ideals find an effective advocate, and a path is shown for the union (*smychka*) between the city and the countryside.

Bondarev's work also betrays its closeness to the novels of refurbished socialist realism of the previous decade. Like Krymov, the protagonist of Bondarev's earlier novel *The Choice* was made to examine the differences between clear ethical choices of the war time and the moral confusion of the seventies. Hesitant forays into fantasy pointed to the hero's dissatisfaction with his society and to a search for an ideal past, eventually found in childhood and the war years. In *The Game* the issues confronting Krymov's society are placed in a global context. The need to paraphrase Bondarev's concerns by means of the traditional devices of fantasy (such as science fiction plots) is no longer there. In the end, what we have in Bondarev's novel is the "battle of the myths," where the myths of socialism are defeated, while the myth of Russia's salvation through personal sacrifice and return to tradition emerges victorious.

The Chronicle of Moral Collapse: Rasputin's *The Fire*

While Bondarev's work accords a lot of attention to the resurrection of the venerable myths of the mighty Russia of old, Valentin Rasputin's contribution to publicistic literature, *The Fire (Pozhar,* 1985), focuses almost exclusively on the fateful effects of Soviet social policy in the countryside.[31] Bondarev's pessimistic vision is counterbalanced to a degree by allusions to Russia's sacred past. Rasputin's work, on the other hand, offers unrelieved documentation of the irretrievability of that past. The novel's plot centers on a fire raging through the storage barns of a state logging farm. The main character, Ivan Egorov, a former villager, helps fight the conflagration and observes the different reactions of his neighbors and coworkers to the disaster. Egorov's thoughts about the fire and about the fate of his community make up most of the novel.

The Fire, obviously a sequel to *Farewell to Matera*, is also a work in the tradition of glasnost.[32] Here nothing is veiled under the cover of legend; the author's ideas are spelled out through the voice of Rasputin's spokesman, Egorov. Rasputin's work analyzes the economic and spiritual costs of the forced and shortsighted dissolution of the peasant community. His uprooted peasants have as little respect for basic values as they do for the forest they are blindly logging on their state farm. The former villagers have become infected with the disease of indifference.

In *Matera* the lives of positive characters, such as Daria, were guided by Christian and pagan beliefs (in the Russian tradition of *dvoeverie*), thereby necessitating the use of fairy-tale and folk elements in the narrative. Now the villagers have no beliefs left, and Rasputin's narrative, stripped of ambiguity, approaches the matter-of-factness of a journalistic account. The accursed "loss of spirituality" *(bezdukhovnost')* has reached the village. In Egorov's view, some of the blame can be placed on the newcomers, former criminals. However, in a sentiment shared by all contributors to the publicistic trend, Egorov assigns primary responsibility for the spiritual malaise to the absence of a tradition, destroyed along with the rightful homes of the villagers, their churches, and the traditional work ethic.

Like Matera in Rasputin's previous work, Egorov's own village, Egorovka, has been submerged to create a hydroelectric station, and the villagers have been resettled on a logging farm. In the beginning, the communal bond is still strong; the entire community takes care of the old and disabled, and the streets of the new settlement are built according to the pattern of the old village. However, as time goes by, as the futility and mindlessness of their work becomes apparent to the former villagers, their values change. They become nomads, moving from one place to another, destroying the forest around them under the exigencies of the work plan. They have been uprooted, both physically and spiritually. Confrontation with the cataclysm of fire reveals the frailty of disintegrating communal bonds. The fire is also a symbol of the spiritual devastation Egorov sees in his villagers. That which constituted the moral foundation of a community has been turned into something abnormal, a thing of the past. As always for Rasputin, indifference to the dead is a sign of the community's collapse; on several occasions Egorov observes newcomers to the settlement, former criminals, urinating in the cemetery. The former villagers themselves are indifferent to the pilfering, heavy drinking, and cheating that occurs on the farm. Egorov is made to feel an outcast when he draws everybody's attention to the immoral behavior of his coworkers. When the doors of the burning barns are opened, both the newcomers and the former villagers help themselves to the goods (food, clothing) inside. A mute from the old village, in charge of guarding the barns (the character akin to the "holy fools" revered in Russian peasant culture), is killed by one of the former criminals. Egorov thinks that good and evil have become confused. The primary reason for this change is the absence of a true home for the former villagers; their former home was sanctified by tradition and ritual, a place where they felt they belonged. The Sosnovka settlement does not fit these requirements; it is a space created as a result of an impulse to destroy—nature, customs, people.

Rasputin provides an alternative, positive model of the resettlement policy: Egorov's son Boris lives in a beautiful, rich settlement where everything is built according to "long-established communal law." Boris urges Egorov to join him; however, for Egorov, to leave Sosnovka is to admit defeat. At the conclusion of the novel, Egorov walks away from the settlement: it is left unclear whether he is to stay and persevere, or leave, abandoning his fight against the loss of traditional values, yet the sense of failure permeating Rasputin's novel is inescapable.

As in modern Russian apocalyptic fiction, an individual in Rasputin's novel is seen to be free to choose between good and evil, and most choose evil. The epic past is shown to guide future personal and national history, yet that past is being fast forgotten. A connection is established between the end of the old world and the personal destiny of the writer's protagonist, and it is the destiny of defeat. In spite of the presence of the positive model of a settlement in this work, the overall impression here is at least as bleak as in the apocalyptic novels of Aitmatov and Bondarev. Egorov's defeat is made to signal the exhaustion of his society's most precious source of moral strength—traditional peasant culture. Both *The Execution Block* and *The Game* offer a similar plan of action: find the people who will spread the new reverence for nature, revitalize the country spiritually, and, perhaps, humanity can be saved. In *The Fire*, Rasputin seems to suggest that the change Russian people have undergone is irreversible, that the essential differences between good and evil have been obliterated in Soviet society, and that there is no hope for the future.

The Traditional Family as the Cure
for the Ills of Society: Viktor Astaf'ev

Viktor Astaf'ev's *The Sad Detective* (*Pechal'nyi detektiv,* 1986) is yet another novel of publicistic literature to raise the issue of the collapse of the moral foundations of Soviet society.[33] The main hero of this short novel, Leonid Soshnin, a policeman-turned-writer recently separated from his wife and daughter, rethinks his sad and lonely life in a series of inner monologues. Soshnin's memories focus on his family life and are supplemented by a catalogue of stark and horrifying incidents from his professional past. After a brief and bloody fight with three drunks on the stairs of his apartment house, Soshnin returns to his family in the hope of a new beginning.

Both the case histories and Soshnin's own family misfortunes serve to underscore several important messages directly offered to the reader through the voice of the conscious hero. Echoing the thoughts of Rasputin's Egorov, Soshnin proposes that for many, evil and good have become indistinguishable. In its harshness, Astaf'ev's catalogue of crimes is reminiscent of Dostoyevsky's lists of atrocities against the "insulted and the injured." Ales Adamovich, a prominent publicist himself, has praised Astaf'ev's insistence in this novel on "not sparing the reader" by "pointedly accentuating the truth" (*zaostriat' pravdu*).[34] And the truth that Astaf'ev accentuates here, the author's gripe list, includes incidents that, until the novel's publication, had been securely hidden from public view.

Soshnin's professional and personal experiences convince him that the disintegration of the traditional family is the reason for all the ills of his society. According to Soshnin, "dynasties, societies, and empires that have not supported the family or have uprooted its foundations would begin to boast about the progress they had achieved, and would rattle their sabers; in such dynasties, societies, and empires, in conjunction with the disintegration of the family, social accord [*soglasie*] collapsed, and evil began to triumph over good."[35] The root of all evil, then, is the severance of traditional family ties, performed under the banner of progress. Progress, a charged word for this "hater of the present" (Venclova's term), is associated with the environmental excesses of socialism, with urbanization, with suppression of religious beliefs, and with the emancipation of women.[36] Disdain for the past leads to war, to the disintegration of the social fabric, and, finally, to the reversal of ethical norms. This is precisely what is happening in Soshnin's society, where people have forgotten their responsibilities toward their environment, their ancestors, and even their children.

Astaf'ev's hero is puzzled over the mindless vandalism wreaked on a new dormitory built for PTU students, destruction committed by the students themselves.[37] He is outraged when he finds out that a funeral procession has forgotten to bury the body, leaving it to rot in the cemetery. Soshnin's own cemetery is almost destroyed when the caretakers burn refuse there. As in Rasputin's works, the destruction of a cemetery is a sign of moral malaise. Another sign of this condition is a profound disrespect for the living. Soshnin witnesses the death of a woman and her little daughter, both run over by a drunken car thief fleeing the police. Soshnin apprehends the murderer of a pregnant woman, killed only because the murderer "felt like" murdering somebody. The most unsettling entries are about children. One child is left unattended for days, and, by the time a neighbor climbs into a window to feed the infant, "it is being eaten by worms." Another child, abandoned by its parents, is found starving to death, eating cockroaches. A baby is left in a locker at a train station; it is saved by a former burglar, who alone is able to open the locker.

The author's culprits are "city-bred intellectuals" (his fellow students and professors at the institute), emancipated women (his editor among them), and Jews (*evreichata*, "little yids"). As in Astaf'ev's earlier story "Fishing for Carp in Georgia,"[38] the present here is associated with an all-pervasive lack of spirituality, the inexorable advent of historical cataclysms, and the demise of the venerable peasant traditions. The past of the preindustrialized Russia, on the other hand, is seen as the only potent source of regeneration. As with other publicistic novels, there occurs in *The Sad Detective* a search for an alternative mythical structure designed to offer clear ethical guidelines for a country that lost its grandeur together with its foundations.

Soshnin calls for the resurrection of the traditional family, which alone in his view can save his society. And Soshnin's ideal family is obviously an extension of the similarly idealized peasant family union, where husband and wife support each other, and the woman's life is devoted to raising children and nurturing close family bonds. Soshnin's understanding of a perfect family relationship is exemplified by a set of proverbs about family life: "Death and wife are given by God," "There is marriage, but no unmarriage," "You die with the one you marry," "A bird is strong for its wings, a wife for her husband," "Behind my husband I am not afraid of anybody," and the equally edifying, "A wife is not a boot, you can't just throw her off." And Soshnin wholeheartedly agrees with this age-old perception of marital obligations, choosing in the end to return to the fold of his own nuclear family. Moreover, Soshnin stresses the importance of loyalty to the people who helped raise him, his extended family. Soshnin's mother, aunt and the woman who took care of him when his aunt was arrested for embezzling money (under the influence of corrupting city values), are presented much like traditional saintly women of village prose. These women are Soshnin's, and Astaf'ev's, hope for the future. Women who insist on their intellectual and personal independence, however, are not spared by the writer.

The Sad Detective is polemically antiurban and anti-intellectual. Astaf'ev is concerned with the loss of viable links with tradition: he laments the severance of generational continuity *(sviaz' vremen)* and he blames it all on the city and its emancipating ways. The writer is convinced that in order to avoid the complete disintegration of society one has to draw inspiration and strength from the Russian peasant tradition and from its understanding of family ties and obligations. The ideal of a return to the sacred past of the village, found in the work of the village utopians of the mid-seventies and in Astaf'ev's own *The King of the Fish* (*Tsar'-ryba*, 1976), is a patchwork of mythological constructs from cosmogonic myths, myth of the Golden Age, and Slavophilism.[39] In the works of the village utopians the idealized past was at the center, shaping the very texture of their narratives, making it essential for the authors to rely on fantasy—be it the creatures out of Russian folklore or the legendary simulacra created by the text itself. Now the hateful present assumes center stage, guiding the reactions of the protagonists and eliciting indignant responses from the hero-author. The standard devices of fantasy give place to mythological entities, where the entire history of Russia is retold with an apocalyptic twist.

Astaf'ev's conscious hero is a typical protagonist of the publicistic literature of glasnost. Aware of the very difficult problems facing his society, he is ready to voice outrage at the path his society has taken. Soshnin is also an eccentric, a truth seeker *(pravdoiskatel')* with very definite moral values, unshakable in the face of personal misfortune. Unlike Rasputin's Egorov, Soshnin is allowed to find a possible, if individual, cure for the spiritual void experienced by his society. And, unlike Bondarev's or Aitmatov's protagonists, Soshnin does not have to sacrifice his own life to save Russia. Yet, in Astaf'ev's scheme, Soshnin can be seen as a martyr as well. He is beaten by criminals, misunderstood by his wife, scorned for his convictions and for his ties with the village. He suffers, and through that suffering comes to understand and accept the rediscovered truth: the collapse of moral values has to be remedied, and Soshnin's country must be saved from extinction. Astaf'ev's protagonist and spokesman is ready to preach this new Gospel to his fellow countrymen.

Publicists as Militants: Vasilii Belov

Vasilii Belov's *Everything Is Ahead of Us* (*Vse vperedi*, 1986), the first "urban" novel of this quintessential village prose writer, is a complete rejection of urban life and of everything commonly associated with the idea of progress.[40] The marriage of two Muscovites, Liuba and Dima Medvedev, the novel's protagonists, is destroyed because of Dima's suspicion that his wife, as a tourist in Paris, could have seen a pornographic film. In addition, Dima's alter ego, doctor Ivanov, suspects Liuba of giving in to the sexual demands of one of her traveling companions on the same ill-fated trip. Liuba's unproven "perversity" is linked to women's liberation, women's liberation in turn to divorce, divorce to alcoholism, alcoholism to crime, crime to prison, and prison to the loss of parental rights.

Like his fellow publicists Astaf'ev and Rasputin, Belov is an antifuturist. His earlier work idealized the glorious past of the Russian village *(lad)*, and folk fantasy was used to shape some of Belov's narratives (as in *Bukhtiny vologodskie*). Here the focus is on the unstoppable evil forces of progress, and the documentation of the decay of morals—or the spiritual void—is cast in mythological terms. The novel can be viewed as a story of the approaching catastrophe (prefigured in the life of its saintly protagonist) brought on by the country's obsession with the future and progress.

Here, as in Astaf'ev's work, *progress* and *future* are charged words, associated with unbridled technological advance and indifference toward nature, with the disintegration of family ties and women's emancipation, with severance of generational continuity, lack of faith, and infatuation with Western culture. In a series of direct statements to the reader, the author claims that his contemporaries idealize the future and, in doing that, reject both the present and the past.

In Belov's view, reverence for the past is immeasurably less dangerous than idealization of the future. All his positive characters have strong ties to the past traditions of Russia. On the other hand, those who falter in this novel (like Liuba, who in the end leaves Russia for the decadent West) have their gaze directed to the future. The close-knit family is disintegrating, poisoned by the noxious amorality of the Westernized metropolis. Belov's city dwellers are "the possessed" *(besy)* brought up in concrete boxes and corrupted by civilization and by its obsession with the idea of progress. His positive characters, Belov's "natural" *(estestvennye)* people, have to fight the pernicious influences of the metropolis. The antagonistic opposition of the possessed versus the natural shapes the entire novel. Certain attributes, acts, and phenomena are established (marked) as negative, while others appear as positive. The following items are presented as wrong: criminals, heavy drinking, the greenhouse effect, loggers, geologists, oil industry workers, the idea that nature is a workshop, lesbians, homosexuals, mass hypnosis, chewing gum, the Voice of America and other "voices," the CIA, Masons, Jews, women who smoke, defection to the West, abortion, disregard for family obligations (such as washing diapers and peeling potatoes), and Nicholas the First (because he burned the first edition of the Bible). In other words, the author rejects everything associated with the idea of modernized Russia. Perhaps because he intends this novel to show the negative aspects of modern life, Belov's list of positive attributes is not as long,: heavy drinking (with male friends); old Muscovites; noblemen; Pushkin; relatives who perished in the war; people who are strong, determined, and aware of their Russian cultural heritage, but also passionate; physical labor; and reverence for nature.

As in other works of publicistic literature, the solution offered by Belov is to go back to the source, which is Russian peasant culture. Not unlike Bondarev's protagonist, Medvedev is a proponent of a resurrected Russia, the end similarly achieved through the return to the sacred pasts of the Second World War and of the preindustrialized village. And, like other representatives of the publicistic trend, Belov needs a martyr who, through his suffering, will demonstrate the enormity of the challenge, face it, and show the way for others to follow. The series of trials Medvedev undergoes (including a prison term and the loss of his parental rights) is designed to do just that.

Belov's ideal vision here is a society of like-minded men (with women staying at home, providing comfort and support), joined by communal brotherly love, nurtured by tradition and love of the country. As in Bondarev's work, Belov organizes his novel around the central battle of the myths: the myth of the advanced socialist state against the myth of the resurrected Russia based on tradition and the past. Belov's tone here is decidedly militant. The novel's conclusion is a call to fight the evils of modern civilization, which has placed all its emphasis on an ephemeral vision of the perfect future, forfeiting in the process all its moral strength.

In its tone and thematic thrust, publicistic literature is clearly an extension of the fantastic trend of the mid-seventies and early eighties; more specifically, of village prose and refurbished socialist realism. One obvious indication of the continuity in themes and concerns is the fact that most of the authors engaged in publicistic literature had written works in the fantastic vein. Another is the publicistic trend's clear indebtedness to the values of village prose. According to the authors of publicistic literature, the spirit of consumerism and indifference pervades Soviet society, which shed its ties with tradition. The senseless use of technology has violated intergenerational continuity and brought about the disintegration of family life and social accord. In most works the blame for the cultural impoverishment of the nation is placed on intellectuals, proponents of Western influences, and city values. And, like village prose before it, this literature is emphatically nationalistic.[41] Paradoxically, even Chingiz Aitmatov, disturbed by the loss of his own national tradition, places his faith in a "second coming" of the Russian Christ—the spiritual void *(bezdukhovnost')* has to be filled with whatever is available.

Publicistic literature's protagonists are akin to the fantastic trend's eccentric seekers, who are aware of the costs of the destruction of traditional values and unrelenting in their search for truth and beauty. But in publicistic literature the seekers, now representing the authors, have to suffer and sacrifice everything they hold dear—sometimes even their lives—to recast the past and present of their country in mythological terms.

In the case of Valentin Rasputin's publicistic work, events in history are presented through the experience and memories of one worthy man. Egorov's confrontation with the present is designed to explain the past and to foreshadow what is yet to come in a carefully shaped tale of a catastrophe. According to this tale, the corrupt present exerts its evil power on the protagonist's world, which (literally) goes up in flames. After submerging the nurturing realm of beauty under water *(Matera)*, the forces of evil again unleash the elements—to destroy everything that had yet been spared *(Fire)*. Aitmatov's and Bondarev's protagonists similarly become characters in a new story of reality lived, the story where only the personal sacrifice of the chosen few can insure change. Belov's urbanized "possessed" and Astaf'ev's decadent intellectuals can be conquered, and Russia cleansed of evil, only through the unwavering adherence to the values that have nurtured the country and insured her greatness for centuries. In a return to Russian messianic tradition, the task of saving the entire world, according to most publicistic literature, should be entrusted to Russia.

If fantastic literature only warned of the dire consequences of the loss of tradition, publicistic literature examined those consequences as established fact. Messages that had been encoded in fantastic literature were now transmitted in "open text"; and the message apparently got through, as evidenced by this literature's sensational popularity with the reader.[42] The practitioners of publicistic literature saw the moral decline of their nation as part of the general process of moral degeneration of humanity. The recurring image of Doomsday, the nuclear end of the world, was only an extreme expression of the pervasive despair with which publicistic literature viewed Soviet reality.

Notes

1. "The Periodicals: Novyi mir," *Times Literary Supplement*, December 4–10, 1987, p. 1350. For more on returned literature see Sergei Chuprinin, "Predvest'e," *Znamia* 1 (1989): 210–224; S. Shvedov, "Chto dal'she? Vozvrashchennaia literatura i obretaiushchii sebia chitatel'," *Literaturnoe obozrenie* 6 (1989): 60–63.

2. For a succinct explanation of the predominance of "old names" in the new thaw see Clark, "Rethinking the Past and the Current Thaw: Introduction," pp. 244–245. See more on the new thaw in Natalia Ivanova, "Zhurnaly v fokuse mnenii," *Literaturnoe obozrenie* 4 (1988): 100.

3. For more on the publicists see Igor Zolotusskii, "Otchet o puti," *Znamia* 1 (1987): 221–240.

4. *Novyi mir* 9 (1985).

5. Notably, the publicistic trend, at least initially, united authors of widely divergent political persuasions. The initial stage of "revelations" of taboo topics was experienced by virtually all writers contributing to publicistic prose, irrespective of their political beliefs. Evtushenko and Voznesensky, poets who are decidedly on the left of the political spectrum, were briefly joined in their fight against stagnation by such writers as Rasputin, Astaf'ev, and Belov, whose allegiance to the ideals of the Russian right-wing nationalists has been amply demonstrated in their public and private statements. See, for example,

Astafiev's correspondence with the historian Natan Eidelman, published in *Syntaksis* 17 (1987).

6. Bethea, *Shape of Apocalypse*, p. 40.

7. Ibid., pp. 39–41.

8. This novel appeared in English translation as *The Place of the Skull* (New York: Grove Press, 1989).

9. Venclova, "Ethnic Identity," p. 324.

10. Aitmatov, *Execution Block*, p. 55.

11. Chingiz Aitmatov, "Tsena-zhizn'," *Literaturnaia gazeta*, August 13, 1986, p. 4. Incidentally, Aitmatov is not the first Soviet writer to establish his positive hero as a "descendant" of Jesus. Christian motifs, particularly the sacrificial aspects of Christianity, play an important role in Dumbadze's *Zakon vechnosti*, 1980 (the novel Aitmatov is most assuredly familiar with). Vladimir Tendriakov's novel *Pokushenie na mirazhi* is yet another Soviet literary attempt to assess Christ's place in history. (See *Novyi mir* 4, 5 [1987]. The novel was submitted for publication in 1982.) The publication of *The Execution Block* set off a controversy about the "God-building" tendency in Soviet writing. For a summary of religious themes in the Soviet prose of the time, see Andrei Nuikin, "Novoe bogoiskatel'stvo i starye dogmy," *Novyi mir* 4 (1987): 245–259. The discussion of the issue was conducted in *Komsomol'skaia pravda* (July 30, 1986, p. 3; December 10, 1986, p. 2; March 12, 1987, p. 2); *Literaturnaia gazeta* (August 13, 1986, p. 4; May 6, 1987, p. 2); *Pravda* (28 September, 1986, p. 1); and *Izvestiia* (December 3 and 4, 1986, p. 3). For more on the controversy see Darrell Hammer, "Glasnost' and 'The Russian Idea,'" *RLRB*, December 1988, p. 16.

12. As in Bulgakov's novel, the action begins with a reference to the oppressive heat in Jerusalem. Other similarities include the bird that is present at the conversation, Pilate's reference to Jesus as a "hapless prophet," Pilate's accusation of Jesus in instigating the mob to revolt, and the idea that Pilate's name will remain in history.

13. Aitmatov, "Tsena-zhizn'," p. 4.

14. See, for example, Alla Latynina and Vadim Kozhinov, "Paradoksy romana ili paradoksy vospriiatiia?," *Literaturnaia gazeta*, October 15, 1986, p. 4. Both call Avdii a "spiritual adolescent" *(dukhovnyi podrostok)*. E. Surkov, in his article "Tragediia v Moiunkumakh: O romane Chingiza Aitmatova 'Plakha,'" *Pravda*, December 22, 1986, p. 3, offers a similar view of Avdii, when he says that "the biblical plot in the novel is not seen by a historian of culture or a poet but by a half-educated seminarian." See also S. Piskunov and V. Piskunova, "Vyiti iz kruga," *Literaturnoe obozrenie* 2 (1987): 54–58.

15. Aitmatov, "Tsena-zhizn'," p. 4.

16. Nikolai Evdokimov's novel *Trizhdy Velichaishii, ili Povestvovanie o byvshem iz nebyvshego* in *Druzhba narodov* 7, 8, 9, (1987) is another "Bulgakovian novel." The protagonists include Christ, the devil and his retinue, the devil's son who becomes human after falling in love with a woman, and a middle-aged Soviet bureaucrat who exchanges his soul with the devil's son. Evdokimov borrows from Bulgakov's satirical-fantastic plot; this novel is much lighter in tone than Aitmatov's tribute to Bulgakov.

17. As E. Surkov proposes in his *Pravda* article on the novel, Aitmatov's discussion of ecological disaster in the Moiunkum savannah is inextricably linked with the general "state of the human soul" ("Tragediia v Moiunkumakh," p. 3).

18. Carol Avins, "The Failure of Perestroika in Aitmatov's *The Executioner's Block*," *Studies in Comparative Communism* 3/4 (1988): 260.

19. The novel was originally called *Krugovrashchenie* (a medieval concept of a wheel of fate present in this version of the title).

20. Some critics found in Boston's story strong elements of the Greek tragedy of fate. (See E. Surkov's article in *Pravda* and Latynina and Kozhinov, "Paradoksy romana," p. 4.)

21. Avins, "Failure of Perestroika," p. 260.

22. Igor' Zolotusskii, "Proiti bezvredno mezhdu chudes i chudovishch," *Literaturnoe obozrenie* 1 (1990): 5.

23. Iurii Bondarev, *Igra* (Moscow: Molodaia Gvardiia, 1985).

24. Some details of the story and the name of the main character bring to mind the events surrounding the real-life drama of the accidental death of the Soviet film director Larisa Shepit'ko, the wife of Elem Klimov (the former head of the Cinema Workers' Union and a controversial director himself) during the filming of Rasputin's novel *Farewell to Matera*.

25. Iurii Bondarev, *Vos'moi s'ezd pisatelei SSSR: Stenograficheskii otchet* (Moscow: Sovetskii Pisatel', 1988), p. 35.

26. *Pravda*, July 1, 1988, quoted in John B. Dunlop, "The Contemporary Russian Nationalist Spectrum," in *RLRB*, special edition, December 19, 1988, p. 7.

27. Bondarev, *Vos'moi s'ezd pisatelei SSSR*, p. 155.

28. Priscilla Hunt: "The reform done on the model of the contemporary Greek Orthodox signalled the beginning of Muscovy's ideological turn to the West, its transformation into an absolute monarchy, and its acceptance of the elitist aesthetic and religious culture of scholastic humanism. The reform indicated a turning away from the traditional messianic penitential ideal which had defined the sacred nature of the Tsar and the redemptive mission of Muscovy since the time of Ivan IV." In Terras, ed., *Handbook of Russian Literature*, p. 29–31.

29. Ibid., p. 30.

30. Ibid.

31. Valentin Rasputin, *Pozhar, Nash sovremennik* 7 (1985): 7. The novel was awarded the State prize for literature in 1987.

32. Svetlana Semenova stresses the point of continuity between the two works in "Talant nravstvennogo uchitel'stva," *Znamia* 2 (1987): 220.

33. *Oktiabr'* 1 (1986): 8–74.

34. Ales' Adamovich, "Urok pravdy," *Literaturnaia gazeta*, March 19, 1987.

35. Astaf'ev, *Pechal'nyi detektiv*, p. 73.

36. Venclova, "Ethnic Identity," p. 324.

37. PTUs are vocational schools, largely regarded as "warehouses" for underachievers, and marked by severe disciplinary problems.

38. In 1986 the Georgian delegation to the Congress of the Union of Writers objected to Astaf'ev's portrayal of Georgians in this story ("Lovlia peskarei v Gruzii," *Nash sovremennik* 5 [1986]: 123–141).

39. Venclova, "Ethnic Identity," p. 322.

40. *Nash sovremennik* 7–8 (1986).

41. Rasputin, Belov, and the critic Vadim Kozhinov have openly defended the right-wing nationalist association Pamiat'. See V. Kozhinov, "My meniaemsia? . . . " *Nash sovremennik*, 10 (1987): 160–174; V. Rasputin, "Vystuplenie na VII s'ezde VOOPIK v g. Gor'kom 8 iiulia 1987 g.," *Zemlya* 3 (unpublished samizdat document); Rasputin's speech was later published in *Nash sovremennik* 1 (1988): 169–176; on Belov see *Russkaia mysl'*, February 27, 1988. This information comes from Hammer, "Glasnost," p. 20 (note 65). On the reaction to Rasputin's statements and the subsequent controversy, see the report on the Plenary Session of the Board of the USSR Writers' Union in *Current Digest of the Soviet Press* 40.12 (1988): 16–19. On Pamiat' under Gorbachev, see Dunlop, "Contemporary Spectrum," pp. 6–8; Hammer, "Glasnost," pp. 19–20; *Novoe Russkoe Slovo*, August 13–15, 1987; G. Kh. Popov and Nikita Adzhubei, "Pamiat' i 'Pamiat','" *Znamia* 1 (1988): 187–203; Vladimir Petrov's article in *Pravda*, February 1, 1988, p. 4; Pavel Gutiontov's article in *Izvestiia*, February 27, 1988, p. 3. On Boris Yeltsyn's meeting with the members of Pamiat', see *Moskovskie novosti* 20 (1987): 4. For a brief history of the association and a list of its members, see *RLRB* 342/87, August 26, 1987 (Julia Wishnevsky).

42. According to John B. Dunlop, under glasnost print runs have been brought into general conformity with readership demand. In 1987 Vasilii Belov's *Everything Is Ahead of Us (Vse vperedi)* had the fifth largest print run of any book published in the USSR (2,700,000 copies); Viktor Astaf'ev's *The Sad Detective (Pechal'nyi detektiv)* was fourth (2,750,000). A novel by conservative Russian nationalist writer Valentin Pikul' was third (2,850,000). Only one liberal writer's novel, Anatolii Rybakov's *Children of the Arbat* has come close to competeing with these figures. Chingiz Aitmatov's *The Execution Block (Plakha)* had the second largest run (3,080,000), and V. Ovchinnikov's *Sakura i dub* had the largest (3,140,000). Dunlop, "Contemporary Spectrum," p. 5.

9

Alternative Literature I: The Thieves of Language

Detective plots, fantasy, games, the erotic—all these function as self-reflective paradigms, making the art of reading into one of active "production," of imagining, interpreting, decoding, ordering, in short of constructing the literary universe through the fictive referents of the words.

—*Linda Hutcheon,* Narcissistic Narrative: The Metafictional Paradox

A CURIOUS FEATURE OF ALTERNATIVE LITERATURE, the central topic of the following two chapters, is the profusion of labels used to describe this trend in Russian fiction. One critic called it "the other prose" *(drugaia proza).*[1] Another, focusing on continuity, invoked the term "alternative prose," thereby equating a trend virtually banned before glasnost with more recent experiments in literature.[2] Yet another saw alternative literature as the new Russian avant-garde.[3]

Andrei Bitov, in his introduction to the first publication of Narbikova's alternative short novel *The Equilibrium of the Diurnal and Nocturnal Rays of the Stars (Ravnovesie sveta dnevnykh i nochnykh zvezd,* 1988), called this young author's peers "the mute generation" *(nemoe pokolenie).*[4] Makanin wrote an entire novel linking the fate of this group of writers to the idea of the "permanent belatedness" of true literature.[5] In the early nineties, literary production in the alternative vein came to be considered in light of postmodernism.[6] Finally, reflections on the literature of the late eighties and early nineties prompted Mikhail Epstein to add the notion of "the last literature" to the ever-expanding menu of terms.[7]

The various labels used in connection with the alternative trend point to different currents within it, as well as to its diverse assessments by the critics. Considered broadly, the terms "alternative prose," or "the other prose," aim at signaling the difference of this literature from established trends—its hard-won independence from socialist realism, village prose, and from the publicistic prose of glasnost. The label "mute generation," on the other hand, brings to mind the social and political conditions of the stagnation period, with its effective suppression of unorthodox works and authors.

Notably, the alternative current was not altogether absent from the literary scene in the late Brezhnev era; intermittently, a handful of texts of the "other prose" were allowed to appear in print in the decade before glasnost. I have in mind that strand of fantastic literature where undisputed and complete knowledge about reality is put into question, the overall message of a work is deliberately camouflaged, and social concerns are present, but accented differently than in other works of the period. Evdokimov, Anar, and the writers of the so-called Moscow school—such as Makanin, Sergei Esin, and Kim—were the published representatives of this alternative trend. They worked in opposition to the officially sanctioned literature, creating a world metaphorically complex, coded, opaque, peopled with characters lost in the uncertainties of everyday existence and plagued by guilt and moral confusion.

The alternative literature of the Moscow school and of its fellow travelers planted the seeds of the "new avant-garde," or "postmodernism," the terms widely used to describe Russian alternative prose of the nineties. It is precisely in the "other prose" before the age of glasnost that we can observe first attempts at articulating, mainly through the devices of fantasy, the concerns of an aesthetic underground. These attempts were characterized by a heightened attention toward the myth-creating propensities of language, by their focus on the previously hidden aspects of human experience, and they were shaped by a desire to give voice to the marginalized segments of what was then still Soviet society.

In the works of the Moscow school and its followers, forays into the realm of the fantastic were a preparation for the war on mimesis and on the tradition of realistic writing in general, the war that would characterize the literary production of the new postmodernists/avant-gardists. Reality portrayed in alternative literature before glasnost was multifaceted, unpredictable, impossible to contain in a transparent language. As a result, in many works of the period language (writing) itself moved into the foreground, attracting attention to its own artifice, its manipulative strategies, and its power.

In the late eighties and early nineties, this preoccupation with language becomes the sole driving force of the alternative trend, leading to a qualitatively new phase—some term it a steep phase *(krutaia faza)*—

in its development. Burrowing into the depths of illusion making is accompanied at this stage by a strong emphasis on being truly alternative, on brandishing the trend's marginal status—by giving voice to an increasing number of underrepresented authors (such as women and homosexuals) and by transgressing traditional norms of writing (in style and themes). Illicit sex, deviant sexual practices, bodily functions, violence for the sake of pleasure are in the foreground of this fiction; investigation of the power of language is its motivating force.

Representation of this striking change in literary practice is the primary aim of the following two chapters. At the center is the progression of alternative literature from its partial dependence on realistic representation to a complete break with mimesis; from its concealed, but still perceivable, "truth-finding mission" to an unequivocal rejection of moralism in literature; from its initial belief in the possibility of articulating meaning to a game with empty signifiers—an illustration of the relativity of all and the meaninglessness of everything; from being different, to becoming avant-garde, to transforming itself into the "last literature."

As before, the fantastic and its uses will serve as a guide through the maze of literary experimentation that characterizes alternative literature as a whole. If, initially, representatives of the trend tended generally to rely on a fantastic situation as the key to some philosophical puzzle, the new generation of alternative writers attempt a fantastic journey into the very nature of language. Here mimetic representation is defied and discourse is shown to be a breeding ground for everything. Texts themselves—refracted, imitated, fractured, and reassembled—come to constitute the world of the new fiction. Intertextuality reigns, and the primary focus of this writing is directed to the process of shaping language to suit various needs, to the way language is able to solidify into myths and then rule the culture. In the end what is mirrored here is not "reality" but verbal-symbolic-mythical structures fixed in a language. These structures are examined, played with, reshuffled, and then dismissed in a defiant act of creative arrogance. As a result, the reality of these narratives (what we visualize when we read) is unverifiable, illusive, fluid—in short, fantastic. The aim of the new alternative writers is to capture the fluidity of represented experience and to demonstrate their control over it by compressing, distorting, and playing with language. The writer becomes the manipulator of interchangeable characters in interchangeable stories in a constantly changing world of discourses.

The critic Sergei Chuprinin's list of writers of alternative prose includes Viktor Erofeev, Venedikt Erofeev, Zufar Gareev, Viacheslav P'etsukh, Sergei Chetvertkov, Valeriia Narbikova, Larisa Vaneeva, Liudmila Petrushevskaia, and Tatiana Tolstaya.[8] This list can be expanded to include such names as Evgenii Popov, Evgenii Kharitonov, and Aleksandr Ivanchenko, whose work clearly belongs to the same trend. Representatives of the later "steep phase" include Tatiana Shcherbina (a poet turned prose writer), F. Erskin (pseudonym of Mikhail Berg), Andrei Levkin, Ruslan Marsovich, Jurii Mamleev, Boris Kudriakov, Vadim Rudnev, Vladimir Sorokin, and Oleg Dark. Narbikova is considered to belong to this group as well.

The following discussion of some of the individual representatives of the trend is arranged generally according to the movement away from mimetic representation into the realm of the postmodernist game with discourses. Makanin, a transitional figure in the trend and a representative of the older generation, and Narbikova, the writer exemplifying most fully the transformation of alternative prose into the "last literature," are given relatively more room than other authors. Makanin, Mikhail Kuraev, and Ivanchenko, considered to belong to the first wave of alternative writers, are discussed in this chapter. The subsequent chapter is devoted to the discussion of the most prominent women representatives of the trend—Liudmila Petrushevskaia, Nina Sadur, Tolstaya, and Narbikova.

The Chronicler of the "Mute Generation": Vladimir Makanin

Vladimir Makanin's novels that appear in the period of glasnost provide a good illustration of the difference between alternative literature and established trends. Experimental in form, employing fantasy to demystify accepted truths, Makanin's work breaks new ground to be further explored by other alternative writers.[9] To the Russian reader of the 1980s, Makanin was both different and familiar; the technique and the philosophical bent of Makanin's prose were relatively new; Makanin's world, however, was easily recognizable. In the seventies Makanin's novels and stories documented the period of stagnation, betraying a close affinity to Jurii Trifonov's harsh portrayal of urban life. In the early eighties he voiced the anxieties of Soviet society (and, particularly, those of the Soviet intelligentsia), on the eve of perestroika.[10] Makanin's work of the mid-eighties provided a summary of sorts, a catalogue of issues to be openly examined by the literature of glasnost in general: the loss of native traditions and history, destruction of the environment, the rootlessness and moral vacuity of city life, and the guilt that members of the Soviet creative intelligentsia experienced when confronted with the seemingly insurmountable problems of their society. These issues, inherited from the literature of the Thaw and, particularly, from village prose and *byt* prose, were probed both by the publicistic and alternative literature of the Gorbachev period. But, in contrast to the publicists, and very much in keeping with the alternative trend, Makanin was interested more in the genesis of mythological thinking, rather than in journalistic accounts of social ills. Moreover, his investigation of the way legends are created and accepted consistently involves the use of the fantastic: the fusion of temporal and spatial planes, hesitation between real and unreal in descriptions of his characters' actions and perceptions, and the act of baring—making literary devices obvious to the reader— used both as a central metaphor and a device designed to draw the attention of the reader to the act of writing.

Like other alternative writers, Makanin actively disliked blaming some social group or policy for the problems experienced by Russian intellectuals and the country as a whole. As one critic has observed, the "mute generation," represented by Makanin, was "alienated from the 'spiritually useful' and 'lifelike' aesthetic almost as much as [it was] from the 'Village Writers' and the 'populists' with their naive experiments in mythologizing the people's age old way of life."[11]

When a solution to social problems is offered in Makanin's work, it is more philosophical than practical or political—for example, the idealized merger of folk and high art, or the miraculous, innocent voice of a child that closes Makanin's novel *Where the Sky Met the Hills*. Overall, Makanin refrains from offering explicit solutions to the problems posed in his works. The authorial message is there, but it is deliberately concealed. Makanin does not help the reader with direct authorial statements, nor can Makanin's attitude be easily derived from the writer's treatment of his characters. Makanin's shifts of temporal planes can confuse his audience even further. The reader is constantly challenged to "narrativize" Makanin, to organize his text according to some chronological or causal consistency, but is unable to do so. The realistic transparency of texture is abandoned, and language becomes viscous, resisting the reader's inclination to frame the narrative within the clearly defined confines of a one-dimensional interpretation.

A good example of Makanin's increasing focus on the vagaries of language is his novel *Loss (Utrata,* 1987*)* which examines the issue of ruptured generational continuity *(sviaz' vremen)*, one of the central concerns of village prose and of the publicistic literature of glasnost.[12] Makanin's novel, however, is a clear departure from the work of the populists—before and during glasnost.[13] If village prose, and the publicists after it, document the demise of the Russian village and offer new myths to substitute for the old ones, the focus of Makanin's work is precisely on the way the mythological consciousness operates and is represented in narratives.

Makanin's approach is based on the fusion of temporal and spatial planes, the borderline between reality and fantasy is never clearly defined, and the text's fictional and linguistic systems are bared to the reader's view. *Loss* begins with the detailed description of the digging of a passage under the Ural River. At a casual reading the initial parts of the narrative might be placed in the present. Only gradually does the reader realize that Makanin is talking about an old Ural legend. The fusion of temporal planes is there to demonstrate the inescapable presence of the past in contemporary time. Makanin supports this idea on a structural level as well: the digging of the passage is newly experienced by another, unnamed hero of the novel in contemporary time. At one point, while in the hospital after a severe trauma, the unnamed hero actually sees the digger, who is able to see him as well. Moreover, certain details from the hero's past mirror the events surrounding the digging of the passage.

For Makanin, a legend begins with an irrational act. The person responsible for this act is the carrier of a creative impulse, a fanatic. The digger's endeavor is irrational, impractical—the passage opens into an impassable swamp. However, it is this fantastic action that gives birth to a legend that in turn becomes imprinted in the popular consciousness. The digger's irrational act is mirrored in the unnamed hero's (and the author's) eagerness to uncover layers of time to get to the roots of the legend. The unnamed hero is a repentant former villager, who calls himself "raised from the dead" *(zagrobnik)* and who, in his attempt to retrieve the past, returns to his dead village and the legendary passage. This standard plot of village prose is transformed in Makanin's novel into an investigation of the essence of human nostalgia for the past, of its symptoms and remedies. If in *Where the Sky* the past is brought back by means of a "situational" miracle, in *Loss* the past is shown to be retrievable through the mythical powers of language.

Anticipating the work of the new wave of alternative writers, Makanin posits at the center language itself, bringing into relief the very mechanism of myth creation. But, in order to get to the core of the myth, the writer has to bare accumulated layers of matter, time, and space. Baring is an organizing metaphor in this novel; when Makanin "bares the device" and comments on the writing process itself, it affects the very texture of the narrative. This is the approach employed by writers of what Linda Hutcheon has termed "narcissistic literature"—literature that "provides, within itself, a commentary on its own status as fiction and as language."[14] Here language "becomes material with which to work, the object of certain transforming operations which give it meaning."[15]

In Makanin's fiction of the seventies we observe a clear dependence on the realistic mode of representation, with language as an inconspicuous conduit of messages. In the eighties, however, Makanin is preoccupied with the way language itself is shaped and, in turn, shapes human behavior. The beginnings of this change can be seen in *Where the Sky*, where Makanin mirrors the merger of the folk and urban sensibilities in the very texture of the narrative ("narrative polyphony").[16] As was common in alternative literature before glasnost, this crucial event is represented by means of a fantastic situation. But the miraculous here is the birth of a new voice, a new language.

A similar hybridization of content and form occurs in *Loss*, where a fantastic situation (the protagonist's ability to live the past in the present) serves as a means of probing the creative potential of language. Most of Makanin's work of the eighties is about creative processes, where the writer, or an artist in general, is seen as a medium—first an unwitting conveyor, then a deliberate organizer, and, finally, a privileged possessor of meaning.

The process of writing is at the center of Makanin's attention in *Left Behind (Otstavshii*, 1987).[17] Here the fusion of temporal and spatial planes serves to articulate the issues of "belatedness" of true literature and of its authors' position in the middle of creative and political processes. The narrator (Gena) is an author whose engagement with writing dates back to the time of Khrushchev's Thaw. The focus is on Gena's juvenile novel written in the late fifties, a retelling of an old Ural legend about little Lyosha, who could sense gold with his hands. The time of the legend, the Thaw, and contemporary time are fused in the vision of the narrator.

While writing his first novel, Gena falls in love with a young woman whose father perished in the Gulag. Gena follows the woman on her journey to visit her father's grave in the Urals. The settlement around the camp becomes a "fused" space shared by virtually all characters in the novel. Gena was born and raised not far from where his friend's father served time. And little Lyosha used to roam the nearby mountains in search of gold.

Temporal and spatial fusion is designed to foreground the state of being left behind, the predicament of all characters here. Lyosha of the legend is forced to stay behind by his fellow prospectors because gold attracts him, and to them his path and overnight stops are a treasure map. Gena's friend is too late to see her father or have a meaningful relationship with any man. In contemporary time, Gena's father is tormented by dreams of trying to catch up to a moving truck but falling behind. Gena's primary condition is one of being left behind. He is too late to mend his relationship with the woman he loves, too late to submit his first novel, and now unable to help his father or daughter—unable to catch up with them, to use another of the novel's key notions.

The ubiquitous state of falling behind (and its reverse condition of constantly catching up) is complemented here by the protagonist's position in the middle. In this novel the two situations are interdependent—being in the middle is predicated on falling behind. Nightmares come and important conversations occur in the middle of the night, and the narrator (Gena) is caught between generations, unable to catch up with the future or grasp the past:

> Father's call (from the previous generation) and my daughter's call (from the next generation) are like waves rolling in opposite directions, counteracting one another. However, for a second, both trills sound in my ears simultaneously, having merged and locked onto my ego like dates of a life put there by some higher power. They overshadow me, as if "I" is a simple point of contact between these two mutually opposite signals from the past and the future.[18]

Here the condition of being in the middle and, simultaneously, lagging behind is given its visual and auditory embodiment. In the opening passage of the book, which describes Gena's father's nightmare, the narrative attempts to recreate the sensation itself. We see the elderly man first when he is irrevocably late to get on a truck leaving for some unknown destination, which, he feels, is so important to do. We go backward, against the current of time, against the logical sequence of events—first, to the last moment, then to the beginning of the nightmarish sequence. Together with the character, we join the action when it is too late to do anything and are forced to become one of those "left behind" in the novel.

Makanin's readers are forced to face their "responsibility toward the text, that is, toward the novelistic world [created] . . . through the accumulated fictive referents of literary language."[19] There is no escape from being in the middle and lagging behind. Being—living—means being in the middle. Or, as Makanin himself puts it in another work, being is a dash between the dates of birth and death. Lagging behind, on the other hand, appears to be vitally important for the ability of Makanin's writer to mediate, organize, and represent what is around him (past, present, and future) in a literary text. Gena records a legend from the past (Lyosha's story), then creates and lives his own legend (a rejection of Stalinism and compassion for its victims); then, from the present, he parodies his own youthful enthusiasm and fascination with the legend. And each time the writer is at one remove from what he is describing.

Being in the middle and lagging behind enables one to create texts. But this central condition is not perceived as a triumph for the writer; rather it is seen as a burden. Being in the middle suggests an emptiness (a dash between the dates) and a certain kind of passivity where the forces that act on one are impossible to identify or fight against. This emptiness and passivity engender guilt. Gena feels guilty about existing—as a son, a father, or a writer. He feels oppressed by being in the middle of what is an obliterating and terrifying everyday existence—neither here nor there, neither with sons nor with fathers, left behind.

Makanin himself is a writer who lagged behind the events of the sixties; he is also a chronicler of the "generation in the middle," recording its history and identifying the philosophical reasons for the inability of this generation to "catch up." Makanin accomplishes this task of historical transcription by investigating the very processes of human creativity, moving into the heart of how and when certain events become fixed and transformed in language and culture. The focus on the mythical power of language through the prism of fantasy is perhaps one of Makanin's weightiest contributions to the development of alternative literature.

History as Language: Mikhail Kuraev

If Makanin's aim is to transcribe the history of his own generation by focusing on the mythological consciousness and its workings in language, Mikhail Kuraev uses fantasy to evaluate historical discourse itself, revealing in the process its dependence on cultural constructs. Representation of history in a novelistic form is a venerable tradition of Russian literature from its beginnings in the eighteenth century to the present. Many writers of the glasnost period as well were moved to offer novelistic accounts of history, uncovering in the process the injustices of the Soviet state. The topic is vast, important, and deserves scholarly attention. What I want to address here, in a necessarily limited fashion, is the contribution of one alternative author, Mikhail Kuraev, to the tradition of writing about historical events, an example that will illustrate the trend's increasing concentration on the whims of representation.

Kuraev's meteoric rise to brief prominence occurred after the publication of his novel about the Kronstadt uprising of 1921, *Captain Dikshtein: A Fantastic Narrative* (1987), followed by *The Night Watch: A Nocturne for Two Voices with the Participation of VOKhR Rifleman Comrade Polubolotov* (1989).[20] Born in 1939 to a family of prerevolutionary intelligentsia, he belongs to an older generation of alternative writers. Trained at the Leningrad Institute of the Arts with a focus in cinematography, Kuraev devoted his energies to writing film scripts for the Lenfilm studios before embarking on an independent writing career. The writer's intimate familiarity with the world of visual effects and his unflagging interest in history were partly responsible for the main topic and the form of *Dikshtein*.

On the surface, *Captain Dikshtein,* is simply a story about an exchange of identities during the uprising, when the appropriation of another person's name saves the life of the protagonist. However, the act of renaming leads to an unforeseen development anticipated in the suggestive subtitle *(A Fantastic Narrative)*: the impostor gradually changes into the person who perished in his stead. The change is not presented here as a just retribution for the sin of cowardice, just the opposite is true. After calling himself Captain, the protagonist has to adhere to the moral and ethical code of an officer. The impostor's personality, as well as his eventual death in the story, come to mirror the personality and fate of the true Captain Dikshtein. This merging of personalities, put in motion by the action of renaming, is particularly vividly underscored in the mirror image of the two men's deaths—a body slowly collapsing on the white snow.

Clearly, Kuraev, like Makanin before him, is concerned with the power of language. But here it is the numerous possibilities of naming and telling that are explored. In Kuraev's work, history is simply a story whose primary vehicle is naming; in the end, all depends on how events are represented through the medium of language. Kuraev's title, subtitle, and epigraphs are his textual guides into the land of literary and historical illusion explored in the body of the novel. If the title, *Captain Dikshtein*, identifies the protagonist of the story as a concrete person, the subtitle *(A Fantastic Narrative)* puts the veracity of the title in doubt and undermines the reader's traditional inclination to interpret the narrative that follows as a true representation of events. The first epigraph comes from a popular song *(chastushka)* and is dated 1921, the time of the uprising: "From the Sevastopol they're firing,/ Too short and too wide!/ And cadets keep on diving/ Beneath the ice, beneath the ice." The second is a quote from Nikolai Gogol's *Dead Souls*: "But then, what a backwoods and what a nook!" The first epigraph gives the reader a precise indication of the historical period to be described and of its one possible representation, in folklore. In the second, Kuraev alludes to the locus of the narration (the provincial town of Gatchina) and to the fantastic nature of the events he is about to portray, placing his narrative in a Gogolian context.

As in the above sequence of epigraphs, in the initial portion of the story, the "historically accurate" reality—place, time, and the full name of the protagonist—clashes with fantasy, here the fantastic reality of dreams. But, paradoxically, dreams are shown to be carefully constructed stories with happy endings, while reality is seen as unpredictable, inexplicable, and ruled by chance. It is lived reality that is presented as truly fantastic here, as details of everyday life, such as a broken clock or a lost coin, become fraught with symbolic significance.

The notion of mystery surrounding the protagonist is introduced early on, leading the reader into the familiar direction of a detective story of lost identities, crimes of the past, and the inevitable punishment of the criminal. On closer examination, however, Kuraev's novel plays with a variety of possible genre configurations. *Captain Dikshtein* alludes to Bulgakov's *Master and Margarita* (e.g., the chatty tone of the deliberately mundane beginning, with hints of fantasy to come). It also provides the contours of the *byt* novel (the protagonist's fight for survival in a provincial town), of a Gogolian story, of a cheap mystery novel, and of historical narratives in all shapes and forms.

To sustain the kaleidoscopic quality of this narrative, Kuraev relies on many different voices, alternating a naive one with voices ironic, "objective," and poetic. The alternation of drastically different voices and generic forms of representation helps to articulate the idea that, while in life nothing is predictable, in writing the solidified forms of expression rule the pen, defying the will of the author.

In order to probe the dynamics of historical representation, Kuraev provides an entire panoply of stylistic choices for a singular historical event, the Kronstadt uprising. The following sequence from a lengthy section devoted to the actual storming of the fortress is a good example of Kuraev's technique. Here the clichéd language of the Bolshevik newspapers and slogans alternates with neutral observations and poetic descriptions of the night.[21]

1. A neutral description flanked by clichés:
   The staunchest and most inflexible fighters, the flower of the Party, its vanguard and its leaders . . . all went down onto the ice on the Finnish Gulf as rank and file soldiers, having become the *bearers of a united and inflexible will.*
2. Ironic clash of a cliché with a dramatic introduction:
   This extreme, unbelievable and desperate measure could only be understood by those who realized the *full danger of a petty bourgeois counterrevolution in a country where the proletariat constituted a minority.*
3. Ironic juxtaposition of a cliché and a neutral description:
   The fate of the Revolution was being decided on the soft melting ice surrounding the smallish low-lying island, blocking the entrance to the shallow gulf.
4. Juxtaposition of a poetic metaphor and clichéd high style:
   Swallowed up in the darkness of night, the columns went farther and farther out from the shore. The 300 delegates to the Party Congress walked along with the ranks of the fighters, indistinguishable from them, *inspiring decisiveness and firmness in the advancing army by their example of personal bravery and the spirit of self-sacrifice.*

5. Poetic metaphoric description:
The bluish-white spokes of light passing through the high clouds by search lights on the ships and in the fortress came down and searched over the icy surface of the gulf like the hands of a blind person, seeking victims for their as yet silent cannons and machine guns.

The above is a sequence, interrupted only by paragraph breaks. The impression is of a high condensation of discourses. In the rest of the narrative Kuraev offers samples of various styles and genres as well, but gives each ample space to develop. Here everything is thrown together in the description of the storming, offering the reader a virtual concentrate of writing about history.

Like Makanin's legendary passage in an abandoned village, Kuraev's place of narrative action is one to which history is drawn. Here—in Gatchina, Leningrad, Kronstadt—events that had occurred were labeled historically significant, described, and edited—named and renamed—time after time. Occasionally, Kuraev emphasizes the temporal density of the place by referring to various events from different epochs in the same paragraph. The resulting impression of this technique is akin to the one we get when looking at a stack of transparencies, of superimposed images of the same place taken in different historical periods. The notion of palimpsest (i.e., a manuscript in which a later writing is written over an effaced earlier writing) can also be used to describe Kuraev's method and to link his work to the younger generation of alternative writers.

Kuraev's condensation of narrative power in the portrayal of the storming of Kronstadt, the ironic undercutting of "objective" historical writing, when it is flanked by neutral, poetic, and clichéd descriptions of the same event, shows both the impotence of scribes and the power of poets. Kuraev's choice of his locus demonstrates the submission of writers of history to the needs of the moment and, consequently, the impossibility of accurate historical representation in traditional narratives.

Kuraev undercuts the "objective" historical discourse and, in a remarkably Tolstoyan fashion, focuses on the "black holes of history" (chernye dyry istorii), on what is typically ignored by "scribes"—the blood, dead flesh, the passion and the misery of suffering:

So where are you to look for fantastic heroes and fantastic events if not in the black holes of history, which, one must assume, swallowed more than one careless, curious man who dared look over the edge! Exactly here, where life is compressed into super-dense matter, where cities freeze in the glow of fires, where the bowels of snow-covered battleships burn from desperation, where bandages and blood are indissolubly baked and caked together, where horses, unused to flight, hover over the ice, rearing on their hind legs in the sky from the explosions, becoming the last things seen by the fighter who has gone made from the rumble and the roar, shielded from death by a mother's prayer and a white robe given out before the attack. . . . [97]

Kuraev's work underscores the fluidity and the fantastic unpredictability of human experience, as well as the rigidity of narrative forms designed to contain this reality. Presaging the orientation of the subsequent generation of alternative writers, Kuraev demonstrates the inevitable manipulation involved in the act of writing and ridicules the historian's desire to interpret or affect the course of history. For, as Kuraev says, "there's nothing stupider than to suggest various paths along which history could have developed in the distant past, especially at a time when even its current path isn't influenced in any way by a great many people who not only read but also write"(116).

Patterns of Novelistic Representation:
Aleksandr Ivanchenko

Even though the spirit of their writing is clearly antiestablishment, and the familiar reality they portray is often "defamiliarized" by unorthodox narrative techniques and unusual foci, both Makanin and Kuraev are still tenuously engaged in realism. This is so not simply because of their adherence to some veracity in representation, but mostly because of the two writers' lingering desire to provide a retrievable message in their works. Very broadly speaking, Makanin and Kuraev are fascinated by the power of representation, using the appearance of legends or diverse accounts of history as examples of that power's processes and strategies. The devices of fantasy employed by the two writers alert the reader to the presence of a narrative will and whim, when it is the structures and solidified forms of perceiving and representing, rather than authors themselves, that control writing—any writing. The writer is thus able only to select and recombine what is always already there.

Still, the analyses of this controlling power of language are never impartial here, for both Makanin and Kuraev are involved in a deliberate construction of hierarchy of discourses, where the antiestablishment sentiment in representation, and, consequently, in the overall message of their novels, is strong. In the work of other alternative writers, on the other hand, the self-referential tendency in writing gradually leads to a shift in orientation and purpose. What in Makanin and Kuraev is still colored by a straightforward value approach, in other alternative writers (particularly in representatives of the steep phase) turns into a virtually academic—"objective" by design—investigation of the way culture, through language, manipulates human consciousness and social behavior.

Aleksandr Ivanchenko's short novel *Safety Measures I (Tekhnika bezopasnosti I)* is an important step in this new direction because the author's primary concern is the very patterns of novelistic representation.[22] Ivanchenko's work is a "generic" existentialist novel. Verisimilitude of description is abandoned in favor of the fragmentary, slippery, and grotesque, and the novel's "message" has much more to do with transgressivity as a principle than with probing the hierarchical values of various discourses.

The author's general inclination to work within an established formula is evident when *Safety Measures* is compared to his other writings. *The Apple on the Snow (Iabloko na snegu,* 1986) is written in the mode of an autobiographical novel, focusing, in Proustian fashion, on the recreation of childhood sensations. *Self-Portrait with a Great Dane* is reminiscent of Trifonov's and Makanin's work, while *The Fish Eye* ventures into the area of village prose.[23] Ivanchenko's urban and village prose, as well as his autobiographical piece, are faithful to the requirements of each of these generic modes. The reality portrayed in these works is recognizable, the protagonists familiar, their lives rooted in the Soviet postwar experience. In *Safety Measures,* on the other hand, the focus shifts to the human experience itself, experience pointedly devoid of any connection to a specific culture.

This approach to representation, while making the overall picture highly inclusive and broad, simultaneously requires narrowing the narrative focus to physiological and psychological aspects of human life. This concurrent expansion and contraction of narration is achieved in the novel by means of fantastic metamorphoses and grotesque transformations. Clearly, Ivanchenko's plot operates within prefabricated structures of an existentialist modernist writing. The author's move toward imitation is particularly evident here because the borrowing is from a "foreign" source, from a mode of representation somewhat unfamiliar to the general Russian reader of the time. This "translation from a foreign language" in itself is a transgressive gesture. But Ivanchenko's transgressivity is not limited to rendering, it finds expression also in the formerly taboo themes of the novel, in the way the protagonist's perceptions and actions are shown to embrace both animate and inanimate objects and to have their source in the protagonist's sexuality.

Written in 1979 and first published only a decade later in an iconoclastic issue of the then obscure journal *Ural, Safety Measures* describes the inner world of a nameless man who, pursued by mysterious "people in black," is tortured by unexplained feelings of guilt on a train going to an unknown destination, and who, finally, escapes an unknown threat. The time of the narrative is, very broadly, the twentieth century; the society Ivanchenko describes is a totalitarian state where his man lives in constant fear and cannot be at peace until he finds a pair of handcuffs to put on his own hands. The train the protagonist is riding turns first into a prison, then into a cinema, and finally into a theater. The overwhelming feeling of guilt and despair stays with the main character through all these metamorphoses of locale until the handcuffs are firmly secured on his wrists.

The opposition of concealed (closed, tight, covered, clothed) versus bare (open, unconstrained, uncovered, undressed) shapes the narrative. Ivanchenko's protagonist wants to be "proper," legitimate, covered, but is always exposed and vulnerable. The character's vulnerability is examined primarily through his sexuality, and the text exposes the most minute fluctuations of the hero's sexual desires and frustrations. At the center we find a vulnerable figure, both a voyeur and an exhibitionist. The protagonist's double role, generalized in the narrative to typify the modern condition, is depicted by means of the grotesque. The body becomes dissolved in the realm of things and loses its clearly defined impenetrable contours. This dissolution is represented through the act of seeing (the protagonist's gaze is capable of discerning the animate qualities of inanimate objects). Here Ivanchenko's hero is the voyeur, and his eye is on the concealed—particularly, on the sexual properties of personified objects and of people. Train cars have sphincters in this novel, and a crack in the ceiling becomes an object of sexual desire and, in the end, a means of sexual relief. The last example points to yet another way the body can lose itself among things—through touch. The tactility of Ivanchenko's descriptions is always related to the sexual, to the hidden (e.g., the act of opening a package is described in terms of labor and delivery). This is also the point where the voyeur's passive gaze merges with the exhibitionist's active pleasure. Both positions appear interdependent; the dissolution of the animate into inanimate, of objects into living essences, and the transformation of the feminine principle of receptivity into the male principle of active subjugation and willful uncovering are all predicated on their opposites. The voyeuristic and exhibitionistic aspects of the hero's vision are underscored by the use of locals related to performance—theater, cinema. And here these two ways of self-expression (seeking the hidden and exposing the hidden) are shown to be inseparable from one another, almost interchangeable, but both equally necessary in shaping the hero's personality. There is a leveling of differences here—between genders, between objects and people, between freedom and bondage—that would later characterize such representatives of the steep phase as Narbikova.

Yet another feature of Ivanchenko's novel, linking him to both the older and younger generations of alternative writers is the attention it accords to the medium. Ivanchenko's text itself is "indecently exposed" most of the time, because the writer comments on the process of writing *(obnazhaet priem)* to the point of obsession. Nevertheless, when the fireworks of the unorthodox setting, characters, desires, and narrative devices are over, what is left can be read as a simple allegory of an oppressive society. The transgressivity of the themes, departures from the mimetic transparency of realistic writing, the androgyny and the grotesque inclusiveness of Ivanchenko's hero still seem to be couched here within a recognizable morality tale. Life is a train with an unknown destination; man is always fearful of freedom, and others are in the same situation (the prison walls expand to include families, children, societies). The crowd wants to destroy someone who is different; it is safer to be a prisoner (the ultimate safe haven in modern society) than to be free.

Safety Measures I is an important novel, but neither because of its existentialist bent, nor because of what, for the Soviet public, were daring themes and techniques. Deliberately derivative, it may be a translation, perhaps of an unknown piece by Camus, Kafka, or Nabokov. (At times Ivanchenko seems to be shamelessly rewriting Nabokov's *Invitation to a Beheading.*) For all its shocking digressions into the sexual imagination, the novel may, then, appear rather old-fashioned to any reader familiar with the writers who inspired Ivanchenko.

However, the work can also be read as a simulacrum, a copy of a prefabricated novelistic pattern. Seen in this light, Ivanchenko's endeavor appears much more significant than it might seem initially. If we consider the overall interest of alternative literature in patterns of representation and in their dependence on social myths, then Ivanchenko's work should be viewed in the context of the loss—not only of oneself in modern society, but of the loss of meaning associated with multiplication and overuse of empty signifiers in a culture ruled by representation. The "safety measures" of the title thus acquires an additional ironic meaning, questioning the reliance on tested truths, on the commonplaces of any culture. This position, shared by the most prominent women representatives in the trend, leads Russian literature into a much closer examination of the way language generates cultural paradigms. As with other alternative writers, the focus on language and on phantasmagorical reality frees alternative women authors from the conventions of mimetic writing, such as three-dimensionality, unities of time, space, and characters, the rigid chronology of narratives, as well as distinctions between animate and inanimate objects, self and other, life and death. Playing with mimesis also brings about a revaluation of social and philosophical values associated with canonical texts of Russian and Soviet literature, providing in the process a new perspective on existential truths, new approaches to hierarchical arrangement of gender roles, and a specific dialect for the expression of the new content.

Notes

1. Sergei Chuprinin, "Drugaia proza," *Literaturnaia gazeta*, February 8, 1989, p. 4.

2. Dmitry Urnov, "Plokhaia proza," *Literaturnaia gazeta*, February 8, 1989, p. 4.

3. Evgeniia Shcheglova, "V svoem krugu. Polemicheskie zamechaniia o 'zhenskoi proze,'" *Literaturnoe obozrenie* 3 (1990): 19.

4. *Iunost'* 8 (1988): 15.

5. Vladimir Makanin, "Otstavshii," *Znamia* 9 (1987).

6. See, for example, Oleg Dark, "Razoblachennyi Zuev, ili Apologiia grafomana," *Literaturnaia gazeta*, June 3, 1992; Viacheslav Kuritsyn, "Postmodernizm: Novaia pervobytnaia kul'tura," *Novyi mir* 2 (1992): 225–236; Mark Lipovetskii, "Patogenez i lechenie glukhonemoty: Poety i postmodernizm," *Novyi mir* 7 (1992): 213–223; and a discussion on postmodernism in *Voprosy literatury*, November-December, 1991: Mark Lipovetskii, "Zakon krutizny," pp. 3–36 and Vl. Slavetskii, "Posle postmodernizma," pp. 38–47.

7. Mikhail Epstein, "After the Future: On the New Consciousness in Literature," *South Atlantic Quarterly* 90.2 (Spring 1991): 411.

8. Chuprinin, "Drugaia," p. 4.

9. On Makanin's work of the eighties see V. Kamianov, "Zadacha na slozhenie," *Novyi mir* 3 (1988): 255–259.

10. For more on this see Nadya Peterson, "Vladimir Makanin's Solutions to the Loss of the Past," *Studies in Comparative Communism* 21.3/4 (1988): 349–356.

11. Epstein, "After the Future," pp. 415–416.

12. *Novyi mir* 2 (1987): 96–134.

13. On *Loss* see Nataliia Ivanova, "Illiuziia obreteniia" and Ruslan Kireev, "Obretenie cherez utratu," *Literaturnaia gazeta*, April 1, 1987, p. 4.

14. Hutcheon, *Narcissistic Narrative*, p. xii.

15. Ibid.

16. For more on this novel see Inna Solov'eva, "Natiurmort s knigoi i zerkalom," *Literaturnoe obozrenie* 4 (1988): 46–49; Anatolii Karpov, "Preodolenie ochevidnosti, ili real'noe v irreal'nom," *Literaturnaia gazeta*, November 18, 1987, p. 4. See also Peter Rollberg, *Invisible Transcendence: Vladimir Makanin's Outsiders* (Washington, D.C.: Woodrow Wilson Center, Kennan Institute for Advanced Studies, 1993).

17. *Znamia* 9 (1987).

18. Makanin, *Otstavshii*, p. 7. The translation is mine.

19. Hutcheon, *Narcissistic Narrative*, p. 27.

20. Mikhail Kuraev, "Kapitan Dikshtein: Fantasticheskoe povestvovanie," *Novyi mir* 9 (1987); "Nochnoi dozor: Noktiurn na dva golosa pri uchastii strelka VOKhR tov. Polubolotova," *Novyi mir* 12 (1989).

21. Quotations here are from Mikhail Kuraev, *Captain Dikshtein: A Fantastic Narrative* in Helena Goscilo, Byron Lindsey, eds. *Glasnost: An Anthology of Russian Literature under Gorbachev* (Ann Arbor: Ardis, 1990), pp. 59–185; italics mine.

22. *Ural* 1 (1988): 64–90; also published in Aleksandr Ivanchenko, *Avtoportret s dogom* (Sverdlovsk: Sredne-Uralske Knizhnoe Izdatelstvo, 1990), pp. 279–344.

23. Ivanchenko, *Avtoportret s dogom; Rybii glaz;* both published in the collection *Avtoportret s dogom.*

10

Alternative Literature II: Games Women Play

It is only in a system in which the marginal, the avant-garde, the subversive, all that disturbs and "undoes the whole" is endowed with positive value, [that] a woman artist, [able to] identify these concepts with her own practice and metaphorically with her own femininity, can find in them a source of strength and self-legitimation.

—*Susan Rubin Suleiman,* Subversive Intent

THE CONTRIBUTION OF WOMEN AUTHORS to alternative literature is substantial, the result perhaps of the traditionally marginal status of women writers in Russian society. Alternative literature is marginal by definition; it assaults established truths and speaks from the underground. Consequently, both male and female authors have been engaged in writing aimed at "undoing the whole," yet there are differences between them.[1] Alternative literature's focus on the interior world of its protagonists and its forays into the fantastic (also characteristic of women's writing between the late 1960s and the late 1980s) represent a reaction to the mimetic mode of representation and the teleological orientation of critical and socialist realism. In the late 1980s the avoidance of the obligatory progressions of realistic plots, the abandonment of mimesis in favor of the fantastic, and the bringing of language into thematized content by alternative writers were the steps characterized by the spirit of antiauthoritarianism, subversive purpose, and avant-gardist design.

The aestheticism of all alternative literature, its apolitical stance, and in particular its preoccupation with the transcendence of reality, were perceived by the Soviet literary establishment "as a significant act of symbolic defiance, a declaration of dangerously counter-cultural val-

ues" or, by its advocates, "as a perspective which [was], if not revolutionary, at least bravely oppositional."[2] If aestheticism and transcendence of
reality in writing were shared by all alternative works, alternative
women's writing exhibited greater concern with the interiority of its subjects than the work of male authors; language in general, and expression
in particular, acquired an additional importance. And it is not solely the
"narrative will," or the hold that cultural patterns have over writers, that
women authors begin to explore in their works of the late 1980s. They
also address the issue of a woman's voice and of the place from which a
woman speaks. Women's voices here often represent a specific vernacular of culture, organized around power relations and inseparable from
the hierarchical arrangements of life. The transgressivity of these writings is apparent in their defiance of mimetic representation in favor of
the grotesque and fantastic and in their choice of formerly taboo
themes; it can also be found in the examination of dominance and resistance that characterizes many of these texts.[3]

The Voice of the Crowd:
Liudmila Petrushevskaia

Ivanchenko's contribution to alternative literature lies in a deliberate
imitation of Western classics of modernist literature, Kuraev's in a
panoply of possible discourses on a historical event offered to the
reader. Petrushevskaia is engaged in imitation as well, but hers is an attempt to recreate a specific vernacular of culture—women's language.
This important difference notwithstanding, both Ivanchenko and Petrushevskaia identify particular emotional states of their characters with
the unchanging patterns of human existence. Ivanchenko's hero lives in
fear; so do Petrushevskaia's characters. Ivanchenko's protagonist is ruled
by the demands of his sexuality, Petrushevskaia's women use their sexuality in a struggle for survival. Both authors offer protagonists who are
engaged in self-expression through voyeurism and exhibitionism. And
both authors are interested in the psychological dynamics of people
marginalized by their society.

Petrushevskaia's membership in the exclusive club of alternative writers might appear unwarranted at first glance. Her stories are short vi-
gnettes of experiences only too familiar to the Russian public. Because
of the attention she gives to the quotidian, Petrushevskaia might be considered to belong to the writers of *byt* prose. She does not seem to rely
on the devices of fantasy eagerly employed by the writers I discuss here,
nor does attention to modes of representation appear to be Petrushevskaia's concern. Yet her prominent position in the canon of alternative literature cannot be denied.[4]

Recognized, if grudgingly, for her work in the theater, Petrushevskaia had to wait until the early eighties for her prose to be available to the Russian reading public. She offered the story "Such a Girl" ("Takaia de-vochka") to Alexander Tvardovsky's *Novyi mir* in 1969, only to be told by the editor that the public was not ready for it. The same fate befell her other stories until Gorbachev's glasnost made the publication of under-ground literature possible.[5] The reasons for the virtual ban on Petru-shevskaia's prose before Gorbachev are clear. Her work is subversive in content and innovative in form. Yet the subversiveness of Petru-shevskaia is not political in a direct sense; rather it lies in a renegotiation of established hierarchies in representation, in questioning the official Soviet morality, in the examination of the way power operates in the so-cial arena, and in the rough treatment that the medium itself receives under her hands. Petrushevskaia's stance was perceived as political pri-marily because the descriptions of Soviet life in her stories clashed vio-lently with the ideals then propagated by the state.

In spite of Petrushevskaia's seeming insistence on verisimilitude, the reality of her stories appears fantastic. This is so because of the intense condensation of rhetorical gestures in her narrative and because the narrator in her stories is always unreliable, clearly recognizable, yet de-liberately distanced from the implied author and the reader. The truth of the text, the "message," cannot be easily pinpointed; it is concealed un-der an avalanche of the commonplace, refracted and distorted in the voices of her unreliable women narrators.[6]

The focus on the horrors of living—presented to the reader as stark catalogues of everyday violence, deception, struggle over possessions, and perceived by the characters as a norm—is responsible for Petru-shevskaia's reputation with some as a writer of *chernukha* (black stuff), the prose whose sole raison d'être is to shake up the readers by exposing the filthy side of their society. But there is more to Petrushevskaia's writ-ing than a naive desire to reveal the unseemly. Her condensed descrip-tions of everyday brutality, her avoidance of the psychology of suffering in favor of its physiology, and the elusive reality of her writing come to-gether to point to some unchanging human motives, or to a shared un-derstanding of certain universal existential truths. The image of com-munal harmony acts in Petrushevskaia's fiction as an antithesis to society's "norm" of brutality and "totalitarian pseudo-nurture" (the phrase is Helena Goscilo's).

One of the basic motives ruling the behavior of Petrushevskaia's char-acters, is a fear of complete annihilation, with personal death foreshad-owing the death of the family and, eventually, leading to the disappear-ance of an entire genetic line *(rod)*. Related to this primary motive are her characters' perpetual quest for power and the accompanying violence in pursuit of that power. Since most of Petrushevskaia's characters are women, the power struggle she describes takes place in gender-specific locations and in the ways that characterize marginalized subordinate groups, the groups who employ the subversive strategies of guerrilla warfare rather than engage in an open war against dominance.

Petrushevskaia's existential scheme is deliberately buried in the descriptions of mundane, if horrific, occurrences. Her story "Uncle Grisha" ("Diadia Grisha"), for example, examines the feelings of a lonely, mistrustful, and unloved woman confronted with the death of her landlord, Grisha, who is killed by a group of youngsters for a pack of cigarettes.[7] Events in the story are refracted through the protagonist's consciousness and are shaped by her voice—vulnerable, uncertain about others' motives and their reactions to her. The narrator's unreliability is underscored by her constant qualifications and often contradictory shifts in her evaluation of events and people. The reality portrayed in the story becomes as suspect as the protagonist's motives. It is cluttered with seemingly unimportant events and conversations; it is filled with the garbage of the quotidian.

Petrushevskaia provides anchors for the reader, however. An important opposition is noise versus quiet; noise disrupts the woman's loneliness, her status quo, and engenders fear. Petrushevskaia's character fears intrusion, recognition, and forced silence. *Strashnyi* (terrifying), *boyalas'* (was afraid), *tait'sia* (to conceal oneself), *skryvat'sia* (to hide) are Petrushevskaia's tags for the narrator. Concealment of herself from some anticipated violence rules the woman's behavior. At the same time she exposes her own fears and vulnerability with what seems like perverse enjoyment. She lives in fear, but the reasons for that fear are moot. She also spies on the activities of her landlord and reports on those activities to the reader. As in Ivanchenko's work, the voyeuristic and exhibitionist impulses feed on each other.

The term *tikhii* (meek and quiet), on the other hand, is reserved for Grisha, and it is Grisha's innate quietness that elicits the protagonist's sympathy. Grisha's eventual death is mentioned in virtually every paragraph of this short story and is used to justify, retrospectively, the woman's anxiety. The anticipated violence, however, comes to the wrong person; an innocent victim is sacrificed to assuage the woman's terror of living and dying. Petrushevskaia concludes the story with a macabre detail: Grisha's wife, mad from grief, digs the body of her husband out of the grave to prove that his hands had been bitten. This bizarre action is placed in the context of the wife's insanity; however, it is linked in the story to the appearance of weasels, the first disrupters of the woman's quiet, and another possible frame for the narrative is suggested—that of witchcraft and black magic. Finally, the manipulation of the dead body suggests that in this world violence is inescapable and that fear is a permanent state of being.

Petrushevskaia's story lends itself to multiple interpretations; its reality is slippery and elusive, the characters' actions impossible to interpret within a traditional realistic scheme. What is fixed here is a condition of unrelieved anxiety. A whim of fate demolishes the quiet Grisha instead of the woman narrator, and the immediate result of his death is a complete disintegration of Grisha's family—his wife's insanity and his son's divorce. The woman's fear of annihilation is misplaced, but demonstrated as justifiable.

The same permanent anxiety of being characterizes Petrushevskaia's story "An Intimate Circle" ("Svoi krug"), a fifteen-page condensed rendition of the life histories of multiple characters over a period of two decades.[8] As often happens in Petrushevskaia's work, the issue of dying occupies center stage in this story. The protagonist's husband leaves her for another woman, her parents die, and, when she discovers that she is dying as well, she realizes that her sickly son is going to be left all alone in the world.

It is the threat of a possible severance of a genetic line that organizes the main character's actions. She does everything possible to insure that her son will be raised by the members of "her circle." The woman's relationship to this circle of friends, children, lovers, ex-husbands, and ex-wives is problematic. She belongs to it, but, paradoxically, as an outsider or, rather, as a person speaking from the underground. Since her actions are ruled by her knowledge of her imminent death and by the desire to preserve her own continuation in her son, the woman's insistence on revealing all the repugnant features of her circle, the group of people eventually entrusted with raising her child, is highly ambivalent. She talks about indolence, drunkenness, adultery, abortions, perversion, rape, incest, and death of children; she portrays a complete collapse of moral foundations in her circle. Yet this is the surrogate family she chooses for her son. Petrushevskaia seems to suggest that there are no alternatives. There is no escape from the prison of the circle.

The writer does not present revelations about the main character and her friends in a sequential way. Rather, links between the various parts of the story are associative. This is a technique that Petrushevskaia herself calls "the voice of the crowd" *(golos tolpy)*, where narration attempts to "record" the actual intonation and associative progression of conversational speech.[9] The woman's enraged loneliness and despair are poured out in a disjointed torrent of words. At first, the source of her boundless anger is not identified, but only hinted at in sarcastic asides. But when the character's situation finally becomes clear, it is seen against the background of other similarly disturbing events occurring around her. The collapse of this woman's life (and of those around her) is presented as a norm; the character's action of binding her child to the circle through violence (by casting herself as a child abuser) can be understood only against this norm of outrage.

While fluent in the language of her circle, and therefore capable of manipulating power relations within the small society of her friends, the character wants to establish herself as different. She proclaims herself a tough and cruel person (*zhestkii i zhestokii chelovek*) in the first sentence of the story. As in Ivanchenko's *Safety Measures I*, the opposition of concealing and revealing is the writer's primary narrative vehicle. Petrushevskaia's character provides a version of what James C. Scott has labeled a "hidden transcript"—a "critique of power spoken behind the back of the dominant."[10] Her true intentions are concealed from the authority of her circle; only the reader is allowed to share her thoughts and designs completely.

The all-embracing hatred for her circle is tinged with the woman's envy for its power. For the circle takes away her husband, and tames her fierceness as well, by turning it into a convention. Her role in the circle becomes that of an interrogator, a revealer of hidden truths, and an accuser. If in this story the narrator is practicing the arts of resistance through manipulation, the circle responds with the practiced gestures of domination, with the time-tested device of institutionalizing dissent.

In general, Petrushevskaia's stories focus on critical situations in the lives of her female characters, who speak in voices filled with impotent rage in the face of impending old age, betrayal by friends and lovers, and death. And Petrushevskaia's insistence on the "normality" of this worldview for her women can be seen as a powerful indictment against her society. What she reveals about her women characters is not what Soviet women were taught to think about themselves. The gossipy and often malicious tone of the narrative is presented as the voice of the common woman; the shocking lack of moral foundations, as the norm of her society; and the desperate and hopeless struggle to preserve the family, as woman's unenviable lot.

Yet the social critique, even if it can and has been extrapolated from Petrushevskaia's work, is not intended by the author. Since she often relies on first person narration, many of Petrushevskaia's characters are nameless. Like Ivanchenko's nameless protagonist, Petrushevskaia's heroines are designed to stand in for every woman, and, like Ivanchenko's character, her women have to face the unrelieved and inexorable burdens of living alone. The density of her narratives, their fantastic elusiveness, the unreliability of her narrators, and the constant games of domination and resistance played out by her characters are the means Petrushevskaia uses to make a general statement about the human condition. Unlike Ivanchenko's *Safety Measures I,* Petrushevskaia's writing seems to be firmly anchored in the Soviet reality of the Brezhnev era. But the surface features of that reality are compressed, distorted, then splintered in the voices of her unstable characters, and, finally, rearranged to create a world that has actually little to do with Soviet society. This is the world ruled by perpetual desires, where living is accompanied by anxiety, fear, violence, struggle for domination, and confusion.

The Economy of Female Violence: Nina Sadur

Nina Sadur's professional story mirrors that of Petrushevskaia—recognition first came to Sadur in her role as a playwright. Similarly, her prose, written in the last decade, had to wait for the milder climate of Gorbachev's liberalization to be published and appreciated.[11] Like Petrushevskaia, Sadur is concerned with the subterranean motives that rule people's lives. Her characters are mostly women, and, like Petrushevskaia, Sadur uses unreliable narrators to open her narratives for conflicting interpretations. But the reality of Sadur's stories, although still identifiable within the Russian context, is aggressively asocial, split between the empirically verifiable and the fantastic—more diffuse than that found in Petrushevskaia's narratives. Petrushevskaia's revelations about her women's lives can be seen as a political statement; Sadur's work categorically resists this interpretation. While some of Petrushevskaia's stories offer a hint of a fantastic scheme (the vampire motif in "Uncle Grisha," for example), Sadur uses fantasy as a narrative lever. Sadur openly employs the rhetorical gestures of Russian folklore in her writing, but changes them to accommodate a new reality and to express an existential position.[12] Sadur's world is as unpredictable, confused, violent, and filled with anxiety as that of Petrushevskaia. But, instead of distorting—by condensing and rearranging familiar snippets of reality—Sadur plays with the tension between the real and fantastic, placing both in the context of violence. The issue of violence—a woman's "disorderly conduct" and her furious voice—is important for Petrushevskaia; it is central to Sadur's work.

To recognize violence in women's fiction, both in themes and in representational strategies, is to acknowledge those less often scrutinized forms of political power that operate in and through the modalities of private lives, leisure activities, and literature.[13] Much work in literary criticism, and social sciences in general, has been done to identify and recognize the dynamics of repression and the violent gestures of the dominant groups toward the oppressed. In gender criticism, the commonly held view is that it is the male "enunciative modality" (to use

Michel Foucault's term—i.e., the sociosexual position from which one speaks) that is common to all the accepted discourses in Western culture.[14] According to this argument, the position of a woman in a male-dominated discourse is vacant and cannot be claimed by women. What this view does not address, however, is the dynamics of opposition to dominance, the carefully worked out strategies of resistance (James C. Scott's "arts of resistance," or a dialect of resistance) that have been part and parcel of all those commonly accepted discourses in Western culture.

It has been shown that, in reaction to dominance, subordinate groups (women among them) devise elaborate "public and hidden transcripts"—as tools for the containment or release of their accumulated rage.[15] The space where these arts of resistance are practiced includes both public and private realms. The work of resistance can manifest itself anywhere in a social body where power relations obtain—it can be directed to an outside group or applied within a seemingly homogeneous body. The strategy of resistance is designed to redress the balance of power, or at least to question it.

Sadur's work appears to be an example of such "subterranean" forms of power, an articulation of resistance to dominance, both in the way her characters act and in the way those actions are inscribed in her narrative. The intricate workings of this power, the economy of violence in Sadur, is the key to her writing. In Sadur's play *The Red Paradise*, perhaps the most overt example of her preoccupation with violence, several male characters are mutilated and murdered only to be brought back to life, to be mutilated and murdered yet again.[16] Death becomes a welcome release from the unbearable torture. The orgy of mutilation, murder, and resurrection comes to an end only when, after much experimentation, a secret of death is discovered—drowning in a sea of blood.

A woman, a priestess of death, aided by a male witch, is in charge of orchestrating these mutilations and murders of gullible men. In the logic of the play, this carnival of death is a retribution for the slights and insults that the priestess suffers when in her everyday garb of a demented woman. The object of violence becomes the subject in a carefully staged performance—by the priestess and the playwright. The violence unleashed in the play is graphic, continuous, orchestrated by a woman, directed exclusively toward males, and reactive. A woman is taking revenge on those who had subjected her to humiliation. We witness that humiliation in the first act of the play and are made to identify with the victim. The transformation of a powerless victim into an all-powerful avenger, who punishes arrogance and rewards humility and kindness, is a familiar plot of Russian fairy tales. A female figure is endowed with power, and the stage for the violent attainment of her satisfaction is elaborate, colorful, almost festive. The perpetrators of violence, however, die along with the victims; as in a primitive ritual of sacrifice, a violent rite ends all violence, and the stage is cleansed by torrents of red blood.

Although the priestess of death resides in a castle on top of a faraway mountain, the spectacle we observe is public. In Sadur's *The Discerning* (*Pronikshie*; literally, "the ones who have penetrated") the locus and style of violence are different.[17] In this cycle of stories, the space where violent confrontations occur is not public (i.e., this is not a staged confrontation with many participants) but most private and gender-specific. Violence takes place in kitchens, the hallways of communal apartments, single women's bedrooms, and vegetable gardens. This is the realm of the woman, and it is the workings of power in this setting that interest Sadur. Significantly, the harm that is contemplated, savored, and then often accomplished, also takes place in a specific way—through the dialogue of witchcraft, monologic fantasies of violence, and seemingly innocuous but deadly gestures or words. Moreover, the objects used in performative acts of magic are gender-specific household items (a button, pots and pans, chocolates, a ring, doll clothes).

The violence here, unlike the joyous dismemberment of males in *The Red Paradise*, is mediated, never direct. Perhaps this is so because, in contrast to the play, violent gestures in the stories are aimed mostly at other women. Sadur's female protagonists are engaged in a fierce battle over the objects of their desire—a child, a lover, or simply a private space. Like murders in the play, however, violent acts in Sadur's stories are reactive (done out of desperation, fear, hurt, neglect), premeditated (carefully evaluated in advance), and ritualized (recognized by the female participants as a preestablished procedure).

The narrative clearly articulates the motives for these women's violent behavior. In "Silky Hair" ("Shelkovistye volosy") a mother, desperate over her son's ill health, finds out through a kind witch that her best friend put a spell on her and the child to secure her own offspring's well-being. The struggle over a button containing the life of the sick child ends in the victory of the injured mother. In another story, "Witch's Little Tears" ("Ved'miny slezki"), a young woman uses witchcraft to kill her wayward lover, but the witch assisting in the rite interferes, and the young woman dies instead. In "The Blue Arm" ("Siniaia ruka"), a young woman turns into a witch and strangles her neighbor in a communal apartment as a revenge for perpetual abuse and humiliation.[18] In the middle of the cycle we find "The Wormy Little Son" ("Chervivyi synok"), the single monologic narrative in this work. A cleaning lady, unhinged by her lover's rejection, contemplates revenge, providing in the process a woman's unsettling portrait of a male character.

Overall, Sadur makes the male point of view inaccessible to the reader. Males are presented externally, as an opposition group of sorts. The laws that govern their behavior remain purposefully oblique. The women engaged in performing or reacting to violence, on the other hand, have a mutual understanding, even when the events in the stories are posited as incomprehensible to the uninitiated. Sadur's women appear to have their own network of communications, their own separate society with its distinct language and laws. This is the language of gossip, aggression through magic, rumor, and madness akin to spirit possession. It has been shown that this mode of communication is "the classical resort of vulnerable subordinate groups who have little or no safe, open opportunity to challenge a form of domination that angers them."[19] Sadur's women are forced to engage in violence to stop violence. But that contact with violence is seen to pollute the participants, who then contaminate their community with a desire for revenge and for more violence.[20]

This fear of contamination is expressed directly in a paragraph-long introduction to the cycle. Here, and this is the only instance of a reliable narrator in the narrative, the reader is warned of the dire consequences of "discerning" or "penetrating" It *(eto)*, a state defined as something similar to and yet different from ordinary life, omnipresent yet vague, inexplicable, and frightening. According to the narrator, those who dare penetrate the mysteries of It will either go crazy, drink themselves to death, or die. Sadur's narrative itself is "contaminated" by magic and violence, permeating the cycle's very structure and generating a new language for its expression, the language of Sadur's women protagonists. Sadur uses the fantastic, voice "filtering," *skaz,* and ritualization to represent the language of gossip and rumor, the standard dialect of the dominated.[21] Ritualization also points to the commonality of the violent intent and to the innovative ways it can be accommodated within culture.

In "A Wormy Little Son" the hidden transcript filled with desperation and fantasies of violence toward males is made public. Sadur delineates the male figure through several complimentary images: orality (males consuming everything); dissimulation (they wear masks to cover their own ugliness and pettiness); violence (they trample women); unrestrained sexuality and decay. As in *The Red Paradise*, the desire of the injured woman in this story is to repay violence and reverse the hierarchy of power:

God knows [males] have been stung by the devil of treachery. Of lust. Of escape. Of freedom. Of treachery. How could the devil sting such a snake? It would be better had he stung a woman. Then she would ravish the male, deflower him, rob him of his future, drink him up, and leave him to get old alone. Then males would become females, and females would turn into males.[22]

The essentially masculine gesture of penetration frames the cycle; penetration is presented as aggressive and dangerous, yet it also enables the reader to enter the closed society of women, the society whose language is Sadur's focus. Thus, the sociosexual position of the reader here is masculine, yet the stories themselves are written in the dialect of the dominated—Sadur's women. It is a dialect that utilizes standard folkloric forms, but reshapes them to allude to the recognizable reality of today's world. The power struggle within the closed society of women is articulated by means of this dialect, and the hierarchical structure of this society is acknowledged as a given, unchangeable.

The tensions within the society of women are resolved by means of magic, rumor, and gossip. The woman is generally defined through the gestures of subversive opposition, yet, as we have seen, the laws of her own group remain basically unchallenged. The male, on the other hand, is the quintessential Other in this configuration, and the woman's desire is to reverse the hierarchical arrangement of gender roles. However, Sadur undercuts the woman's aggressive impulse by placing the dreams of direct violence and of reversal of roles into the mouth of an unreliable protagonist—a demented cleaning lady. Thus, the antagonism between the male and female "enunciative modalities" also appears as a constant. Sadur underscores this existential given by presenting, in the introduction to the cycle, the very act of reading as penetration, and the voices of women in the stories (and that includes incantations, chants, gossip) as always expressing resistance.

Sadur's contribution to alternative literature lies in the attention she accords to the essential motives for her characters' actions and to their language. Like Petrushevskaia before her, Sadur seems to work toward a generalized scheme of human interactions, anchored in the unreconcilable conflicts of desire, determined by gender, and articulated in languages of subjugation (male) and resistance (female). Like Ivanchenko, Sadur uses fantasy—her "domesticated folklore" and the tension between real and unreal in her narratives—to express existential concerns. Like Petrushevskaia, Sadur departs from the traditions of realistic representation to examine the strategies of the injured and to suggest a view of life as a perpetual battlefield.

The Phantoms of the Text: Tatiana Tolstaya

Tatiana Tolstaya's[23] interest in the psychology of her characters, the opposition between the spiritual and physical realms that often shapes her stories, the density of her narratives, the focus on the grotesque body, and the attention she accords to the power of memory and imagination are the features that the writer shares with other alternative authors.[24] Tolstaya's fin de siècle ornamentalism (in Catriona Kelly's description), the result of the author's roots in Russian rather than Soviet literature, is what distinguishes her from others in the trend. Tolstaya's is "a luxurious, sonorous prose saturated with expressive metaphors and metonyms that enable radical condensation—a prose rich in rhetorical devices, intertexts, echoes from folklore, and erratic shifts in mood, tone, perspective, and diction that is marked by irregular rhythms and intense poetic energy."[25] The comparison with poetry is particularly valid, although Tolstaya's unrestrained style is capable both of radical condensation and expansive generosity. So much so that in Russia Tolstaya's work has earned her a dubious label of "the talent that squanders" *(rastochitel'nyi talant)*.[26]

Tolstaya uses of fantasy are propelled by an animistic impulse. She expands reality to include the physical and the spiritual; she animates inert matter and creates phantoms out of living people, dissolves differences between genders, and seeks the ideal in the childlike naiveté of her marginalized protagonists. Tolstaya's narrative strategies point to the whims and power of imagination and writing. Ultimately, however, the author's store of rhetorical gestures is based on a Romantic matrix and used for emotional impact—to create a certain mood, and to engage the reader.

Like other alternative writings, Tolstaya's fiction is asocial, or, more precisely, the social critique cannot be easily extrapolated from her narratives. The avoidance of blunt messages is symptomatic of a direction that Russian literature has taken in the last two decades, particularly obvious in Tolstaya's case, whose voice as a literary critic and social historian is loud, biased, and shaped by strong convictions and firm ideas. Similarly, like other representatives in the alternative trend, Tolstaya pays a lot of attention to the medium. Her prose, while being tremendously engaged with the reader, is, nevertheless, self-referential, offering an examination of the way imagination works. Like Kuraev, for example, Tolstaya shapes her narratives around a number of representational patterns. Yet Tolstaya's motives for this strategy differ from those of Kuraev (and of the representatives of the "steep phase"). The autoeroticism of those alternative writings, their exclusive preoccupation with self-generation, is absent in her work.

Tolstaya's prose engages with the reader intimately by making use of the cultural assumptions shared by her audience. Cultural clichés in Tolstaya serve, simultaneously, to demonstrate the power of writing, to delineate her characters, engage the reader, and to show the participation—of readers, protagonists, and writers—in cultural mythologies. For this writer, the medium is all-important, and the way it is used draws attention to the limited way language operates in the social. In Tolstaya's work the author is shown to possess a measure of freedom—to select and recombine bits of visible reality, to animate matter, and to play with patterns of representation. Yet she also seems to be doomed to be working with what is always already there. The writerly predicament—the writer's power and limitations—is best expressed in Tolstaya's description of the Okkervile River (in the story by the same name), the river that "flows on, narrowing and widening feverishly, unable to select a permanent image for itself."

In "Okkervile River" Tolstaya uses cultural clichés to gain insight into the psychology of her character and to show how they affect the character's transformation. Simeonov, the protagonist, has constructed a romantic story of the fleeting fame, failure, "sadness and decay" of his idol—the long-forgotten singer Vera. It is Simeonov who shapes the young Vera's plot, and Tolstaya delineates Simeonov as a character in *her* story by concentrating on the way he constructs his own. Romantic tales of the beautiful Vera's demise or graceful decay, created by Simeonov, are a formidable presence in the story, but so is the tale of Simeonov's own life—the tale of an incurable dreamer, loner, and failure—as it emerges through Simeonov's fantasies, the details of his bachelor existence, and his reaction to the revelation that Vera is still alive yet very different from the woman he imagined.

Various versions of Vera's life compete in Simeonov's imagination. It is here that Tolstaya provides a glimpse into the way a writer reuses and recombines bits of culture:

No, no reason to be disillusioned by going to Okkervil River, it was better to mentally plant long-haired willows on its banks, set up steep-roofed houses, release slow-moving residents, perhaps in German caps, striped stockings, with long porcelain pipes in their mouths . . . even better to pave the Okkervil's embankment, fill the river with gray water, sketch in bridges with towers and chains, smooth out the granite parapets with a curved template, line the embankment with tall gray houses with cast iron grates on the windows—with a fish-scale motif on top of the gates and nusturtiums [sic] peeking from the balconies—and settle young Vera Vasilevna there and let her walk, pulling on a long glove, along the paving stones, placing her feet close together, stepping daintily with her black snub-toed slippers with apple-round heels, in a small round hat with a veil, through the still drizzle of a St. Petersburg morning; and in that case, make the fog light blue.[27]

This version of the young Vera's story is a pastiche constructed from her songs (the Russian "romances"), the visual details of St. Petersburg gleaned from photographs and old movies, and from other visual clichés, such as the happy Germans and windows decorated with flower boxes. Svetlana Boym finds the cultural subtext for Tolstaya's prose in Soviet urban folklore, especially slightly outmoded urban romances and sentimental songs. According to Boym, the writer both engages and distances herself from the banal discourse of the romances. To transcend the banality designated as such, to endow its representations with this power of transcendence, Tolstaya has to involve herself fully in the discourse of sentimentality and to abandon, if briefly, the distance between the narrator and character. A banal object, such as Sonya's pin in "Sonya," can be transcended. Tolstaya's banal object can become a metaphor, in this case for the power of love and writing, problematizing in the process the customary denigration of everyday life *(byt)* and elevation of spiritual being *(bytie)*. In order for that transcendence to take place, however, Tolstaya's characters have to undergo personal transformations and profound crises of imagination. For the protagonist of "Okkervile River," such crisis is brought about by a confrontation with a clichéd representation of womanhood, radically different from the ones he himself had concocted. A producer of images, Simeonov is shown to recombine visual and discursive paradigms in a continuous creative endeavor—infinite in its potential and dangerous to the manufacturer.

Ivanchenko and Kuraev offer the reader an exercise in imitation of various discourses, an effort chiefly determined by an impulse to display the artifice of writing and of cultural constructs in general. Tolstaya, similarly, uses clichés, cultural myths, and literary allusions to demonstrate the inevitability and limitations of reliance on cultural myths. Yet in her writing one also finds a strong argument for the power of the author. The surface plot of "Sweet Shura" ("Milaia Shura"), for example, is a story of the narrator's friendship with a very old woman, a relationship that comes to its natural end when Shura dies. At the center is Shura's unconsummated affair with a young suitor, Ivan Nikolaevich, sixty years earlier. In this plot, Shura never goes to see Ivan, although she has her ticket and her belongings are packed. In the story that Tolstaya constructs, however, Shura is on her way to Nikolai in the end:

And Alexandra Ernestovna, sweet Shura, as real as a mirage, crowned with wooden fruit and cardboard flowers, floats smiling along the vibrating crossing, around the corner, southward to the unimaginably distant shimmering south, to the lost platform, floats, melts, and dissolves in the hot midday sun.[28]

Tolstaya seems to confirm the power of the author by suggesting that it is only a writer who can bestow this character with the fulfillment of her most cherished dreams.

In Tolstaya's "Sonya," the writerly impulse is responsible for the creation of another phantom of the text—a love-stricken Nikolai—the result of a practical joke played on the gullible, ugly Sonya by the cunning and beautiful Ada. Love letters that Ada writes to Sonya on behalf of the nonexistent Nikolai change the lives of both women: the writer (Ada) becomes indistinguishable from her own protagonist (Nikolai), and Sonya sacrifices her life to save the phantom lover from starvation during the war. Not only does Tolstaya "restore Sonja to her rightful role as the triumphant, sublime (if externally ridiculous) agent of those spiritual values that reassert their mysterious power in a world of skeptical materialism and cynical indifference," she also shows how writing can overtake the writer.[29]

Games with patterns of representation do not exhaust Tolstaya's store of narrative strategies. The chorus of voices populating her stories, as well as the grotesque, work together to create a fantastic androgynous animistic world. Tolstaya's narrator is immediately accessible to the reader; there are no obstacles impeding the reader's identification with the voice of the storyteller–a voice playful, sharp, irreverent, and youthful. However, her reliance on Erlebte Rede for her characters establishes a distance between the storyteller and her protagonists, the distance essential for the writer's comic intent. Tolstaya's comic heteroglossia points to the writer's power to manipulate objects, people, and meanings; and so does Tolstaya's use of the grotesque—personification through metonymy and metaphor, and depersonification.

The crude physical reality of dead things loses its sharply defined contours; it is "overgrown" and reanimated by seemingly superfluous associative details. Phantoms of the past are fully engaged in the events of the present, gender differences become blurred, and objects become alive, participating equally in an opulent, vibrating, fantastic universe of colors, sounds, and smells. Bathing suits in "Sweet Shura" dream of mischief, and lovely transparent dresses languish in a woman's trunk, ready for the warm breezes of the Black Sea. As in a medieval torture, a photograph of Shura's beloved Ivan Nikolaevich is stretched and squashed (raspialen) under the weight of other images in the picture album. And it is Ivan Nikolaevich's phantom who, after sixty years of anguished anticipation, is still pacing the dusty platform of a Crimean railway station, waiting for Shura to arrive.

Tolstaya's technique of poetic condensation, her use of the grotesque, and the principle of association that structures her narrative brings to mind Gogol's style more than that of any other writing in Russian literature. Tolstaya's links to Gogol do not stop on the level of style, however. Her posture is essentially Romantic. The opposition between the spiritual and the physical realms is at the center of her writing, and the omnipotence of the author—its dangers and rewards—stands at the heart of her concerns as a writer of fiction. In "A Clean Sheet" Tolstaya examines a fantastic situation, a Gogolian pact with the devil (a soul surgeon) that the protagonist strikes to relieve his depression. Here and elsewhere, Tolstaya presents ungracefulness, ludicrous behavior, and inability to adapt to the status quo as indications of a special kind of sensitivity pointing to an unorthodox spirituality. When the tormented protagonist of "A Clean Sheet" sheds his depression-soul-difference, he, quite predictably, becomes an ordinary Russian bourgeois—crude, greedy, and boring.

As in Gogol, torment and disharmony are inseparable from true creativity and spirituality, while complacency, symmetry, and visual perfection point to some spiritual fault. Physical beauty is always suspect in Tolstaya; it is either a phantom of imagination, or a mask covering an inner void. Physical decay and overall incongruity in appearance, on the other hand, even though ridiculed at first, are often sublimated. In "Okkervile River" it is the physicality of the true Vera—loud, old, fat, and mannish—that clashes with the phantom of the fragile feminine beauty that Simeonov had created to relieve his depression. The repulsion toward this excessive body is the reverse side of the attraction the Romantic hero of Tolstaya feels toward "acceptable" manifestations of death and decay. Simeonov is consumed with visions of disintegration, yet the reality of disintegrating flesh does not fit the sadly sweet world of the Russian fin de siècle he chooses for his protagonist. In Tolstaya's tale, the old ugly Vera becomes Simeonov's harshest literary critic.

As in other alternative writings, we find in Tolstaya a fantastic reality which, by its very existence, points to the irrelevance, or limitations, of mimesis. And, like other alternative authors, Tolstaya draws attention to the way language operates in the social sphere by showing a writer's dependence on cultural clichés. Yet in Tolstaya's work the author is also shown to possess a great measure of freedom—to select and recombine bits of reality, to play with patterns of representation, to animate dead matter, and to create a chorus of her protagonists' resonant voices openly and playfully manipulated by the narrator-author herself.

Eroticism Rediscovered: Valeriia Narbikova

Tolstaya's Romantic juxtaposition of the finite and infinite, which structures her prose, is concealed behind comic heteroglossia. Another obstacle to a neat interpretation of her work lies in Tolstaya's use of an overarching ironic orchestrator, her narrator. Thus, as in other alternative writings, Tolstaya's narratives are designed to trigger multiple interpretations, and the "truth" of the text becomes as illusive as its reality.

With Valeriia Narbikova we enter the steep phase of alternative literature, where language becomes the sole protagonist, and manipulations
with refractions of empirical reality occupy center stage.[30]

Narbikova, a young Russian author of "erotic prose," was ushered into
the literary limelight by the Russian writer Andrei Bitov in 1988.[31] "Discovered" and praised by one important man of letters, she was deni-
grated and verbally abused by another, the prominent Soviet critic
Dmitry Urnov.[32] As in Narbikova's own stories, the woman appeared at
the center of a controversy, at the apex of a triangle, between two men.

To Bitov, Narbikova's world appeared "astonishingly, enchantingly
transparent and tender."[33] To Urnov, Narbikova's density and unusual
technique were proofs of the author's inability to deal with erotic
themes. In Urnov's opinion, in Narbikolva's writing, in order to compensate for a lack of philosophical depth, "a trivial situation, which,
however, does not want to appear trivial . . . is made complex by purely
verbal gymnastics."[34] Other critics joined in the fight over the significance and value of Narbikova's contribution to Russian literature, generally echoing the arguments of the two principals.[35] Critics have
tended to agree on the main features of Narbikova's work—its complexity, its deliberately shocking, insatiable interest in sex and physiology,
and the triviality of some of its situations and language. They have dis-
agreed, vehemently, on the general worth of such literature—a clash of
opinions indicative of the traditional value-oriented ways of Soviet criticism, which has very little to do with Narbikova as a serious writer or
innovator.

What is immediately apparent to anyone attempting to make sense
of Narbikova's work is that the author does everything possible to resist
such an endeavor. The critic embarking on deciphering Narbikova's
convoluted language of ostensible eroticism is a critic engaged in a labor of love. And this is not to imply that her prose aims at exciting one's
libidinal impulses (it generally does not—an issue addressed in greater
detail below) but, rather, to emphasize the arduousness of the critical
task at hand.

Narbikova's work is a permanent exercise in transgression, which, by
virtue of its predictability, subverts its own transgressive intent. The first
reaction to Narbikova's prose is an intense involvement with the shocking distortions in her compacted language; her narrative configurations
are an inducement to guess, to "crack the code," to find the rules of the
game she is playing with the reader. Then, inevitably, the novelty wears
off, her devices become predictable and automatized; the cross-fertil-
ization of other texts within her text, Narbikova's "intertextuality," is no
longer a refreshing revelation, and the deliberately meager story line can
no longer sustain interest.

The principal player defeats herself at her own game: the work becomes too dull to read. This is a predicament that a modernist writer faces when her text becomes "all too readable—not in the sense of readability imposed on [it] by the traditional reader, but in the sense in which [it itself has] codified [its] own transgressive procedures, and codified as well the commentary on those procedures."[36] However, if one views Narbikova's work in the context of the contemporary Soviet avant-garde, precisely as a modernist work aimed at upsetting artistic standards and challenging the dominant ideology, then the automatization of her transgressive procedures is a price she has to pay for being subversive. The questions I pose below may thus yield a broader view of Narbikova's work—not as an isolated incident, but as a trend within alternative literature, the result of intense cross-pollination of ideas and techniques between East and West, between the visual and narrative arts.

What is the significance of Narbikova's innovative focus on the commonplace? How important are the clichés of Soviet speech in Narbikova's writing? Why does the author constantly engage in what Urnov called verbal gymnastics? Equally intriguing is the issue of her work as an example of "erotic" prose written by a woman. What norm does Narbikova use as a platform for transgression in the language she employs and the situations she describes? Is her prose erotic, pornographic, or realistic in some new sense? Does her work have a message, and if so, what kind?

In Narbikova's view, socially oriented literature (what she calls the literature of great ideas) turns ideas into stale slogans. In contrast, alternative literature tends to mask its message to avoid the obvious presence of a social agenda.[37] In Narbikova's debut work, *The Equilibrium of Diurnal and Nocturnal Stars*, which can serve as a paradigm for her writing in general (particularly because her narratives emphasize their "uninterruptedness" and elasticity), ideas are not spelled out directly.[38] Instead the author, following her own prescriptions for writing alternative prose, conceals her message by weaving it into the dense fabric of the narrative.

At the core of *Equilibrium* we find a familiar love triangle, a standard arrangement for Narbikova's stories. The main character, Sana, is married to Avvacum but is seeing Otmatfeian (an allegorical name with allusions to Matthew's gospel—"Ot Matfeiia"). The names of Sana's men are deliberately recognizable quotes whose significance, however, is limited to their recognizability. Neither Archpriest Avvacum's famous "Life," nor Matthew's rendition of biblical events contribute in any way to an understanding of the characters or of the author's philosophical position. Rather, the allusions are aimed to discompose the readers, to jolt them out of the complacent attitude of passively consuming "easy" texts. (Such empty allusions, snares, abound in Narbikova's writing; as is evident in her use of the name False Dmitrii for one of the characters in *Rally about Running (Probeg—pro beg)*, or Dodostoyevsky (which can be loosely rendered as Foredostoyevsky) and Toest'lstoy (I. E. Tolstoy) in *First Person. And Second (Plan pervogo litsa. I vtorogo)*.[39]

After a bitter argument with Sana, her lover escapes to a seaside resort under the pretext of a business trip. She and her husband follow and find themselves in the same house with Sana's lover and his friend. The group discovers a Sleeping Beauty and, after unsuccessful attempts to rouse her from her sleep, chooses to take her along. Sana abandons her husband, gives birth to a child conceived over the telephone, and lives with her lover in an old museum. In the end, the Sleeping Beauty is released back into the sea, Sana's lover returns to his wife, and Sana reunites with her husband.

The above summary is but a skeleton of the journal version of the novel. In the expanded version, the veiled messages are elaborated on, and certain themes are more directly expressed as the plot dissolves into a series of very loosely related episodes (in fact, the last part of the expanded version was published as a separate piece in the émigré publication *Strelets*).[40] Narbikova's style is very dense, aware of its own literariness, and seemingly aimed at puzzling the reader. The author's principle of narration has a lot in common with one strand of the Soviet avant-garde—that of conceptual art (*kontseptualizm*)—associated primarily with such artists as Ilya Kabakov and Erik Bulatov and such poets as Dmitry Prigov and L. Rubinstein. (Narbikova is Kabakov's close friend and repeatedly refers to his work in her writing).

In Soviet conceptual art, as Mikhail Epstein has pointed out, "everything existing is transcribed in the mode of banality, all utterances appear as quotations."[41] In this process, according to Epstein, the author-artist does not simply use the ready-made clichés of speech, but imitates, consciously and skillfully, entire worldviews, situations, characters, elements of plot, and ideas (*suzhdeniia*) about life. This "humiliation of speech" is seen by the critic as a means of debunking the myths of Soviet society, as a "solemnly cheerful interment of those ideas that for a long time have tortured the soul of the people with vain dreams (*tsheta*) of unbounded power, happiness, unity, and victory."[42]

It should be noted that Russian conceptualism is a blend of indigenous and extrinsic trends, namely American Pop art and conceptualism on the one hand, and Soviet Sots art on the other. Sots art as a movement began with the work of Vitaly Komar and Alexander Melamid and a group of underground artists of the Aptart (apartment exhibitions) of the early 1970s. Epstein's definition of conceptualism ("everything existing transcribed in the mode of banality, all utterances appearing as quotations") is perhaps too narrow for conceptualism itself; it defines Sots art, however, with utmost precision. Here, as Elisabeth Sussman explains, banality appears as a "signifier of the social" and the artifacts of the Soviet politicized mass culture are used for avant-garde purposes.[43]

Sots art and Pop art both employ the proliferating signs of their respective mass cultures to subvert the process of "naturalization" in which, as Roland Barthes has shown in his work on modern mythologies, artificial constructs of dominant cultures strive to appear as "Nature." But, if Pop art reacted aesthetically to the mass consumption of Western culture and its clichés, Sots art was a reaction to the social advertising of socialism and to the redundancy and overabundance of ideological propagandistic graphic production (slogans, quotes, and posters).[44]

The postwar cross-influences in art between East and West have created what Sussman calls a "state of hybridity."[45] According to the critic, one can find parallel descriptions of a shift from expressive to conceptual attitudes in the writings of Soviet conceptual artists and some American critics. The Soviet conceptualist Sergei Anufriev refers to "artistic pathos" being replaced by "investigative pathos," while the American Hal Foster, writing in 1983, points to the existence of the "anti-aesthetic" gestures of Western art in which "a poem or picture is not necessarily privileged, and the artifact is likely to be treated less as a work in modernist terms—unique, symbolic, visionary—than as a text in a postmodernist sense—"already written," allegorical, contingent."[46] According to these observers, the shared tendencies in Western and Soviet art of the last twenty years point to an art layered with meanings, organized by strategies of irony and parody—art that is self-referential, resisting a single meaning or interpretation. The above assessment can very easily be applied both to the conceptualist art of Ilya Kabakov and to Valeriia Narbikova's narratives.

Ilya Kabakov's early work might be seen as an example of Sots art, but in the seventies acquires the more depoliticized elastic dimensions of Russian conceptualism. Kabakov's mature art, then, can no longer be easily contained within the ironic boundaries of quotational Sots art. Writing becomes an important element of his artistic design, linking Kabakov's work to the Western conceptualism of the late sixties (Joseph Kosuth, Douglas Huebler, and Lawrence Weiner). Here concept, information, language, and system are foregrounded through the use of narrative texts, photographs, and objects.[47]

Through installations and narratives Kabakov creates a fictional cosmos—a communal Soviet apartment shared by ten fictional characters—in the process constructing, in his own words, a "metaphysics of the commonplace."[48] Kabakov's purpose here is to expand the limits of Sots art, to move from a straightforward ironic undercutting of the myths of socialist realism to an almost existentialist worldview where the emptiness, purposelessness, and wastefulness of life occupy center stage. If garbage in Kabakov's art has been interpreted to signify the waste of ideology, of words, of the environment—the failure of the human "experiment"—then the always white last page of Kabakov's albums is there to undercut any attempt at one-dimensional interpretations of anything.

Narbikova's work is similarly constructed to resist a single interpretation. Mikhail Epstein has noted that in the works of the avant-garde (i.e., Soviet experimental art of the last three decades) the absurd dominates over the meaningful, the individual is alienated from self, and we observe "a crisis of reality impossible to contain in forms available to humans, reality that melts, disappears, becomes less perceptible and knowable."[49] In Narbikova this "barely perceptible and knowable reality" emerges through the defamiliarization of the quotidian, through the deliberate debunking of the mythology of the Soviet and Russian state.

The waste of ideology and environment in Narbikova is presented, exemplified, and amplified as the waste of words. Trivial languages are mimicked, forcibly stripped of their logic, and torn out of the normalized system of speech:

You know, she wanted to "do it" and with the one you know. But "the one you know" didn't call, and the one who called no one knew. No one knew what was happening outside either. Yesterday they promised something and it happened the way they promised.[50]

Or:

They had an unhappy marriage: while she was his mistress, she wanted him to love her as a wife; when she became his wife, she wanted most of all for him to love her as a mistress; he couldn't do this; he loved her as he could; when she was his mistress, he loved her as a mistress; when she became his wife, he loved her as his wife.[51]

Narbikova rearranges clichés in striking combinations and reaccents set expressions to reveal the texture of the language they are composed of—in order to defamiliarize notions about reality embedded in effaced truisms of everyday life. As one prominent Soviet critic has recently noted, this technique betrays the direct influence of Sasha Sokolov's prose in Narbikova's work.[52] Furthermore, like Sokolov, Narbikova likes to upset the standard hierarchy of styles by trivializing attributes of high culture while placing the vernacular of culture on a pedestal. For example, Boileau and Aristotle are brought in to support the notion that for an act of physical love one needs the unity of time, place, and action. Since the main woman protagonist is married, it is rather complicated to satisfy two of the prerequisites—of time and place—to arrange a rendezvous with her lover. A similar, and striking, reaccentuation occurs when a discussion of mythologies and religious beliefs appears next to a description of dirty underwear. Or when the biblical story of Madonna's journey to Egypt is retold in the gossipy tone of a communal apartment discussion:

> He left his son in the care of people. What can one say, then, about the young girl, the mother of his son, whom he left in the care of her husband, her son's stepfather; he didn't even take her to Egypt himself, but just told Iosif Iakovich to take her to Egypt, didn't even say it himself, just left a message with the holy ghost. If he could do that to the people close to him, what then about the people completely unknown to him? Although, people he didn't know he sometimes treated better than those close to him. People often treat those they don't know better than those close to them.[53]

Rearrangement, reaccentuation of clichés (what Helena Goscilo refers to as reversed syllogisms), "empty" allusions (historical tags used to disorient rather than orient in meaning), and the deliberate triviality of situations and actions work together in Narbikova's writing to create a sense of plasticity and transparency that has nothing to do with mimesis. The word I want here is interchangeability—of characters, sexes, situations, spaces, interpretations, even historical periods. The following two passages from *Ad kak Da aD kak dA* (as well as the title itself, which translates as *Hell as Yes HeLL as yeS*, with an allusion to Dadaism imbedded in it) can serve as good illustrations of the above point:

> parts of her face were arranged to created an illusion of complete interchangeability: where she had her nose, her mouth could have been easily located; where she had her eyes, she could have had her ears; the chin could have been where the forehead was; no matter how the parts of her face were moved around, the face itself retained its natural harmony. . . . [326]

Or:

> It was precisely Popoff; and only Popoff who could attract by this rare combination of the plebeian and the refined; and women (men) were won over by the refinement he inherited from his father (mother), and the men (women) were won over by his plebeian qualities given to him by his

mother (father): for women (men) he was an absolute whore, for women—
a gentleman, for gentle women—a man [dlia zhenshin—dzhentl'menom, a
dlia dzhenshchin—zhentl'menom]. [358–359]

Nothing changes, there is no tangible plot in which to anchor one's
readerly expectations, yet everything can and does change. Banality,
Kabakov's trivial constant garbage of life, becomes an object of contem-
plation, an aesthetic object; the component parts of this refuse of life,
however, can and do undergo an infinite number of transformations.
Narbikova's spaces shrink and expand, and her characters merge and
emerge; they surface in the time of Napoleon or go back to the period of
Henry the IX in France, then suddenly appear in a new guise in contemporary Leningrad. The guidelines are elusive, the movement is perceived
not on the level of plot, but on the level of words—in the incessant game
with meaning that leads one to the conclusion that there can be no
meaning because the author can always rephrase, reaccentuate, and
laugh at the reader's willingness to narrativize, make sense:

What are they talking about? It's hard to catch the meaning. This meaning
has another meaning hiding behind it, which reaches zero and then
changes its sign to the opposite one: she attempts to convince him about
something he has been trying to propose just a while ago, she denies that
which she has asserted just a minute ago, he denies what he has just asserted, they are talking simultaneously, and when she is the voice he is
the background, and when he is the voice she is the background, and
then it is one voice over another and one background against another
background. . . .[54]

The woman author is in complete control over these permutations of
the story's meaning. Prohibitions are broken, norms transgressed—
through the violation of the word, the defamiliarization of the commonplace, the infinite game of reaccentuation. That is why Narbikova's love
triangles are narratively "unanchored"; certain situations transcribed in
traditional narratives do occur, but also could occur, and do, somewhere
else, at other times. Thus, what is stated needs always to be restated in a
different way.

The few fixed areas of representation are love sickness, wives-hus-
bands-lovers, adulterous situations, sex, eating, nature, water, body flu-
ids and waste, certain mythological characters (e.g., the Beautiful Helen
of Troy), certain historical figures (e.g., Peter the Great), writers (e.g.,
Pushkin—he stands for God in literature), and God. The present tense
environment is recognizable; it is probably in Soviet Russia, probably in
Leningrad, probably within the last ten years.

The only departure from the overall movement of Narbikova's prose into unintelligibility and dissolution of meaning as a philosophical stance is her directly expressed indignation with what can be called the fruits of civilization. Narbikova emphasizes the notion that people are part of nature by recasting human bodies and the attributes of everyday life in terms of nature. Instead of personifying nature—a familiar device of traditional narratives—she "naturalizes" persons and their environment. This imparts a surrealistic quality to Narbikova's descriptions. For example, in *Equilibrium* the main character adorns her legs with brooks and covers herself with clouds. Similarly, human clothes are compared to mountains and forests protecting the earth.

The device of "naturalization of persons" serves to underscore several philosophical points in *Equilibrium*. If one were to disregard the novel's innovative technique for a moment, the closeness of Narbikova's position to that of the ecologically aware village prose of Valentin Rasputin or Sergei Zalygin, or to the prose of her discoverer Andrei Bitov, for example, becomes startlingly apparent. In addition, the emphasis on the absurdity of humanity's attempts to mold nature to suit its own purposes is consistent with the views espoused by Soviet conceptualists, namely Ilya Kabakov, and can also be found in the recent paintings of Komar and Melamid (the New Jersey cycle).

In *Equilibrium* Narbikova's narrator points out that although people have been part of nature from the very beginning, in assuming divine powers, they have lost their sense of belonging to it. People have become poor imitators of God; they have been able to create, but on a much smaller scale. Having imbued nature with their own petty desires, they have defiled it. Peter the Great, the great imitator of nature, built his city on a swamp, but nature has not been conquered—it is always there. In Narbikova's view, human attempts to tame nature are absurd. That absurdity is demonstrated through the striking image of people living, like animals, on little hills or under bushes, but provided with electricity and telephones.

A note of warning is sounded in the final pages of the journal version of *Equilibrium*, evocative of the apocalyptic pronouncements of Soviet publicistic literature. The atmosphere will soon leave the earth as the soul leaves a dying body; we are living the first of those millions of minutes before the end of the world.

The ecological anxiety that pervades the journal version of the novel is even stronger in the expanded book version. Here we find one of those rare instances when Narbikova's narrator insists on her "reliability," and the points expressed are not completely embedded in the maze of reaccentuated clichés. Rather the tone is bitter and ironic:

We live in a society where everything is fine: it's raining radioactive waste, and everything is fine; birds will fly over us and die over Finland, and everything is fine; tomatoes are picked, brought somewhere and thrown away, and bread too is thrown away; potatoes and sausage they won't throw away because those won't be delivered in the first place. Everything that grows well on its own we throw away, and that which we have to do ourselves, we do badly, but everything is fine with us. [80]

For Narbikova—and here her position begins to veer away from the solutions offered by village prose and publicistic literature—only love can make the earth more noble and only lovers are able to perceive fully their links to, and dependence on, nature. Narbikova's ideal love is the spiritual and physical connection, almost an interchangeability, between a man and a woman. This idea, consistent with Narbikova's philosophical emphasis on the principle of substitution, is elaborated on in the expanded version of *Equilibrium,* where the two lovers become one to the point where all gender differences between them disappear.

What, however, appears unusual at first in Narbikova's representation of spiritual and physical love, ostensibly the central topic in her writing, is the absence of directly expressed pleasure (or any other feelings) by the participants about their emotional connection and sexual activities. The approach is to show the actions of characters during a sexual act in an estranged, disembodied way. Within this defamiliarizing description the narrative is organized by means of what might be called associative jumps. For example, in *Equilibrium* the characters' lovemaking is presented, quite predictably, as an act of riding. Then the narrative shifts into a discussion of a dead palm tree, possibly covertly alluding to the state of the man's sexual organ after intercourse. The image of a dead palm tree resonates with allusions to Mikhail Lermontov's poem ("Three Palm Trees," 1839). Reference to the poem leads the narration toward a discussion of the phenomenon of subtext, which then turns into a dissection of the word *subtext.* Subtext is perceived by the author as a text laboring under the weight of all other existing texts; the idea acquires sexual overtones.

Feelings of uncertainty, of the desire to possess the object of one's love, or of suffering are generally expressed in cliché-spiked dialogues or dealt with by silence—the two strategies that serve to neutralize emotions traditionally associated with infatuation. Pleasure is absent in descriptions of sexual acts; rather, the basic organizing principle of representing sexual contacts in Narbikova is the woman's surrender to the male's aggressive force:

Semiodin raised her arms, they froze in this position; he bent her head to the side, and the head froze like this. Lena was obedient, like a doll, and equally indifferent; when he moved her body forward a little, she didn't lose her balance. . . .

. . . her face remained calm, like a mask, no matter what he did to her, no matter what position her body assumed. All his embraces rolled off her, not one kiss stayed on her cheeks. He sprained his neck examining her from all sides. Looking at her, he hit her to break her into pieces, and she fell to the floor; but there was no punch, she just rocked smoothly and slowly went down to the floor, like a wave.[55]

I have stated earlier that Narbikova's prose is deliberately transgressive. The transgressive intent is immediately apparent in the distortions of Narbikova's narrative—in the reaccentuation of clichés, the use of "empty" allusions, the continuous deliberate reversals of the plot line, in the interchangeability of the general philosophical and narrative principle. To understand Narbikova's violation of the norm in terms of sexual practices and their descriptions we have to consider the very issue of this norm in traditional narratives.

Narbikova's prose touches on aspects of sexual behavior avoided by the traditional Russian, and particularly Soviet, literary discourse. In her writing we find descriptions of various unorthodox sexual positions, of homosexual love, and of incest. Narbikova's characters engage in oral sex, make love under water and during the woman's menstruation, they masturbate and urinate in each other's presence. There is also a considerable degree of violence in her prose, directed primarily at men: one male character is turned into a hedgehog, cooked, and eaten by his former mistress and her lover; another's head is torn from his body; yet another character's limbs are severed; a male character dies, but comes to life again.

However, the intent here does not seem to be the arousal of the libidinal or the erotic-sadistic impulse in the reader, the aim of traditional pornographic and erotic literature. Admittedly, the reception of any narrative, even of a such prudish mode of writing as a socialist realist novel, can be viewed as a process in which the initial narrative foreplay leads to the conflictual climax at the center, and, finally, to a narrative release in the denouement. The reading of fiction, as has been correctly pointed out, is akin to an onanistic sexual activity. What differentiates erotic and pornographic literature from all other types, however, is the primary thematic focus of the former on sexual practices, as well as the obvious intent of such literature to arouse the reader sexually. One can find neither the former nor the latter aspects of erotic and pornographic literature in Narbikova's work.

Moreover, in pornographic literature, as Vladimir Nabokov points out in his "On a Book Entitled Lolita," the aim of arousal is achieved through the description of an action that is "limited to the copulation of clichés."[56] Nothing—style, structure, imagery—should ever distract the readers from their "tepid lust." Nabokov notes that the pornographic novel must consist of an alternation of sexual scenes that "must follow a crescendo line, with new variations, new combinations, new sexes, and a steady increase in the number of participants."[57] In Narbikova, Nabokov's "copulation of clichés" is the general focus of the narrative. However, if what Nabokov means here is actualizations (performances) of a certain erotic code, Narbikova takes the notion literally, and the "alternations, variations, and new combinations" in her work occur on the level of clichés embedded in everyday speech, related to commonplace occurrences, and not limited to sexual situations.

Another important vehicle for the transmission of the pornographic intent is the obscene word (understood here as the word belonging to the vulgar linguistic register, employing anatomical vocabulary and clinical terminology avoided in polite conversation). As Lucienne Frappier-Mazur has observed, in order to achieve the pornographic effect most fully, the obscene word has to appear in a particular context: the pornographic impact is enhanced when crude and polite registers of language are "inappropriately" attributed (i.e., when crude words are put in the mouths of aristocratic or female characters); the effect of the obscene word is stronger in prose than in poetry, since so much depends on the narrative line here (Nabokov's "copulation of clichés"); first person narration engages the reader more than other forms of narration because it promotes the reader's voyeurism; even dialogues in pornographic literature have to be "padded" with stories.

Erotic literature, while employing many of the same devices as its pornographic counterpart, is less formulaic, more open to interpretation. The obscene word here becomes polysemic, and clinical terminology in its vulgar form is generally avoided. There is more emphasis on style, structure, and imagery, which (I agree with Nabokov) distract the reader from the blunt arousal techniques of pornographic literature.[58]

Narbikova breaks taboos of traditional nonerotic literary practice by representing violations of established norms of sexual intercourse and, even more importantly, by distorting the rules of literary discourse related to sexuality. Occasionally, the latter purpose is achieved by the innovative use of the obscene word. Obscene words in Russian literature are normally represented with the initial letter and an ellipsis. Narbikova plays with this norm in the following way: the norm is confirmed by the traditional usage (for example, the word *bliad'* [whore] first appears as *b* . . .), then is transgressed by the use of the same word in its full form. Or the transgressive intent is established by the use of the full form of the word, and then, unexpectedly, the same word is offered in its customary abbreviation.

In Narbikova the obscene word as such appears extremely rarely; most often the anatomical parts involved in sexual activity are described metaphorically (e.g., "hedgehog" *[ezhik]* for a woman's genitals, and a "masculine finger" *[muzhskoi palets]* for a penis). Sexual acts are represented in third person narration, also metaphorically rephrased and "defamiliarized." Thus scenes of sexual activity can be interpreted on various levels, and the pornographic impact is subverted. The crescendo arrangement of pornographic and erotic literature is absent, as is the acknowledgment of pleasure.

All its uninhibited representation of sexual activities notwithstanding, Narbikova's prose cannot be considered pornographic or even erotic. The central tendency of her narrative to avoid straightforward interpretation, her focus on interchangeability, the deliberately polysemic nature of erotic words and sexual situations in her writing—all these work together to dampen and almost nullify the erotic impact.

Erotic situations in Narbikova serve to propagandize transgression of norms (I can do it with anybody at any time, in any way I choose, and, if I love one, I love all). The text reigns—I name, I distort; the only meaning here is that there is no meaning beyond my power to effect change and substitution (what Robbe-Grillet has termed the writer's "will to intervention" *[volonte d'intervention]*). I, as a writer, can go into free association; being in charge, I can embody in language my own, woman's, desires of violation, my own fantasy of voyeurism. And the pleasures I offer to the reader have much more to do with intellectual than with sexual prowess.

The resulting effect of Narbikova's prose is not erotic, but, curiously, didactic, indicative of a desire to instruct readers about the nature of prohibition and control rather than to arouse them sexually. Overall, her work fits into the category of modernist, or perhaps postmodernist, writing much better than into the narrow confines of "erotic prose," suggested by her Soviet critics and accepted by Narbikova herself. This is the case because, like the work of her conceptualist counterparts, Narbikova's writing privileges "heterogeneity, play, marginality, transgression, the unconscious, eroticism, excess" over "representation, the unitary subject, linear narrative, paternal authority, and Truth with a capital T."[59]

Like conceptualist art, Narbikova's writing—self- referential, resisting a single meaning or interpretation—is layered with meanings, organized by strategies of irony and parody. Sex is just one of many instruments Narbikova chooses to challenge the norms of her society with, to break the taboo which "power" uses to regulate it, and which, as Michel Foucault has demonstrated, "plays on the alternative between two nonexistencies" (where the existence of sex is maintained only "at the cost of its nullification").[60]

Paradoxically, Narbikova's desire to engage in erotic play with language, thereby severing her ties to societal and representational norms, simultaneously plays into the hands of Foucault's "power," by virtually eliminating the erotic effect of her narrative. Nevertheless, the use of sex as a transgressive gesture is a powerful strategy, as powerful as the threatening "unreadability" of Narbikova's texts. Both aim to upset, to disorient the reader, thereby exposing the fragility of the commonplace, of the norm, embodied in the language we all use, and, possibly, in the lives we all lead.

Narbikova's work strives to be what Barthes has called "writerly prose"—a process of production in which "the reader becomes a producer, infinitely plural and open to the free play of signifiers and of difference, unconstrained by representative considerations, and transgressive of any desire for decidable, unified, totalized meaning."[61] At the center of this writerly prose we find the unpredictability, fluidity, and oppressive emptiness of existence seen through the eyes of a woman narrator, shaped in an unorthodox narrative by a woman author—a doubly subversive gesture in a writing that privileges the marginal over the norm.

The game Narbikova plays with the reader is governed by the rules of transgression, the theme is prohibition, and the result is a narrative that titillates at first, but ultimately numbs. The reader dies a little death, satiated and fulfilled until that time when the author finds yet another way to challenge the reader's solidified expectations. Narbikova's avant-gardist aim of disrupting the status quo, of arousing indignation and fear in some, curiosity and appreciation of her boldness in others, is, nevertheless, accomplished. The woman here does not want to be constrained by norms, reduced to a simplistic interpretation, or contained in the predictability of a traditional story line and language. She is at the center, a powerful manipulator and generator of meaning: referring to the patriarchs of Russian literature and history, but undercutting their importance by using them as empty signifiers; submitting to male desire, but confirming her ultimate control through violence directed toward males; absorbing the clichés of Soviet life, but playfully exposing their mythological underpinnings. The woman author plays freely, and the reader must join in the game.

The modernistic tendency to involve the readers in "the production of the text"—to play with them—can be observed, in different degrees, in all works of alternative literature discussed in the present work. Another shared feature of this fiction is its privileging of heterogeneity, marginality, transgression, the unconscious, eroticism, and excess over those strategies of writing commonly associated with the tradition of realism. Alternative literature declares a virtual war on mimesis, and the battleground is the medium of representation itself. Most alternative writers are the "thieves of language" who, through skillful imitation of discourses, offer an examination of how mythical consciousness operates, how certain commonly accepted truths become accepted as such, and how culture, through language, can shape perception and expression.

For many of these writers, the focus on writing and the imitation of discourses serve to articulate existential truths. For Ivanchenko, simulation is a key to demonstrating the unpredictability, fluidity and oppressive emptiness of existence. For Sadur and Petrushevskaia, the mimicking of the common woman's voice is a means of revealing the power of the instinct for survival and of exposing the strategies of resistance, which alone, after more than seventy years of the existence of the "people's state," are shown to direct the actions of their characters. For Kuraev, imitation is essential to underscore the impossibility of pinpointing the "final truth" about reality in any text, or of containing that reality in writing. For Tolstaya and Narbikova, the game with patterns of representation is a way to transgress norms, to escape simplistic interpretations, and to claim a writer's position as a powerful manipulator and generator of meaning. The fantastic reality of these texts is a result not so much of the devices of fantasy per se, as of a general uninhibited playfulness that generates new truths, new forms of expression, and thrusts marginality and novelty forward.

Narbikova's work, designed to transform old perceptions by imitation of clichéd languages and shocking descriptions of sexual acts, marks a new stage in Russian literature. Her focus on clichés allows Narbikova to demonstrate the loss of meaning inherent in the overuse and misuse of commonplaces of culture, and of Soviet culture in particular. At the same time, when language becomes the sole protagonist of fiction, when a plot is not much more than a story of a conflict between disembodied signifiers, playfully and openly arranged by an omnipotent author in a game of hide-and-seek, then there is nothing left for literature to do but to lapse into silence.

Representatives of the "steep phase," and Narbikova among them, belong to what Epstein so aptly termed "the last literature," not definable in terms of the category of time, the literature that "remains the last even if the flow of history is to be renewed thereafter."[62] It is "last" because of its makeup, its essential "beyondness," since it has no attachment to the image of this world and does not even attempt to imitate it.[63] The language and mythologies of the Soviet state are at the center of this literature, and by irreverently deconstructing this language, by showing the artifice of its mythologies, this Russian fiction of the early nineties bids a true farewell to Soviet literature and to the society that brought it into being.

Notes

1. For a brief discussion of all authors mentioned in this chapter in the context of sexuality and gender, see Costlow, Sandler, and Vowles, *Sexuality and the Body*, pp. 28–36; also Helena Goscilo, "Inscribing the Female Body in Women's Fiction: Cross-Gendered Passion à la Holbein," in Marianne Liljestrom et al., eds., *Gender Restructuring in Russian Studies* (Tampere, Finland: University of Tampere, 1993), pp. 73–86.

2. Catriona Kelly, *A History of Russian Women's Writing, 1820–1992* (Oxford: Oxford University Press, 1994), p. 372.

3. On the use of fantasy in women's writing, see Nancy Walker, *Feminist Alternatives: Irony and Fantasy in the Contemporary Novel by Women* (Jackson: University Press of Mississippi, 1990); Rae Beth Gordon, *Ornament, Fantasy, and Desire in Nineteenth-Century French Literature*, (Princeton: Princeton University Press, 1992); and Jean Wyatt, *Reconstructing Desire: the Role of the Unconscious in Women's Reading and Writing* (Chapel Hill: University of North Carolina Press, 1990).

4. For more on Petrushevskaia's style see Natalia Ivanova, "Bakhtin's Concept of the Grotesque and the Art of Petrushevskaia and Tolstaia," in Helena Goscilo, ed., *Fruits of Her Plume: Essays on Contemporary Russian Women's Culture* (Armonk, N.Y.: M. E. Sharpe, 1993), pp. 21–32; also in the same collection, Nicholas Zekulin, "Soviet Russian Women's Literature in the Early 1980s," pp. 33–58.

5. Petrushevskaia's first publications were "The Storyteller" ("Rasskazchitsa") and "The Story of Clarissa" ("Istoriia Klarissy") in *Avrora* in 1972. Only seven of Petrushevskaia's many stories written between 1963 and 1983 appeared in print. Her first published collection was *Bessmertnaia liubov': Rasskazy* (Moscow: Moskovskii Rabochii, 1988).

6. For more on the difficulty of Petrushevskaia's narratives see Josephine Woll, "The Minotaur in the Maze: On Liudmila Petrushevskaia," *World Literature Today* 1 (Winter 1993).

7. *Neva* 7 (1987): 85–87.

8. *Novyi mir* 1 (1988).

9. Liudmila Petrushevskaia, interview by author, Louisville, Ky., October 1989.

10. James C. Scott, *Domination and the Arts of Resistance: Hidden Transcripts* (Yale University Press, 1990), p. xii.

11. On Sadur's literary beginnings see T. Khoroshilova, "Zagadka Niny Sadur," *Komsomol'skaia pravda*, June 1, 1989. See also "Dramaturg iz kommunalki," *Sobesednik* 4 (1990): 14; Aleksandr Denisenko, "I rozy, i ved'miny slezki," *Sudarynia* 8 (May 28, 1991); and Vladimir Tuchkov, "Cherti, suki, kommunal'nye kozly," *Paritet*, 4 (1992): 8.

12. See more on Sadur's own brand of folklore and on her use of language in Serafina Roll, "The Death of Language and the Language of Death in Nina Sadur's 'Echai,'" *Russian Literature* 34 (1993): 187–206.

13. Nancy Armstrong and Leonard Tennenhouse, eds., *The Violence of Representation: Literature and the History of Violence* (London: Routledge, 1989), p. 4.

14. This is the point of view articulated in Teresa de Lauretis, "The Violence of Rhetoric: Considerations on Representation and Gender," in Armstrong and Tennenhouse, *Violence of Representation*, pp. 239–258.

15. Scott, *Domination and the Arts of Resistance*, pp. 2–28.

16. Nina Sadur, *Krasnyi paradiz*, in Svetlana Vasilenko, ed., *Novye Amazonki* (Moscow: Moskovskii Rabochii, 1991), pp. 255–274.

17. The cycle appeared in a collection of Russian women's fiction, Larisa Vaneeva, comp., *Nepomniashchiaia zla* (Moscow: Moskovskii Rabochii, 1990), pp. 217–248.

18. This story, according to the writer, is a fantastic rendition of Sadur's own experiences of living in a communal apartment. Nina Sadur, interview by author, June 20, 1991.

19. Scott, *Domination and the Arts of Resistance*, p. 144.

20. Pollution by violence is a concept that also operates in primitive societies. On the functions of violence in primitive societies see René Girard, *Violence and the Sacred* (Baltimore: Johns Hopkins University Press, 1977), esp. chap. 1, "Sacrifice."

21. Sadur's fantastic lies in the hesitation between real and unreal, when events described can be put in a rational scheme or attributed to the influence of magic. Voice "filtering" occurs when the narrated event is the result of several retellings by several characters. The technique of *skaz* underscores differences between the voices of the narrator and the implied author-reader. All these devices serve to distance the implied author and the reader from the narrator and to provide another barrier for the reader to penetrate. Ritualization occurs when certain commonly used objects unexpectedly become objects in performative acts of magic and certain common words or gestures are used in what appears like acts of magic.

22. Sadur, *Pronikshie*, pp. 235. The translation is mine.

23. A granddaughter of Alexei N. Tolstoi and a graduate of Leningrad State University, Tatiana Tolstaya is perhaps the best known representative of alternative literature in the West. She has been writing for about a decade, yet her publications are relatively few. Her first story, "On the Golden Porch" ("Na zolotom kryl'tse"), appeared in 1983, and the first collection of stories under the same title followed in 1987 and in 1989 (in translation). The second volume of Tolstaya's stories, which previously appeared in various journals in Russia, has been published in translation as *Sleepwalker in a Fog* (New York: Alfred A. Knopf, 1992).

24. See, for example, Lucy Hughes-Hallett, "Tatiana Tolstaya: *Sleepwaker in a Fog*," *Literary Review* 4 (1992); also Helena Goscilo's sketch of the writer in Helena Goscilo and Byron Lindsey, eds., *Glasnost: An Anthology of Literature under Gorbachev* (Ann Arbor: Ardis, 1990), pp. 465–466. On Tolstaya's use of banality and grotesque see Ivanova, "Bakhtin's Concept," and two articles in Helena

Goscilo, ed., *The Fruits of Her Plume: Essays on Contemporary Russian Women's Culture* (Armonk, N.Y.: M. E. Sharpe, 1993): Svetlana Boym, "The Poetics of Banality," pp. 59–84 and John Givens, "Reflections, Crooked Mirrors, Magic Theaters," pp. 251–268.

25. Goscilo and Lindsey, *Glasnost*, p. 466.

26. Coined by another prominent woman writer, I. Grekova, in "Rastochitel'nost' talanta," *Novyi mir* 3 (1988): 252–256.

27. Tatiana Tolstaya, *On the Golden Porch* (London: Virago, 1988), p. 21.

28. Ibid., p. 40.

29. Helena Goscilo, "Tolstajan Love as Surface Text," *SEEJ* 34.1 (Spring 1990): 42.

30. A version of this section appeared as "Games Women Play: The 'Erotic' Prose of Valeriia Narbikova," in Goscilo, *Fruits of Her Plume*, pp. 165–184.

31. Andrei Bitov, introduction to Valeriia Narbikova, "Ravnovesie sveta dnevnykh i nochnykh zvezd" (Equilibrium of diurnal and nocturnal stars), *Iunost'* 8 (1988): 15.

32. Urnov, "Plokhaia proza," p. 4.

33. Bitov, Introduction, p. 15.

34. Urnov, "Plokhaia proza," p. 4.

35. For Soviet assessments of Narbikova's work see also Chuprinin, "Drugaia proza," p. 4; Shcheglova, "V svoem krugu," p. 25; Viacheslav Kondrat'ev's remarks in "Sovetuem pochitat'," *Znamia* 1 (1990): 235–238; A. Vasilevskii, "Bespredel'," *Literaturnaia gazeta*, September 12, 1990, p. 4.

36. Suleiman, *Subversive Intent*, p. 43.

37. Valeriia Narbikova, "Dunovenie erosa: Beseda s Valeriei Narbikovoi (Elena Veselaia)," *Moskovskie novosti* 13 (April 1, 1990): 14. In the same interview Narbikova professes her fascination with emigré literature and lists Gogol', Vladimir Nabokov, and Fyodor Sologub among her most important literary influences.

38. Narbikova, "Ravnovesie."

39. In addition to the works I quote from in the body of this chapter, Narbikova's bibliography includes: "Probeg—pro beg," *Znamia* 5 (1990): 61–87; "Plan pervogo litsa: I vtorogo," in T. V. Del'sal', comp., *Vstrechnyi khod: Sbornik* (Moscow, 1989), pp. 119–156; "Okolo ekolo . . . ," in *Iunost'* 3 (1990): 10–25, published also in *Okolo Ekolo . . . povesti* (Moscow: Exlibris, 1992); "Velikoe knia . . . ," *Iunost'*, 12 (1991): 54–64. Her first written work, the novel *Skvoz' (Through)* was still unpublished at the time of my interview with the author in March 1991. The latter is perhaps the most sexually transgressive of all Narbikova's narratives.

40. Published as "Vidimost' nas" (what is chapter four of *Equilibrium* in book form, pp. 161–191), *Strelets* 3.63 (1989): 119–135.

41. Mikhail Epstein, "Iskusstvo avangarda i religioznoe soznanie," *Novyi mir* 12 (1989): 229.

42. Ibid., p. 235.

43. Elisabeth Sussman, "The Third Zone: Soviet 'Postmodern,'" in D. A. Ross, ed., *Between Spring and Summer: Soviet Conceptual Art in the Era of Late Communism* (Cambridge, Mass.: MIT Press, 1991), p. 64.

44. This is the point made in Elena Izumova, "Breaking All Barriers," *Ogonek*, July 1989.

45. Sussman, "Third Zone," p. 64.

46. Hal Foster, "Postmodernism: A Preface," in Hal Foster, ed. *The Anti-Aesthetic: Essays on Postmodern Culture* (Port Townsend, Wash.: Bay Press, 1983), pp. x–xi.; Sussman, p. 64.

47. Ibid., p. 65.

48. Ilya Kabakov, interview by Byron Lindsey, in *Novostroika/ New Structures: Culture in the Soviet Union Today,* ICA Documents 8 (London, 1989); quoted in Sussman, "Third Zone," p. 65.

49. Epstein, "Iskusstvo avangarda," p. 226.

50. Narbikova, *Equilibrium* (*Iunost'* version), p. 15. This and all subsequent translations from Narbikova are mine.

51. Narbikova, *Ad kak Da aD kak dA*, in Larisa Vaneeva, ed., *Ne pomniashchaia zla* (Moscow: Moskovskii Rabochii, 1990), p. 319.

52. Marietta Chudakova, "Put' k sebe. Literaturnaia situatsiia–89. Beseda korrespondenta LO Evgeniia Kanchukova s Mariettoi Chudakovoi," *Literaturnoe obozrenie* 1 (1990): 34.

53. Narbikova, *Ravnovesie*, p. 105.

54. Ibid., p. 140.

55. Narbikova, *Ad kak*, p. 321.

56. Vladimir Nabokov, *The Annotated Lolita* (New York: McGraw-Hill, 1970), p. 315.

57. Ibid.

58. Lucienne Frappier-Mazur, "Pornography and the Obscene in the Eighteenth Century," from a tape-recorded version of the paper delivered at the Conference on "The Invention of Pornography," University of Pennsylvania, October 4, 1991. My definition of the obscene word comes from Mazur as well.

59. Suleiman, *Subversive Intent*, p. 13.

60. Michel Foucault, *The History of Sexuality*, vol. 1, *An Introduction* (New York: Vintage Books, 1980), p. 84.

61. Barbara Johnson, "The Critical Difference: Barthes/Balzac," in Robert Con Davis, ed., *Contemporary Literary Criticism* (New York: Longman, 1986), p. 441.

62. Epstein, "After the Future," p. 411.

63. Ibid.

11

Conclusion

M AJOR CHANGES IN POST-STALINIST Soviet society led to the gradual disintegration of the cultural and political myths that are encoded in socialist realism and that supported that society's structures. The last decade of the Soviet Union witnessed the emergence of a new Russian literature that used the paradigms of Soviet culture and language as building blocks for qualitatively new literary works. In a gesture of self-examination and self-reinvigoration, prompted in part by the cataclysmic occurrences within society, literature began to feed on itself, recombining in its narrative the simulacra of its culture, and demonstrating in the process its own limitations and powers. The mythological underpinnings of the Soviet mentality were examined in painstaking detail, the language of Soviet society defamiliarized, and the absurdity of most commonly held beliefs exposed as such. Soviet culture was now perceived as an artificial construct, a scholarly dialect that could be learned, understood, and abandoned, since the society that brought forth this culture, and literature, was fast disappearing.

Although rooted in the first Thaw, the transformation of Soviet letters gained momentum in the seventies and eighties, prompted by the expansion of the limits of the permissible and by the desire of writers to contribute to the emerging dialogue with the state. Writers in the fantastic decade used utopian motifs and gestures of fantasy to couch their political, social, and personal concerns in an acceptable form. In the process of that examination a new mentality was emerging, a mentality that was able to accept the revelations of glasnost and to express directly its dissatisfaction with the bankrupt ideology of Communism.

Literature, like society itself, was shaped by the Soviet redistributive state, yet the distinctive relationship between the writer and the reader continued to enshrine the writer as both social prophet and moral conscience of the nation, guaranteeing a large and serious audience for his or her writings. That audience was dominated by the middle classes, the principal consumers of literature. Before the collapse of the Union, mainstream writers were both insulated from the market and virtually assured of an audience, as long as they spoke to the concerns of this "middle," the stratum to which they themselves belonged and whose feelings, anxieties, and desires they expressed.

In what has become a classical assessment of Soviet prose before the Thaw, Rufus Mathewson noted the absence there of several general themes present in the modern European novel. These include movement into the workings of consciousness, a central concern with authorial self, exploration of the sexual dimension of experience, an existentialist approach and posing of religious questions, the examination of mystery, and the problematic hero.[1] The Thaw was instrumental in moving Soviet fiction one step closer to the complex and rich literature of modernity. A continuous dialogue with the traditions and mentality underlying the aesthetics of socialist realism marked this transition. *Byt* prose and youth prose both explored human actions and emotions and portrayed "new Soviet people" as alienated and lost in their urban environment. Village prose focused on the unimaginable in socialist realism and rejected the portrayal of the village as a realized utopia. Science fiction of the Thaw approached the issue of alternative social practices and addressed the notion of coercive benevolence inherent in changing a stable social order. In the mid-seventies, fantastic fiction continued the process of self-revaluation, exploring the themes Mathewson considered essential for the entry into the world community of literatures. Soviet literature broadened its scope; its spatial and temporal limits expanded, and a variety of popular genres were incorporated into the mainstream novel. The artist's self became an object of investigation in the works of Bondarev, Kim, and Makanin. The workings of human consciousness and sexuality were investigated by Evdokimov, Anar, Makanin, and Kim. Aitmatov attempted to pose and answer religious questions. The examination of mystery became a central concern for the majority of Soviet writers of fantastic fiction.

Writers in the fantastic decade attempted to answer Andrei Sinyavsky's call for a literature "with hypothesis instead of a Purpose." At the same time their writing offered a proof of the sustaining power of the traditional. Fantastic fiction was both new and old, linked to the immediate social and cultural dilemmas of the day and steeped in the traditions of Russian fantastic literature. In a society where all aspects of creative endeavor were controlled by censorship, fantasy and utopian dreaming served as the most convenient, relatively safe, and easily accessible vehicle for the expression of the public's dissatisfaction with the regime. Under the guise of myth and legend, writers articulated such important issues as the disappearance of tradition and the search for a national identity, the fear of nuclear war and of ecological catastrophe, and the loss of moral foundations in contemporary Soviet life.

Even though the literature of the fantastic decade made giant strides toward an accommodation of the themes and techniques of modern letters, it did not divorce itself completely from the traditions of Realism, and of socialist realism in particular. The surface features of the modern novel, its focus on human consciousness, sexuality, existential and religious issues, and on the alienation of its protagonist, appeared in most fantastic fiction in the context of a palpable moralistic scheme. Monosemy, univocity of purpose, clarity and coherence of presentation still characterized most of fiction written in the late Brezhnev era. Fantastic devices were employed as an embellishment on a mimetic mode of writing that had clear affinities with the canon of socialist realism. It is only in alternative writing that we observe earnest attempts to revalue the very premises of socialist realistic writing—its purported ability to reflect reality faithfully, its monological character and square protagonists. Here the ideas of an aesthetic underground are first given their expression, and pluralistic discourse replaces the certitudes of *zakonomernost'*.

Experimentation with literary language, probing of the very notion of mimesis, "baring" of the mythmaking propensity of Soviet culture, and examination of its utopian impulse in fantastic prose prepared the ground for the appearance and enthusiastic reception of glasnost literature. Innovations in glasnost literature did not arrive miraculously as a result of a transformation in the political situation but originated in the preceding period, when the "rigid scheme of the 'classic' plot was broken, the former balance between reality and fantasy upset, the arsenal of representational resources broadened indefinitely, and entire continents of virgin lands in language cultivated [by Soviet writers]."2 Yet glasnost did mark a definite change of course for Soviet society and for its literature. As a result of the newly found openness in expression, the mythical History of the Soviet Union was replaced by history, a faithful if horrific account of what really happened in the country. The grand Purpose immortalized in socialist realism lost its monopoly on culture, and the myths nurturing the idea of the Great Society were shown to be illusory.3

In alternative fiction of glasnost and post-Gorbachev era, Soviet culture appears as a text, and writers recombine its pieces in new and intricate arrangements. Alternative literature engages ideological totalities of utopian thinking in an attempt to "open a neutral space that permits the emergence of other possible patterns of social practice."[4] At the same time, alternative writing insists on its apolitical stance, pointing, through transgressivity of its representational techniques and themes, to its disconnectedness from the real world. With this literature we enter "a region of dissipating structure and evaporating reality." This is the literature that "has found itself in the beyond—without a top or a bottom, without a left or a right— any kind of directedness 'for' or 'against' is alien [to it]."[5] It is the literature of the end.

This book has centered on the cracking and final demolition of the mythology of the Great Society, from the beginning of that process in the literature of the first Thaw to its conclusion, after the fall of the Soviet Union. The roots of change go back to the fifties and sixties, when the first hesitant steps away from the literature of Purpose were first made. In the fantastic decade, the dialogue with the state continued in the language of fantasy, through prosthetic memories of an unattainable past in legends, examination of alternative patterns of social practice in science fiction plots, and through the subversion of the socialist realist view of history and the world as knowable and hierarchical.

Under glasnost, publicists, still firmly grounded in the either-or mentality of Stalinist and post-Stalinist culture, sought to find a new set of mythological anchors to replace the now discredited myths of Soviet society. Alternative writers, on the other hand, focused on the mythological impulse itself, the ability of myths to manipulate meaning to serve ideological needs of the moment, showing in the process the overall arbitrariness of cultural constructs, as well as their irrelevance to fluid, uncontainable, fantastic reality. It is only now that we can say that Russian letters has finally gained entrance into the literature of modernity—by divorcing itself from the certitudes of realism, by ironically distancing itself from its own culture, by deconstructing the language of Soviet society, and by celebrating the end of its literature.

Notes

1. Mathewson, "The Novel in Russia and the West," pp. 9–10.

2. Valentin Luk'ianin, "Ustarevshie formuly i nezyblemost' suti," *Literaturnaia gazeta*, April 1, 1987, p. 2. The translation is mine.

3. For an early and highly perceptive assessment of the changes in Soviet literature under perestroika see Donald Fanger, "The Two Perestroikas," in *New Republic*, October 22, 1989, pp. 26–30.

4. Clowes, *Russian Experimental Fiction*, p. 5. See also in the same mono-graph, "Play with Closure in Petrushevskaia's 'The New Robinsons' and Kabakov's 'The Deserter,'" pp. 198–207. Here Clowes argues convincingly: "Glasnost is a time of 'pluralist' debate: it is deeply meta-utopian in that many ideologies—utopian, anti-utopian, and counterutopian—are being subjected to needed critique, but on the relatively neutral ground of journal pages, literary fiction, and unprecedented peaceful street demonstrations. And yet it is a time of deep skepticism and distrust of all rhetoric, all grand schemes" (p. 206).

5. Epstein, "After the Future," pp. 411–412.

Selected Bibliography

Adamovich, Ales'. 1987. "Urok pravdy." *Literaturnaia gazeta* (March 19): 4.
Aitmatov, Chingiz. 1980. "I dol'she veka dlit'sia den'." *Novyi mir* 11.
_____. 1986. "Plakha." *Novyi mir* 6,8,9.
_____. 1986. "Tsena-zhizn'." *Literaturnaia gazeta* (August 13): 4.
Aleksin, Anatolii. 1983. "Kak zhe ty mog?: 'Vybor' Iuriia Bondareva na stsene Malogo teatra." *Komsomol'skaia pravda* 4 (April 15).
Anar. 1978. "Kontakt." *Druzhba narodov* 12.
Anninskii, Lev. 1978. "Zhazhdu realizma!" *Literaturnaia gazeta* 4 (March 1).
_____. 1980. "Mne by vashi zaboty!" *Literaturnoe obozrenie* 5: 43–45.
_____. 1986. "Struktura labirinta." *Znamia* 12: 218–226.
Apter, T. E. 1982. *Fantasy Literature: An Approach to Reality*. Bloomington: Indiana University Press.
Arkhangel'skii, Aleksandr. 1991. *U paradnogo pod'ezda: Literatura i kul'turnye situatsii perioda glasnosti (1987–1990)*. Moscow: Sovetskii Pisatel'.
Armstrong, Nancy, and Leonard Tennenhouse, eds. 1989. *The Violence of Representation: Literature and the History of Violence*. London: Routledge.
Astaf'ev, Viktor. 1986. "Pechal'nyi detektiv." *Oktiabr'* 1.
Avins, Carol. 1988. "The Failure of Perestroika in Aitmatov's *The Executioner's Block*." *Studies in Comparative Communism* 21.3/4: 255–261.
Bakhtin, Mikhail. 1981. *The Dialogic Imagination: Four Essays*. Ed. Michael Holquist. Austin: University of Texas Press.
Baranskaia, Natalia. 1968. "Provody." *Novyi mir* 5.
Barratt, Andrew. 1987. *Between Two Worlds: A Critical Introduction to* The Master and Margarita. Oxford: Clarendon Press.
Beitz, W., H. Conrad, D. Kassek, and P. Rollberg. 1987. "Prosa und Dramatik der Generation der 'Vierzigjährigen.'" *Weimarer Beitrage* 33.10: 1701.
Belaia, Galina. 1978. "Tsennostnyi tsentr." *Voprosy literatury* 2: 27–32.
_____. 1985. "O prirode eksperimenta: K sporam o khudozhestvennykh poiskakh v sovremennoi literature." *Literaturnoe obozrenie* 7: 21–26.
_____. 1986. "Vse vperedi." *Nash sovremennik* 8
_____. 1987. "Pereput'e." *Voprosy literatury* 12: 75–103.
_____. 1988. "In the Name of Common Culture." *Soviet Literature* 9: 132–138.
_____. 1990. "Ugrozhaiushchaya real'nost.'" *Voprosy literatury* 4: 3–38.
Belov, Vasilii. 1969. "Bukhtiny vologodskie." *Novyi mir* 8.
Bethea, David M. 1989. *The Shape of Apocalypse in Modern Russian Fiction*. Princeton: Princeton University Press.
Bialer, Seweryn. 1980. *Stalin's Successors: Leadership Stability, and Change in the Soviet Union*. Cambridge: Cambridge University Press.

Bitov, Andrei. 1988. Introduction to "Ravnovesie sveta dnevnykh i nochnykh zvezd," by Valeriia Narbikova. *Iunost'* 8: 15.

Bocharov, A. 1982. *Beskonechnost' poiska.* Moscow: Sovetskii Pisatel'.

_____. 1985. "Kak slovo nashe otzovetsia?" *Voprosy literatury* 11: 115–154.

Bondarenko, Vladimir. 1981. "Otchuzhdenie." *Don* 7: 149–153.

_____. 1985. "Avtoportret pokoleniia." *Voprosy literatury* 11: 79–113.

Bondarev, Iurii. 1981. *Vybor.* Moscow: Molodaia Gvardiia.

_____. 1985. *Igra.* Moscow: Molodaia Gvardiia.

Boym, Svetlana. 1993. "The Poetics of Banality." In *Fruits of Her Plume: Essays on Contemporary Russian Women's Culture,* ed. Helena Goscilo, 59–84. Armonk, N.Y.: M. E. Sharpe.

Brandis, Evgenii. 1979. "Gorizonty fantastiki." *Neva* 10: 171–181.

_____. 1981. "Fantastika i novoe videnie mira." *Zvezda* 8: 41–49.

Brine, Jenny, Maureen Perrie, and Andrew Sutton, eds., 1981. *Home, School and Leisure in the Soviet Union.* London: Allen and Unwin.

Britikov, A. F. 1970. *Russkii Sovetskii nauchno-fantasticheskii roman.* Leningrad: Nauka.

_____. 1971. *Zhanrovo-stilevye iskaniia sovremennoi prozy.* Moscow.

_____. 1980. "Problemy izucheniia nauchnoi fantastiki." *Russkaia Literatura* 1: 193–202.

Brooks, Jeffrey. 1985. *When Russian Learned to Read: Literacy and Popular Literature, 1861–1917.* Princeton: Princeton University Press.

Brown, Deming. 1993. *The Last Years of Soviet Russian Literature: Prose Fiction, 1975–1991.* Cambridge: Cambridge University Press.

Brown, Edward J. 1982. *Russian Literature since Revolution.* Rev. ed. Cambridge, Mass.: Harvard University Press.

_____. 1988. "Trifonov: The Historian as Artist." In *Soviet Society and Culture. Essays in Honor of Vera S. Dunham,* ed. Terry L. Thompson and Richard Sheldon, 109–123. Boulder: Westview Press.

Brudny, Yitzhak, M. 1988. "Between Liberalism and Nationalism: The Case of Sergei Zalygin." *Studies in Comparative Communism* 21.3/4: 331–340.

Buckley, Mary. 1993. *Redefining Russian Society and Polity.* Boulder: Westview Press.

Busch, R. L. 1989. "The Contexts of Bulgakov's Master and Margarita." In *Aspects of Modern Russian Literature: Selected Papers of the Third World Congress for Soviet and East European Studies,* ed. Arnold McMillin, 55–78. Columbus, Ohio: Slavica Publishers.

Bushnell, John. 1980. "The 'New Soviet Man' Turns Pessimist." In *The Soviet Union since Stalin,* ed. Stephen F. Cohen, Alexander Rabinowitch, and Robert Sharlet, 179–199. Bloomington: Indiana University Press.

_____. 1988. "A Popular Reading of Bulgakov: Explication des Graffiti." *Slavic Review* 47.3: 502–511.

_____. 1990. *Moscow Graffiti: Language and Subculture.* Boston: Unwin Hyman.

Byrnes, Robert F., ed. 1983. *After Brezhnev: Sources of Soviet Conduct in the 1980s.* Bloomington: Indiana University Press.

Chanady, Amaryll Beatrice. 1985. *Magical Realism and the Fantastic: Resolved versus Unresolved Antinomy.* New York: Garland.

Chernysheva, T. 1972. *V mire mechty i privideniia: Nauchnaia fantastika, ee problemy i khudozhestvennye vozmozhnosti.* Kiev: Naukova Dumka.

———. 1975. "Potrebnost' v udivitiel'nom i priroda fantastiki." *Voprosy literatury* 5: 211–232.

Chertkov, A. 1990. "Fenziny, ili samizdat fantastiki." *Sovetskaia bibliografiia* 1: 114–122.

Chudakova, Marietta. 1990. "Put' k sebe. Literaturnaia situatsiia–89. Beseda korrespondenta LO Evgeniia Kanchukova s Mariettoi Chudakovoi." *Literaturnoe obozrenie* 1: 34.

Chuprinin, Sergei. 1989. "Drugaia proza." *Literaturnaia gazeta* (February 8): 4.

———. 1989. "Predvest'e." *Znamia* 1: 210–224.

Clark, Katerina. 1981. *The Soviet Novel: History as Ritual.* Chicago: University of Chicago Press.

———. 1983. Introduction to *The Day Lasts More than a Hundred Years,* by Chingiz Aitmatov. Bloomington: Indiana University Press.

———. 1988. "Rethinking the Past and the Current Thaw: Introduction." *Studies in Comparative Communism* 21.3/4: 241–253.

Clowes, Edith W. 1993. *Russian Experimental Fiction: Resisting Ideology After Utopia.* Princeton: Princeton University Press.

Cohen, Stephen F., Alexander Rabinowitch, and Robert Sharlet, eds. 1980. *The Soviet Union Since Stalin.* Bloomington: Indiana University Press.

Colton, Timothy. 1986. *The Dilemma of Reform in the Soviet Union.* Rev ed. New York: Council on Foreign Relations.

Condee, Nancy, and Vladimir Padunov. 1988. "The Frontiers of Soviet Culture: Reaching the Limits?" *Harriman Institute Forum* 5.

Cook, Linda J. 1993. *The Soviet Social Contract and Why It Failed: Welfare Policy and Workers' Politics from Brezhnev to Yeltsin.* Cambridge, Mass.: Harvard University Press.

Cornwell, Neil. 1990. *The Literary Fantastic: From Gothic to Postmodernism.* New York: Harvester Wheatsheaf.

Costlow, Jane T., Stephanie Sandler, and Judith Vowles, eds. 1993. *Sexuality and the Body in Russian Culture.* Stanford: Stanford University Press.

Dark, Oleg. 1993. "Razoblachennyi Zuev, ili Apologiia grafomana." *Literaturnaia gazeta* (June 3): 4.

Davis, Robert Con, ed. 1986. *Contemporary Literary Criticism: Modernism Through Poststructuralism.* New York: Longman.

Dumbadze, Nodar. 1979. *Zakon vechnosti.* Tbilisi: Merani.

Dunham, Vera S. 1976. *In Stalin's Time: Middle-Class Values in Soviet Fiction.* Cambridge: Cambridge University Press.

Dunlop, John B. "The Contemporary Russian Nationalist Spectrum." *RLRB*, special ed. (December 19): 7.

Easter, Gerald M., and Janet E. Mitchell. 1989. "Cultural Reform in the Soviet Union." In *Toward a More Civil Society? The USSR Under Mikhail Sergeevich Gorbachev,* ed. William Green Miller, 79–119. New York: Harper and Row.

Edwards, T.R.N. 1982. *Three Russian Writers and the Irrational: Zamyatin, Pil'nyak, and Bulgakov.* Cambridge: Cambridge University Press.

Efremov, Ivan. 1958. *Tumannost' Andromedy.* Moscow: Molodaia Gvardiia.

Eklof, Ben. 1989. *Soviet Briefing: Gorbachev and the Reform Period.* Boulder: Westview Press.

Eliade, Mircea. 1961. *The Sacred and the Profane: The Nature of Religion.* New York: Harper and Row.

Epstein, Mikhail. 1989. "Iskusstvo avangarda i religioznoe soznanie." *Novyi mir* 12.

_____. 1991. "After the Future: On the New Consciousness in Literature." *South Atlantic Quarterly* 90.2: 409–444.

Epstein, Mikhail, and E. Iukina. 1981. "Mir i chelovek." *Novyi mir* 4: 236–247.

Ermolaev, Herman. 1989. "The Theme of Terrorism in *Starik.*" In *Aspects of Modern Russian and Czech Literature: Selected Papers of the Third World Congress for Soviet and East European Studies,* ed. Arnold McMillin, 96–109. Columbus, Ohio: Slavica Publishers.

Erofeev, Viktor. 1990. "Pominki po sovetskoi literature." *Literaturnaia gazeta* (July 4): 8.

_____. 1991. *Zhizn's idiotom.* Moscow: SP "Interbruk."

Evdokimov, Nikolai. 1983. *Izbrannye proizvedeniia v dukh tomakh.* Moscow: Khudozhestvennaia literatura.

_____. 1987. "Trizhdy Velichaishii, ili Povestvovanie o byvshem iz nebyvshego." *Druzhba narodov* 7, 8, 9.

Evtushenko, Evgenii. 1982. *Iagodnye mesta.* Moscow: Sovetskii Pisatel'.

_____. 1985. "Fuku." *Novyi mir* 9: 30–58.

Foster, Hal, ed. 1983. *The Anti-Aesthetic: Essays on Postmodern Culture.* Port Townsend, Wash.: Bay Press.

Foucault, Michel. 1980. *The History of Sexuality.* Vol 1., *An Introduction* New York: Vintage Books.

Franz, Norbert. 1988. *Moskauer Mordgeschichten: Der Russisch-Sowjetische Krimi 1953–1983.* Mainz: Liber.

Gasparov, B. 1978. "Iz nabliudenii nad motivnoi strukturoi romana M. A. Bulgakova 'Master and Margarita.'" *Slavica Hierosolymitana* 3: 198–251.

Geller, Mikhail. 1982. *Andrei Platonov v poiskakh schast'ia.* Paris: YMCA Press.

Gillespie, David. 1986. *Valentin Rasputin and Soviet Russian Village Prose.* London: Modern Humanities Research Association.

_____. 1992. *Iurii Trifonov: Unity Through Time.* Cambridge: Cambridge University Press.

Girard, René. 1977. *Violence and the Sacred.* Baltimore: Johns Hopkins University Press.

Givens, John. 1993. "Reflections, Crooked Mirrors, Magic Theaters." In *Fruits of Her Plume,* ed. Helena Goscilo, 251–268. Armonk, N.Y.: M. E. Sharpe.

Gordon, Rae Beth. 1992. *Ornament, Fantasy, and Desire in Nineteenth-Century French Literature.* Princeton: Princeton University Press.

Goscilo, Helena. 1990. "Tolstajan Love as Surface Text." *SEEJ* 34.1: 40–52.

_____. 1993. "Inscribing the Female Body in Women's Fiction: Cross-Gendered Passion à la Holbein." In *Gender Restructuring in Russian Studies,* ed. Marianne Liljestrom, Eila Mantysaari, and Arja Rosenholm, 73–86. Conference Papers, Helsinki, 1992. Tampere, Finland: University of Tampere.

_____, ed. 1993. *Fruits of Her Plume: Essays on Contemporary Russian Women's Culture.* Armonk, N.Y.: M. E. Sharpe.

Goscilo, Helena, and Byron Lindsey, eds. 1990. *Glasnost: An Anthology of Literature under Gorbachev.* Ann Arbor: Ardis.

Green, Barbara B. 1994. *The Dynamics of Russian Politics: A Short History.* Westport, Conn.: Praeger.

Grekova, Irina [Elena Venttsel']. 1965. "Letom v gorode." *Novyi mir* 4.

_____. 1988. "Rastochitel'nost' talanta." *Novyi mir* 3: 252–256.

Hammer, Darrell P. 1988. "Glasnost' and 'The Russian Idea.'" *RLRB* December.

Hayward, Max, and Edward L. Crowley, eds. 1964. *Soviet Literature in the Sixties: An International Symposium.* New York: Praeger.

Hoisington, Sona. 1981. "Fairy-tale Elements in Bulgakov's *The Master and Margarita.*" *SEEJ* 25.2: 44–55.

Hosking, Geoffrey. 1980. *Beyond Socialist Realism: Soviet Fiction since Ivan Denisovich.* New York: Holmes and Meier.

Hume, Kathryn. 1984. *Fantasy and Mimesis: Responses to Reality in Western Literature.* New York: Methuen.

Hutcheon, Linda. 1984. *Narcissistic Narrative: The Metafictional Paradox.* New York: Methuen.

Idashkin, Iurii. 1983. *Grani talanta: O tvorchestve Iuriia Bondareva.* Moscow: Khudozhestvennaia literatura.

Il'ina, Natal'ia, and Arkadii Adamov. 1975. "Detective Novels: A Game and Life." *Soviet Literature* 3: 142–150.

Iukina, Elena. 1984. "Dostoinstvo cheloveka." *Novyi mir* 12: 245–248.

Ivanchenko, Aleksandr. 1986. *Iabloko na snegu.* Moscow: Sovetskii pisatel'.

_____. 1988. "Tekhnika bezopasnosti I." *Ural* 1: 64–90.

_____. 1990. *Avtoportret s dogom.* Sverdlovsk: Sredne-Ural'skoe Knizhnoe Izdatelstvo.

Ivanova, Natal'ia. 1983. "Vol'noe dykhanie." *Voprosy literatury* 3: 179–214.

_____. 1987. "Illiuziia obreteniia." *Literaturnaia gazeta* (April 1): 4.

_____. 1987. "Ispytanie pravdoi." *Znamya* 1: 198–220; 1988. "Trial by Truth" (English trans.). *Soviet Studies in Literature* (Summer): 5–57.

_____. 1988. *Tochka zreniia: O proze poslednikh let.* Moscow: Sovetskii pisatel'.

_____. 1988. "Zhurnaly v fokuse mnenii." *Literaturnoe obozrenie* 4: 97–100.

_____. 1993. "Bakhtin's Concept of the Grotesque and the Art of Petrushevskaia and Tolstaia." In *Fruits of Her Plume: Essays on Contemporary Russian Women's Culture,* ed. Helena Goscilo, 21–32. Armonk, N.Y.: M. E. Sharpe.

Ivasheva, V. 1976. "O granitsakh poniatii." *Literaturnoe obozrenie* 1: 72–75.

Jackson, Rosemary. 1981. *Fantasy: The Literature of Subversion.* London: Methuen.

Jameson, Fredric. 1971. *Marxism and Form: Twentieth-Century Dialectical Theories of Literature.* Princeton: Princeton University Press.

Johnson, Barbara. 1986. "The Critical Difference: Barthes/Balzac." In *Contemporary Literary Criticism,* ed. Robert Con Davis, ed., 439–446. New York: Longman.

Joravsky, David. 1989. *Russian Psychology: A Critical History.* Oxford: Basil Blackwell.

Kamianov, V. 1988. "Zadacha na slozhenie." *Novyi mir* 3: 255–259.

Kamyshev, Vitalii. 1989. "Beskonechnost' sud'by: Zametki o proze Anatoliia Kima," *Dal'nii Vostok* 6.

Karpov, Anatolii. 1987. "Preodolenie ochevidnosti, ili real'noe v irreal'nom." *Literaturnaia gazeta* (November 18): 4.

Karyakin, Yurii. 1987. "Stoit li nastupat' na grabli?" *Znamya* 9: 200–224.

Kazintsev, Aleksandr. 1983. "Igra na ponizhenie." *Literaturnoe obozrenie* 10: 29–32.

Kelly, Catriona. 1994. *A History of Russian Women's Writing, 1820–1992.* Oxford: Clarendon Press.

Kim, Anatolii. 1980. "Lotos." *Druzhba narodov* 8.

———. 1981. *Nefritovyi poias.* Moscow: Molodaia Gvardiia.

———. 1984. *Belka.* Moscow: Sovetskii Pisatel'.

Kireev, Ruslan. 1987. "Obretenie cherez utratu." *Literaturnaia gazeta* (April 1): 4.

Klitko, Anatolii. 1983. "Geroi i ego zhiznennaia pozitsiia." *Literaturnaia Rossiia* (January 14): 8.

Koehler, Ludmila. 1979. *N. F. Fedorov: The Philosophy of Action.* Pittsburgh: Institute for the Human Sciences.

Kolchevska, Natasha. 1988. "White Garments: Retrieving the Past Through Science and Literature." *Studies in Comparative Communism* 21.3/4: 275–282.

Kondrat'ev, Viacheslav. 1990. "Sovetuem pochitat'." *Znamia* 1: 235–238.

Koniaev, Nikolai. 1983. "Vtoraia zhizn' Petra Kornilova." *Zvezda* 7: 199–201.

Korol'kov, Aleksandr. 1986. "Zrelost' zrelosti (Filosofskii roman S.P. Zalygina)." *Sever* 5: 107–113.

Kozhinov, V. 1987. "My meniaemsia? . . . " *Nash sovremennik* 10: 160–174.

Kozlov, V., A. 1983. *Kul'turnaia revoliutsiia i krest'ianstvo, 1921–1927.* Moscow: Nauka.

Krasnov, Vladislav. 1991. *Russia Beyond Communism: A Chronicle of National Rebirth.* Boulder: Westview Press.

Kuraev, Mikhail. 1987. "Kapitan Dikshtein: Fantasticheskoe povestvovanie." *Novyi mir* 9.

———. 1989. "Nochnoi dozor: Noktiurn na dva golosa pri uchastii strelka VOKhR tov. Polubolotova." *Novyi mir* 12.

———. 1990. "Captain Dikshtein: A Fantastic Narrative." In *Glasnost: An Anthology of Russian Literature Under Gorbachev,* ed. Helena Goscilo and Byron Lindsey, 59–185. Ann Arbor: Ardis.

Kuritsyn, Viacheslav. 1992. "Postmodernizm: Novaia pervobytnaia kul'tura." *Novyi mir* 2: 225–236.

Kustanovich, Konstantin. 1991. "Monologue of the Anti-Hero: Trifonov and the Prose of the Last Decade." *Slavic Review* 1 (Winter): 978–988.

LaCapra, Dominick. 1985. *History and Criticism.* Ithaca: Cornell University Press.

Lakshin, Vladimir. 1981. "O dome i o mire." *Literaturnoe obozrenie* 9: 38–43.

———. 1989. "Mir Mikhaila Bulgakova." *Literaturnoe obozrenie* 11: 17–27.

Lane, David. 1985. *Soviet Economy and Society.* New York: New York University Press.

Lanshchikov, A. 1984. "Nameki ili metafory?" *Literaturnaia gazeta* (June 6): 5.

Lapidus, Gail W. 1983. "Social Trends," in *After Brezhnev,* ed. Robert F. Byrnes, 186–249. Bloomington: Indiana University Press.

———. 1988. *Gorbachev's Reforms: Redefining the Relationship of State and Society.* Washington, D.C.: Wilson Center, Kennan Institute for Advanced Russian Studies.

Latynina, Alla. 1979. "Forma dlia mysli?" *Literaturnoe obozrenie* 7: 55–58.

———. 1982. "Beg v zazerkal'e." Literaturnoe obozrenie 9: 22–26.

———. 1986. "Tsep' chelovecheskoi pamiati." *Oktiabr'* 5: 203–208.

Latynina, Alla, and Vadim Kozhinov. 1986. "Paradoksy romana ili paradoksy vospriiatiia?" *Literaturnaia gazeta* (October 15): 4.

Lauretis, Teresa de. 1989. "The Violence of Rhetoric: Considerations on Representation and Gender." In *The Violence of Representation,* ed. Nancy Armstrong and Leonard Tennenhouse, 239–258. London: Routledge.

Lévi-Strauss, Claude. 1963. *Structural Anthropology.* New York: Basic Books.

Levinson, A. G. 1987. "Starye knigi, novye chitateli." *Sotsiologicheskie issledovaniia* 3: 43–49.

Liapunov, B. V. 1975. *V mire fantastiki: Obzor nauchno-fantasticheskoi i fantasticheskoi literatury.* 2d ed. Moscow: Kniga.

Likhachev, D. S. 1981. *Zametki o russkom.* Moscow: Sovetskaia Rossiia.

Liljestrom, Marianne, Eila Mantysaari, and Arja Rosenholm, eds. 1993. *Gender Restructuring in Russian Studies.* Tampere, Finland: University of Tampere.

Lipovetskii, Mark. 1989. "Svobody chernaya rabota." *Voprosy literatury* 9: 3–45.

———. 1991. "Zakon krutizny." *Voprosy literatury* 12: 3–36.

———. 1992. "Patogenez i lechenie glukhonemoty: Poety i postmodernizm." *Novyi mir* 7: 213–223.

Lukashevich, Stephen. 1977. *N. F. Fedorov (1828–1903): A Study in Russian Eupsychian and Utopian Thought.* Newark: University of Delaware Press. London: Associated University Press.

Lykoshin, Sergei. 1981. "Vybor pokoleniia." *Don* 7: 154–157.

Maguire, Robert. 1968. *Red Virgin Soil: Soviet Literature in the 1920s.* Princeton: Princeton University Press.

Makanin, Vladimir. 1982. *Golosa.* Moscow: Sovetskaia Rossiia.

———. 1987. "Otstavshii." *Znamia* 9.

Markov, Georgii. 1981. "Sovetskaia literatura v bor'be za kommunizm i ee zadachi v svete reshenii XXV-go s"ezda KPSS." Doklad pervogo sekretaria pravleniia Soiuza pisatelei SSSR G.M. Markova. *Literaturnaia gazeta* 27 (July 1): 2.

Marsh, Rosalind, J. 1986. *Soviet Fiction Since Stalin: Science, Politics and Literature.* Totowa, N.J.: Barnes and Noble.

Mathewson, Rufus. 1964. "The Novel in Russia and the West." In *Soviet Literature in the Sixties: An International Symposium,* eds. Max Hayward and Edward L. Crowley. New York: Frederick A. Praeger.

McGuire, Patrick, L. 1985. *Red Stars: Political Aspects of Soviet Science Fiction.* Ann Arbor: UMI Research Press.

McLaughlin, Sigrid. 1988. "A Moment in the History of Consciousness of the Soviet Intelligentsia: Trifonov's Novel Disappearance." *Studies in Comparative Communism* 21.3/4: 303–312.

Mikhailov, Alexandr. 1981. "Taina dushi." *Literaturnaia ucheba* 5: 127–137.

_____. 1986. "Stereotip ili kharakter?" *Literaturnaia Rossiia* 13 (March 28): 17.

Mikhailova, L. 1983. "Fakt v zerkale voobrazheniia." *Literaturnoe obozrenie* 6: 9–14.

Miller, Arthur H., William M. Reisinger, and Vicki L. Hesli, eds. 1993. *Public Opinion and Regime Change: The New Politics of Post-Soviet Societies.* Boulder: Westview Press.

Miller, William Green, ed., 1989. *Toward a More Civil Society? The USSR Under Mikhail Sergeevich Gorbachev.* New York: Harper and Row.

Morson, Gary, Saul. 1981. *The Boundaries of Genre: Dostoyevsky's Diary of a Writer and the Traditions of Literary Utopia.* Evanston: Northwestern University Press.

Mozur, Joseph. 1987. *Doffing "Mankurt's Cap": Chingiz Aitmatov's* The Day Lasts More than a Hundred Years *and the Turkic National Heritage. Carl Beck Papers in Russian and East European Studies,* no. 605. Pittsburgh: University of Pittsburgh Center for Russian and East European Studies.

Murikov, Gennadii. 1986. "Poedinok s sud'boi." *Zvezda* 5: 191–200.

Nabokov, Vladimir. 1970. *The Annotated Lolita.* New York: McGraw-Hill.

_____. 1981. *Strong Opinions.* New York: McGraw-Hill.

Narbikova, Valeriia. 1989. "Plan pervogo litsa: I vtorogo." In *Vstrechnyi khod: Sbornik,* comp. T. V. Del'sal', 119–156. Moscow.

_____. 1989. "Vidimost' nas." *Strelets* 3.63: 119–135.

_____. 1990 "Ad kak Da aD kak dA" In *Ne pomniashchaia zla,* ed. Larisa Vaneeva. Moscow: Moskovskii Rabochii.

_____. 1990. "Probeg—pro beg." *Znamia* 5: 61–87.

_____. 1990. *Ravnovesie sveta dnevnykh i nochnykh zvezd.* Moscow: Vsesoiuznyi molodezhnyi knizhnyi tsentr.

_____. 1991. "Velikoe knia . . . " *Iunost'* 12: 54–64.

_____. 1992. "Okolo ekolo . . . " *Iunost'* 3: 10–25.

_____. 1992 *Okolo Ekolo . . . povesti.* Moscow: Exlibris.

Natov, Nadine. 1978. "Structural and Topological Ambivalence of Bulgakov's Novels Interpreted Against the Background of Baxtin's theory of 'Grotesque Realism' and Carnivalization." In *American Contributions to the Eighth International Congress of Slavists,* 536–549. Columbus, Ohio: Slavica Publishers.

Nerler, Pavel. 1982. "Otrazhenie istiny: Molodye kritiki obsuzhdaiut." *Literaturnoe obozrenie* 3: 41–43.

Nikolaev, P. 1983. "Trudnoe vremia: Liudi, sud'by." *Literaturnaia gazeta* (March 30): 4.

Novikov, Vladimir. 1985. "Pod sudom vechnosti." *Literaturnaia gazeta* (February 13): 4.

Nudelman, Rafail. 1989. "Soviet SF and the Ideology of Soviet Society." *Science Fiction Studies* 16, pt. 1 (March): 39–48.

Nuikin, A. 1982. "Ot mozaiki k panorame." *Literaturnoe obozrenie* 12: 50–53.

_____. 1987. "Novoe bogoiskatel'stvo i starye dogmy." *Novyi mir* 4: 245–259.

Orlov, Vladimir. 1980. "Al'tist Danilov." *Novyi mir* 2, 3, 4.

_____. 1981. *Al'tist Danilov.* Moscow: Sovetskii pisatel'.

Ospovat, Lev. 1981. "Oboianie mifa, besstrashie smekha: Zametki o novom latinoamerikanskom romane semidesiatykh godov." *Literaturnoe obozrenie* 12.

Ostriker, Alicia. 1985. "The Thieves of Language: Women Poets and Revisionist Mythmaking." In *The New Feminist Criticism: Essays on Women, Literature, and Theory,* ed. Elaine Showalter, 314–338. New York: Pantheon.

Ovcharenko, Aleksandr. 1981. "Novyi uroven' khudozhestvennogo myshleniia." *Novyi mir* 6: 231–253.

Panchenko, I. 1983. "Voproshaia proshloe—zaglianut' v budushchee." *Voprosy literatury* 6: 83–108.

Pankin, Boris. 1982. "Dobrota, nedobrota." *Druzhba narodov* 9: 249–254.

Paperno, Irina. 1988. *Chernyshevsky and the Age of Realism: A Study in the Semiotics of Behavior.* Stanford: Stanford University Press.

Parkhomenko, Mikhail. 1981. "Masshtabnost' vzgliada." *Novyi mir* 6: 244–253.

Parnov, E. 1968. *Sovremennaia fantastika.* Moscow: Znanie.

Parthé, Kathleen. 1987. *Time, Backward! Memory and the Past in Soviet Russian Village Prose.* Washington, D.C.: Wilson Center, Kennan Institute for Advanced Russian Studies.

_____. 1992. *Russian Village Prose: The Radiant Past.* Princeton: Princeton University Press.

Partridge, C. J. 1990. *Yuri Trifonov's* The Moscow Cycle: *A Critical Study.* Lewiston, N.Y.: E. Mellen Press.

Peterlin, Viktor. 1981. "Korni." *Ogoniok* 12 (March): 19.

Peterson, Nadya. 1988. "Vladimir Makanin's Solutions to the Loss of the Past." *Studies in Comparative Communism* 21.3/4: 349–356.

Petrushevskaia, Liudmila. 1988. *Bessmertnaia liubov': Rasskazy.* Moscow: Moskovskii Rabochii.

_____. 1988. "Svoi krug." *Novyi mir* 1: 116–138.

Piskunov, V., and S. Piskunova. 1986. "Mezhdu byt' i ne byt'" *Novyi mir* 5: 238–246.

_____. 1987. "Vyiti iz kruga . . . " *Literaturnoe obozrenie* 2: 54–58.

_____. 1988. "Uroki zazerkal'ya" *Oktyabr'* 8: 188–198.

_____. 1988. "Vse prochee—literatura." *Voprosy literatury* 2: 38–77.

Pittman, Riita, H. 1992. "Writers and Politics in the Gorbachev Era." *Soviet Studies* 4: 665–685.

Popov, Evgenii. 1990. *Prekrasnost' zhizni: Glavy iz "Romana s gazetoi," kotoryi nikogda ne budet nachat i zakonchen.* Moscow: Moskovskii rabochii.

Porter, Robert. 1989. *Four Contemporary Russian Writers.* New York: St. Martin's Press.

Potapov, N. 1981. "Mir cheloveka i chelovek v mire: Zametki o romane Chingiza Aitmatova." *Pravda* (February 16): 7.

Powell, David E. 1983. "A Troubled Society." In *The Soviet Union Today: An Interpretive Guide,* ed. James Cracraft, 317–331. Chicago: University of Chicago Press.

Proffer, Ellendea. 1984. *Bulgakov: Life and Work.* Ann Arbor: Ardis.

Rabkin, Eric S. 1976. *The Fantastic in Literature*. Princeton: Princeton University Press.

Rasputin, Valentin. 1985. "Pozhar." *Nash sovremennik* 7: 3–38.

_____. 1989. *Siberia on Fire: Stories and Essays*. DeKalb: Northern Illinois University Press.

Remnick, David. 1994. "Exit the Saints." *New Yorker* 70 (July 18): 50–55.

Revich, Vsevolod. 1983. "Eta real'naia fantastika." *Literaturnaia gazeta* (February 9): 4.

Riabchuk, Mikola. 1984. "Sindrom Bashilova." *Literaturnoe obozrenie* 11: 43–45.

Robin, Regine. 1992. *Socialist Realism: An Impossible Aesthetic*. Stanford: Stanford University Press.

Rodnianskaia, Irina. 1986. "Neznakomye znakomtsy." *Novyi mir* 8: 230–247.

Roll, Serafina. 1993. "The Death of Language and the Language of Death in Nina Sadur's 'Echai.'" *Russian Literature* 34: 187–206.

Rollberg, Peter. 1989. "Anatoli Kim: Einhornchen." *Weimarer Beitrage* 35.7: 1174.

_____. 1993. "Between Beast and God: Anatolii Kim's Apocalyptic Vision." *World Literature Today* 67.1: 100–106.

_____. 1993. *Invisible Transcendence: Vladimir Makanin's Outsiders*. Washington, D.C.: Woodrow Wilson Center, Kennan Institute for Advanced Studies.

Rothberg, Abraham. 1972. *The Heirs of Stalin: Dissidence and the Soviet Regime, 1953–1970*. Ithaca: Cornell University Press.

Rougle, Charles. 1990. "On the 'Fantastic Trend' in Recent Soviet Prose." *Slavic and East European Journal* (Fall): 308–321.

Sadur, Nina. 1990. "Pronikshie." In *Ne pomniashchaia zla*, ed. Larisa Vaneeva. Moscow: Moskovskii Rabochii.

_____. 1991. "Krasnyi paradiz." In *Novye Amazonki*, ed. Svetlana Vasilenko, 255–274. Moscow: Moskovskii Rabochii.

Scott, James C. 1990. *Domination and the Arts of Resistance: Hidden Transcripts*. New Haven: Yale University Press.

Seifrid, Thomas. 1992. *Andrei Platonov: Uncertainties of Spirit*. Cambridge: Cambridge University Press.

Seleznev, Iurii. 1977. "Fantasticheskoe v sovremennoi proze." *Moskva* 2: 198–206.

Semenova, Svetlana. 1987. "Talant nravstvennogo uchitel'stva." *Znamia* 2.

Sergeev, Evgenii. 1986. "Poisk schastliveishego sluchaia." *Znamia* 3: 205–215.

Shcheglova, Evgeniia. 1990. "V svoem krugu: Polemicheskie zamechaniia o 'zhenskoi proze'." *Literaturnoe obozrenie* 3.

Shklovskii, Evgenii. 1986. *Proza molodykh: Geroi, problemy, konflikty*. Moscow: Znanie.

Shneidman, N. N. 1989. *Soviet Literature in the 1980s: Decade of Transition*. Toronto: University of Toronto Press.

Shragin, Boris. 1977. *Protivostoianie dukha*. London: Overseas Publications Interchange.

Shukshin, Vasilii. 1975. "Do tret'ikh petukhov." *Nash sovremennik* 1: 28–61.

Shvedov, S. 1988. "Literaturnaia kritika i literatura chitatelei." *Voprosy literatury* 5: 3–30.

_____. 1989. "Chto dal'she? Vozvrashchennaia literatura i obretaiushchii sebia chitatel'." *Literaturnoe obozrenie* 6: 60–63.

Simmonds, George W., ed. 1977. *Nationalism in the USSR and Eastern Europe in the Era of Brezhnev and Kosygin.* Papers and Proceedings of the Symposium held at the University of Detroit, October 3–4, 1975. Detroit: University of Detroit Press.

Sinyavskii, Andrei [Abram Tertz]. 1960. *On Socialist Realism.* New York: Pantheon Books.

Skuratovksii, V. 1984. "Real'nost' mysli." *Literaturnaia gazeta* (June 6): 5.

Slavetskii, Vl. 1991. "Posle postmodernizma." *Voprosy literatury* (November–December): 38–47.

Sokolova, Natal'ia. 1981. *Ostorozhno, volshebnoe!* Moscow: Sovetskii Pisatel'.

Solov'eva, Inna. 1988. "Natiurmort s knigoi i zerkalom." *Literaturnoe obozrenie* 4: 46–49.

Sorokin, Vladimir. 1992. *Sbornik rasskazov.* Moscow: Russlit.

Starr, S. Frederick. 1983. *Red and Hot: The Fate of Jazz in the Soviet Union, 1917–1980.* New York: Limelight Editions, 1983.

_____. 1988. "Soviet Union: A Civil Society." *Foreign Policy* 70 (Spring 1988).

_____. 1989. "Civil Society and the Impediments to Reform." In *Toward a More Civil Society? The USSR Under Mikhail Sergeevich Gorbachev,* ed. William Green Miller, 304–309. New York: Harper and Row.

Stel'makh, Valeriia. 1973. "Kakaia kniga u vas v rukakh." *Literaturnoe obozrenie* 5: 100–104.

Stites, Richard. 1989. "Fantasy and Revolution: Alexander Bogdanov and the Origins of Bolshevik Science Fiction." In *Red Star: The First Bolshevik Utopia,* by Alexander Bogdanov, ed. Loren R. Graham and Richard Stites, 1–16. Bloomington: Indiana University Press.

_____. 1989. *Revolutionary Dreams: Utopian Vision and Experimental Life in the Russian Revolution.* Oxford: Oxford University Press.

_____. 1992. *Russian Popular Culture: Entertainment and Society Since 1900.* Cambridge: Cambridge University Press.

Strugatsky, Arkadii, and Boris Strugatsky. 1964. *Dalekaia raduga: Trudno byt' bogom.* Moscow: Molodaia Gvardiia.

_____. 1972. *Ulitka na sklone: Skazka o troike.* Frankfurt am Main: Posev.

_____. 1981. *Les.* Ann Arbor: Ardis.

Suleiman, Susan. 1983. *Authoritarian Fictions: The Ideological Novel as a Literary Genre.* New York: Columbia University Press.

_____. 1990. *Subversive Intent: Gender, Politics, and the Avant-Garde.* Cambridge, Mass.: Harvard University Press.

Surganov, Vs. 1985. "Energiia dobra." *Literaturnaia gazeta* (February 13).

Surkov, E. 1986. "Tragediia v Moiunkumakh: O romane Chingiza Aitmatova 'Plakha.'" *Pravda* (December 22): 3.

Sussman, Elisabeth. 1991. "The Third Zone: Soviet 'Postmodern.'" In *Between Spring and Summer: Soviet Conceptual Art in the Era of Late Communism,* ed. D. A. Ross, 61–72. Cambridge, Mass.: MIT Press.

Suvin, Darko. 1976. *Russian Science Fiction 1956–1974.* Elizabethtown, N.Y.: Dragon Press

———. 1979. *Metamorphoses of Science Fiction: On the Poetics and History of a Literary Genre.* New Haven: Yale University Press.

———. 1979. "The Utopian Tradition of Russian Science Fiction." *MLR* 66: 139–159.

Tendriakov, Vladimir. 1987. "Pokushenie na mirazhi." *Novyi mir* 4, 5.

Terras, Viktor. 1985. *Handbook of Russian Literature.* New Haven: Yale University Press.

Teskey, Ayleen. 1982. *Platonov and Fyodorov: The Influence of Christian Philosophy on a Soviet Writer.* Amersham, England: Avebury Publishing.

Thompson, Terry L., and Richard Sheldon, eds. 1988. *Soviet Society and Culture. Essays in Honor of Vera S. Dunham.* Boulder: Westview Press.

Todorov, Tzvetan. 1973. *The Fantastic: A Structural Approach to a Literary Genre.* Cleveland: Press of Case Western Reserve University.

Tolstaia, Tatiana. 1988. *On the Golden Porch.* London: Virago.

———. 1992. *Sleepwalker in a Fog.* New York: Alfred A. Knopf.

Tolstaia, Tatiana, and Karen Stepanian. 1988. ". . . Golos, letiashchii v kupol." *Voprosy literatury* 2: 78–105.

Trifonov, Jurii. 1968. "Golubinaia gibel'." *Novyi mir* 1.

———. 1969. "Obmen." *Novyi mir* 12.

———. 1970. "Predvaritel'nye itogi." *Novyi mir* 12.

———. 1971. "Dolgoe proshchanie." *Novyi mir* 8.

———. 1975. "Drugaia zhizn'." *Novyi mir* 8.

———. 1978. *Povesti.* Moscow: Sovetskaia Rossiia.

———. 1985. *Kak slovo nashe otzovetsia.* Moscow: Sovetskaia Rossiia.

Tucker, Robert. 1987. *Political Culture and Leadership in Soviet Russia: From Lenin to Gorbachev.* New York: Norton.

Turbin, V. 1981. "O khudozhestvennoi fantastike: Iskaniia i mel'tesheniia." *Oktiabr'* 9.

———. 1983. "I igra i bor'ba." *Literaturnoe obozrenie* 5: 45–49.

Updike, John. 1985. "Books: Back in the USSR." *New Yorker* (April 15).

Urban, Adolf. A. 1972. *Fantastika i nash mir.* Leningrad: Sovetskii Pisatel'.

Urnov, Dmitrii. 1983. "Bor'ba ili igra so zlom?" *Literaturnoe obozrenie* 5: 43–45.

———. 1989. "Plokhaia proza," *Literaturnaia gazeta* (February 8): 4.

Vail', Petr, and Aleksandr Genis. 1982. *Sovremennaia russkaia proza.* Ann Arbor: Ermitazh.

Vaneeva, Larisa, comp. 1990. *Ne pomniashchaia zla: Novaia zhenskaia proza.* Moscow: Moskovskii Rabochii.

Vasilenko, Svetlana, ed. 1991. *Novye Amazonki.* Moscow: Moskovskii rabochii.

Vasilevskii, A. 1990. "Bespredel'." *Literaturnaia gazeta* (September 12): 4.

Vasil'eva, I. 1981. "Stilisticheskoe svoeobrazie romana Chingiza Aitmatova 'I dol'she veka dlitsia den' kak proizvedeniia sovetskoi internatsional'noi literatury." *Russkii iazyk v shkole* 5: 79–84.

Venclova, Thomas. 1988. "Ethnic Identity and the Nationality Issue in Contemporary Soviet Literature." *Studies in Comparative Communism* 21.3/4: 319–329.

Veselaia, Elena. 1990. "Dunovenie erosa: beseda s Valeriei Narbikovoi." *Moskovskie novosti* 13 (April 1): 14.

Walker, Nancy. 1990. *Feminist Alternatives: Irony and Fantasy in the Contemporary Novel by Women.* Jackson: University Press of Mississippi.

Weiner, Douglas. 1988. *Models of Nature: Ecology, Conservation, and Cultural Revolution in Soviet Russia.* Bloomington: Indiana University Press.

Woll, Josephine. 1991. *Invented Truth: Soviet Reality and the Literary Imagination of Iurii Trifonov.* Durham: Duke University Press.

_____. 1993. "The Minotaur in the Maze: On Liudmila Petrushevskaia." *World Literature Today* 1 (Winter): 125–130.

World Congress for Soviet and East European Studies. 1989. *Aspects of Modern Russian Literature: Selected Papers of the Third World Congress for Soviet and East European Studies.* Ed. Arnold McMillin. Columbus, Ohio: Slavica Publishers.

Wyatt, Jean. 1990. *Reconstructing Desire: The Role of the Unconscious in Women's Reading and Writing.* Chapel Hill: University of North Carolina Press.

Young, George M., Jr. 1979. *Nikolai F. Fedorov: An Introduction.* Belmont, Mass.: Nordland Publishing.

Zalygin, Sergei. 1982. 3d ed. *Literaturnye zaboty.* Moscow: Sovetskaia Rossiia.

Zamyatin, Yevgeny. 1982. *A Soviet Heretic: Essays by Yevgeny Zamyatin.* Ed. Alex M. Shane. Chicago: University of Chicago Press.

Zarin', Marger. 1981. *Fal'shivyi Faust ili perepravlennaia popolnennaia povarennaia kniga.* Moscow: Sovetskii pisatel'.

Zekulin, Nicholas. 1993. "Soviet Russian Women's Literature in the Early 1980s." In *Fruits of Her Plume: Essays on Contemporary Russian Women's Culture,* ed. Helena Goscilo, 33–58. Armonk, N.Y.: M. E. Sharpe.

Zhukov, I. 1980. "Ispytanie zhizn'iu." *Komsomol'skaia pravda* (December 13).

Zolotusskii, Igor'. 1987. "Otchet o puti." *Znamia* 1: 221–240.

_____. 1989. "Krushenie abstraktsii." *Novyi mir* 1: 235–246.

_____. 1990. "Proiti bezvredno mezhdu chudes i chudovishch." *Literaturnoe obozrenie* 1.

About the Book and Author

In response to the profound changes in Soviet society in recent years, the author considers the demise of Soviet literature and the emergence of its Russian progeny through the prism of the writers' engagement with fantasy.

Viewing the mutual interaction of Soviet/Russian literary output with aspects of the dominant culture such as ideology and politics, Nadya Peterson traces the process of mainstream literary change in the context of broader social change. She explores the subversive character of the fantastic orientation, its utopian and apocalyptic motifs, and its dialogical relationship with socialist realism, as it steadily gathered force in the latter Soviet decades. The shattering of the mythic colossus did not put an end to these opposing forces, but rather diverted them in various unexpected directions—as the author explains in her concluding chapters on the new "alternative" literatures.

Nadya L. Peterson is assistant professor of Russian language and literature at the University of Connecticut.

Index